2/9/09

The sociology
of old age

The sociology of old age

GRAHAM FENNELL
CHRIS PHILLIPSON
HELEN EVERS

Open University Press
MILTON KEYNES · PHILADELPHIA

HQ
1061
.F46
1988

Open University Press
Open University Educational Enterprises Limited
12 Cofferidge Close
Stony Stratford
Milton Keynes MK11 1BY

and
242 Cherry Street
Philadelphia, PA 19106, USA

First published 1988

British Library Cataloguing in Publication Data

Fennell, G.
    Sociology of old age.
    1. Old age – Sociological perspectives
    I. Title   II. Phillipson, Chris, *1949–*
    III. Evers, Helen
    305.2'6

    ISBN 0-335-15861-7
    ISBN 0-335-15860-9 Pbk

Library of Congress Cataloging-in-Publication Data

Fennell, Graham.
    Sociology of old age / Graham Fennell, Chris Phillipson, Helen
Evers.
        p.   cm.
    Bibliography: p.
    Includes index.
    1. Gerontology.   I. Phillipson, Chris. II. Evers, Helen.
III. Title.
HQ1061.F46   1988   305.2'6—dc19   87-36851
ISBN 0-335-15861-7
ISBN 0-335-15860-9 (pbk.)

Typeset by Rowland Phototypesetting Limited,
Bury St Edmunds, Suffolk
Printed in Great Britain by Biddles Limited,
Guildford and King's Lynn

To our parents, partners and children

Contents

Acknowledgements

Authors commonly acknowledge the disruption to family life which producing a book entails. This one has been no exception. Our geographical dispersion has meant extensive travelling, and absence or preoccupation also disrupts the flow of other work. In addition to the forbearance and support of our families, therefore, we would like to acknowledge the help we have received both directly and indirectly from various individuals in our respective universities.

Among the supporters, our thanks are due to Frances Badger, Elaine Cameron and Karl Atkin at the University of Birmingham for maintaining the research (mentioned in Chapter 7) during Helen Evers's absences. Among direct helpers we wish especially to thank Sue Allingham at the University of Keele, who entered Chris Phillipson's writing onto disc, and Steve Mosley at the University of East Anglia who made our different computing systems compatible: this made it far easier to integrate sections originating from different hands. We all owe a great debt to Ann Way, Research Associate at the University of East Anglia, for her assistance in every aspect of realizing the manuscript to a standard which matched our aspirations.

We thank Souvenir Press for permission to quote from Michael O'Donnell's *The Impossible Virgin*; Cambridge University Press for Table 2.1; Routledge and Kegan Paul for the photograph on p. 9; *New Society* for Figure 4.1 and the Joint Unit for Social Services Research at the University of Sheffield for Figure 4.2. The photograph at the start of Part I is reproduced by permission of the Open University and those at the start of Part III by permission of *Community Care*. Other photographs are by Dave Guttridge.

PART I

1

Towards a sociology of old age

Introduction

Our wish is to write a clear and interesting account of the sociology of old age in Britain today. We aim at two different types of reader. On the one hand are those who want to know more about old age and have no immediate preference for a sociological – as compared with a medical, psychological, geographical or historical – approach to it: they want a readable and helpful introduction without worrying about subject boundaries. To them we hope to provide the introduction and also convey the particular interest and excitement of the sociological imagination (Mills 1959). On the other hand are those who study our subjects professionally – some gerontologists (not necessarily sociologists); and some sociologists, who may not previously have examined this field. To gerontologists we hope to show the distinctive contribution of sociological analysis; to sociologists we hope to demonstrate the vitality and importance of this neglected topic.

To satisfy such different readers is bound to be difficult, although not necessarily impossible. One difficulty is put like this by Bertaux and Bertaux-Wiame:

> During the sixties, thousands of students in many countries came to sociology because they wanted to find out how people live and what social life is like concretely. But instead of finding what they are hoping for, they found academic sociology. Is it necessary to make any further comment? The disillusion was as great as the expectations had been. (1981 : 173)

This problem, of a latent reservoir of interest and enthusiasm which is 'turned off' by academic sociology, is a nettle which has to be grasped. It arises in our view because sociology is an academic discipline, and the very notion of a discipline implies tensions and restraints. Sociology is motivated by two powerful human impulses. One is simple curiosity, as Berger acknowledges in his *Invitation to Sociology*:

We would say then that the sociologist . . . is a person intensively, endlessly, shamelessly interested in people's doings. The sociologist's natural habitat is all the human gathering places of the world, wherever people come together. . . . What interests us is the curiosity that grips any sociologist in front of a closed door behind which there are human voices. A good sociologist will want to open that door, to understand these voices. (Adapted from 1966 : 29–30)

The other well-spring is a form of compassion. It appears in various guises – a concern with injustice, a wish to champion the underdog, an urge to call attention to the unseen and the invisible, an itch to establish more rational social policies, a drive to redress the balance in society a little against the powerful. This drive is well-captured in an autobiographical reflection by Peter Townsend:

I work as a sociologist. I should like this to mean that I explore, and write about, present-day society so that others may understand it better. I should like it to mean that I spend a good deal of time observing and interviewing small cross-sections of the population before writing detailed reports which aim to keep human beings to the forefront. Above all, I should like it to mean studying very carefully the life of the poorest and most handicapped members of society. (1958 : 103)

Most sociologists, in private, acknowledge these two sorts of motivations. They find human behaviour endlessly interesting and fascinating to study and they think there is some point in studying it beyond merely gratifying a curiosity: they hope, in some shorter or longer term, that their studies will contribute to a better world.

The problem for academic sociologists is that, in public, they have to deny themselves. To establish their scientific credentials they have to keep their emotions under restraint; to establish their political legitimacy, they have to assert their 'objectivity'. This may mean pretending to a greater neutrality about their subject than they feel. Yet, to the enemies of sociology, this pretence of objectivity, this claim to disinterested scientific study, was always too thin, too transparent. Those hostile to sociology argue two things: either that society can never be reformed, human nature being what it is; or that it should not be, because whatever injustices and inequalities are revealed, they are inherently natural in a competitive world (Lenski 1966 : 22–3). These (and opposing) positions are more a matter of deeply held belief rather than being subject to argument or disproof, so it is possible that the restraint or denial of feeling both fails to impress the sceptics and contributes to some of the 'disillusion' with academic sociology among those who come to it with their emotions and reforming enthusiasms untarnished. However, it is integral to our approach that arguments and evidence *are* subject to critical examination and that issues are not *pre*judged.

If one of the sources of disillusion with academic sociology is the requirement to keep emotions damped down, another is the accusation that sociologists write obscure, jargon-filled prose. Examples of this may certainly be found, but we must remember that any field of study has its technical terms. Electricians need to know about polarity and phase, blood technicians about plasmaphoresis, musicians about syncopation and harmony. To outsiders, technical terms sound like 'jargon' – either meaninglessly verbose or a deliberate attempt to erect a barrier to understanding; yet to insiders such terms are used for precision and speed.

There are two problems with jargon. One is that terms which are crystal-clear to professionals become obscure when we communicate across a professional boundary; the other is that, on some occasions at least, jargon is unnecessary. This can be seen clearly in the following extract from a Modesty Blaise adventure. In *The Impossible Virgin*, Modesty performs a field operation to remove an appendix under the direction of an injured doctor, Giles Pennyfeather. He, in turn, is refreshing his memory by reference to a medical textbook. The operation has been going well:

> Scalpel, appendix and forceps dropped together on to her discarded sheet of oilskin. She wanted to relax, but knew that the longest part of the work lay ahead, the sewing up. Pennyfeather said, 'Super. Now invaginate the stump into the caecum.' She lifted her head to stare at him. 'Do *what?*' 'Push the stump inside the tube.' (O'Donnell 1971 : 237)

Here we can see that Pennyfeather lapses into jargon, not to obscure, but because the operation has been going so well that he forgets he is not talking to another doctor. We can also see that a robust vernacular translation can be supplied if necessary but that it offers scope for ambiguity, whereas the jargon is precise and unambiguous.

It would be folly to write on any technical subject without recourse at all to its specialist vocabulary. It is sometimes sensible to use less accessible terms, either for their precision or because they convey a whole world of meanings and actions which it is cumbersome to spell out in words every time (like the word 'service' to a mechanic). However, we try to keep such usages to a minimum. In a further attempt to avoid the 'disillusion' with academic sociology we also outline our theme in broad brush strokes, using few, rather than many, sources and drawing on vivid, concrete examples from our own and others' research to illustrate our observations.

These tensions or difficulties which we have identified – the urge to objective dispassionate enquiry, the need for scientific credentialism, the choice of an appropriate vocabulary – are not the only ones which have to be restrained in the academic discipline of sociology. Another important tension is that experienced between the urge to generalize, to make sense of human experience and to identify patterns and the fact that we study unique, idiosyncratic individuals at particular moments in time.

The sociologist is always seeking the pattern, the rule, the generalization, when all around exceptions to the rule spring to mind and the world dissolves again into formlessness. Yet the drive to make sense of the social world, to impose order on it, is part of the professional task. To do this, we are driven to 'run ahead of the data': we want to understand the pattern *now*, to have the answers *now*. But, often, we do not yet have the evidence.

These are creative tensions which are common to many fields of enquiry, not just sociology, and they can be resolved partially by making a candid confession of them. In what follows we want to retain the human interest and allow feelings of compassion or injustice to be explored: this means we draw on certain types of source in particular, 'personal-involvement studies' as Douglas (1970) calls them, where a single investigator or small team have come physically and emotionally close to the elderly people they are writing about. Other types of studies are left in the background – on the one hand, the large-sample surveys carried out by teams of anonymous interviewers and, on the other, the desktop analysts who have hardly met an elderly person in the flesh. [For a review of material derived from such studies, see Victor (1987).]

Some common difficulties

In our work over the last two decades we have introduced several hundred students to the sociological study of old age and a suitable point of departure is to join such a group of intellectual travellers and consider what they carry in their baggage: typically they do not know much about the subject to begin with, but they do have their share of common beliefs and stereotypes about old age. The students are generally well-disposed towards elderly people and are anxious to learn about their problems. They often have one elderly person in mind whom they know something about: they test what we say and what they read against their image of that person, like biting on a coin to test for counterfeit.

Ignorance is remediable. Being well-disposed to 'the elderly', however, and wanting to know about 'their problems' can present difficulties less easy to remedy, even supposing that were our wish. Sympathy may be necessary for empathy; but to take a benign interest in other people's problems involves a number of risks. First, there is the risk of 'welfarizing' the group under study, which involves a subtle mixture of diminution and patronage. Sykes (1985) says that 'welfarization' includes a focus on action to meet need rather than an attempt to discover the social processes which produce need; the creation of agencies whose role is to define need and direct action at people in need, rather than at the causes of need; the generation of statistics about need (such as demographic statistics) and a tendency to assume that ameliorative action is 'the role of specialized agencies with expert competence upon the problem, people or needs so defined'.

There may be nothing wrong with welfare, as such, but there is a risk that the people we welfarize, we do not allow fully human stature: they are not quite whole people, not people like us. They are only one step removed from the 'poor dears' in nursing homes whom other elderly people are said to patronize in the subtle stratification systems of the disadvantaged (Hochschild 1973).

Secondly, to approach the study of old age in terms only of problems and needs involves what Johnson (1976) has rightly termed a pathology model. We are prevented from seeing the whole picture and focusing it correctly, because we see elderly people only in terms of their diseases, disabilities and deprivations. We focus unerringly on poverty, bereavement, social isolation, loneliness, role loss, illness, handicap, apathy and abuse. Elderly people who do not fit into the pathology model (the rich, fit, active elderly person, the assertive elderly person, the political leader, the quiet, healthy busy elderly person, anyone getting on with a purposive existence) are almost defined out of frame. They are not a problem, they have no obvious needs, hence they cannot really be elderly. Within the pathology model, elderly people must *need* something, they must be worse off in some respect than we are. If not, they do not fit the image and, therefore, cannot be regarded as elderly.

Thirdly, and most difficult to handle, is the 'thing-status' of 'the elderly'. Students want to know about 'them'; they are well-disposed towards 'them'; they want to know what can be done for 'them'. There is, in other words, a real thing to study, a problem to resolve and hence an expertise or specialism which can be mastered and acquired. Anything unproblematic is regarded as natural, self-evident and not the realm of experts. This is what Marx was driving at when he said that, when we try to appreciate the world, we appreciate it in its mystified sense. What he meant by this important insight was that for much of the time the social world seems immensely *natural* to us, so natural that we do not question it and do not seek to modify or control it. Conversely, controlling the natural or physical world, modifying the environment, has attracted human interest and effort throughout history. 'Old people suffer from poverty – well, that's inevitable, there is nothing you can do about that.' 'Old people die of cold – that's terrible, we must make sure it never happens again.' Among the 'natural' arrangements examined as questionable later in this book are arguments about the association between old age and ill-health, between old age and unemployment and between domesticity, subordination and being a woman.

To say people first appreciate the social world in a mystified sense means also that they may think they do not need sociologists to tell them how society works because they know already, indeed they may even not be able to see the point of sociology at all. Social knowledge lies in the realm of common sense, things everybody knows. Even sociologists, who spend their lives trying to demystify society, find that its immense present reality distorts their vision constantly. While we strive towards a clear, timeless and objective view of old age, we can manage only brief glimpses of it. We always find ourselves slipping back into a more conventional, easier vision – conceptually, linguistically and in the way we reason with ourselves.

One simple example is the stigmatizing use of adjectives as nouns. We try, wherever possible, not to talk of 'the elderly', 'geriatrics' (as applied to people), 'the elderly mentally infirm', 'the old' or 'the confused'; but, when we do have to generalize, we refer to 'elderly people', 'older people', 'ill people', 'people in old age' or 'confused elderly people'. This is not to deny the physical realities of ageing, disability or dementia, but to try, linguistically, to remind ourselves constantly of human variety in the groups we are categorizing and to underline the 'people-status' (people like us, in other words) of elderly people as opposed to the 'thing-status' (objects inferior to us) of 'the elderly'.

Our students and readers may ask, however, 'what is wrong with talking about "the elderly"? After all, there are masses of books and statistics about "them" – Tinker's *The Elderly in Modern Society* (1981), or the OPCS study by Hunt, *The Elderly at Home* (1978), to name but two – surely the usage is commonsensical and natural?'

We reply that many things which seem natural are, in fact, socially constructed and the language we use is woven into this social construction. We need to think carefully about such details as whether we are using adjectives as nouns to refer to people; and whether we write habitually in a passive rather than active voice ('old people need help', in preference to 'old people fight for their rights'). Hence, in this book, we shall attempt not to refer to 'the elderly' again.

Images and the social construction of old age

The imagery of old age as desolation is found graphically in the cover photograph for Marris's *Loss and Change* (1974): an elderly person is depicted as an urban waif, lost in a concrete jungle she never made. An example of welfarist imagery, with its pathological overtones and emphasis on needs is found in the following word-picture from Shaw's *On Our Conscience, the Plight of the Elderly*. This type of image can easily become a stereotype:

> The old woman's deterioration was such that her condition was desperate. She was found slumped in a broken, urine-saturated armchair in front of an empty firegrate. The day was bitterly cold and she had no fuel for the fire and no other means of heating. Nor had she any food. She gazed from blank, uncaring eyes and gave all the appearance of waiting for death to overtake her. (1971:27)

In social gerontology itself, a rival imagery has been developing, one which explicitly challenges the welfarist approach – that of old age as opportunity. This is just as appealing as the image of old age as misery, though it can be equally specious. Puner (1974) exemplifies this approach in his book *To the Good Long Life* when he quotes J. B. Priestley's celebrated reply – at the age of 79, on the publication of his ninety-ninth book – to the question of what it was like to be old:

> It was as though walking down Shaftesbury Avenue as a fairly young man, I was suddenly kidnapped, rushed into a theatre and made to don the grey hair, the wrinkles and other attributes of age, then wheeled on-stage. Behind the appearance of age I am the same person, with the same thoughts, as when I was younger. (1974:7)

Later, Puner tells the story about a fellow American keen to visit Puner's local nudist beach in France. The friend is, of course, an 'elderly' man: the general

Peter Marris

Loss and Change

Institute of Community Studies

message of contemporary American social gerontology is that old people are no different from we youngsters, so let's all swing along together.

Counterposing stereotypes may help to loosen preconceptions, but we do not suggest that one should replace the other, that a 'jolly' view of old age is superior to a 'miserable' view. What old age means depends in large measure on who you are. The gulf which separates Shaw's old lady in Sheffield from Puner's Priestley in Shaftesbury Avenue is the gulf of wealth, education, success and social class. Priestley may *feel* the same as he always did, even if people treat him differently, but Shaw's unknown woman undoubtedly feels worse.

Two further notions which our group of travelling students carry in their baggage are usually revealed when searched. They are both versions of an idea that 'fings ain't wot they used to be'; one contrasting 'primitive' with 'advanced' societies, the other contrasting 'today' with what Laslett (1965) calls *The World We Have Lost*. This latter idea we consider in detail in Chapter 2. To do justice to the range of issues raised by cross-cultural studies of old age would require a book in itself, but we give the subject brief consideration before turning our attention to the post-war British scene.

Old age in simple societies

'Simple' as opposed to 'complex' societies have been the traditional subject matter of social anthropology. They show enormous diversity, and the trainee social anthropologist was usually pitched head first into an enormous literature which revealed that no generalizations could be made about anything and all preconceived ideas had to be thrown away. Without this rigorous and extensive reading, contemporary graduates in social science have a blurred and undifferentiated image of simpler societies. Typically, elderly people in such societies are thought to be few in number and revered because (in these societies) knowledge is supposed to accumulate with experience: to achieve old age is meant to indicate practical knowledge and survival skills. However, as Douglas comments:

> The popular idea that tribal societies are dominated by the old is wrong. Tribal societies represent the whole gamut of possible variations in the amount of respect and authority accorded to old age and in the different spheres in which the old are influential. . . .
>
> Often when we read of decisions being taken by the village elders we find that 'elder' is a misleading rendering of a world meaning 'fully responsible adult male'. . . . The elders are vigorous men in their late 40s. Even where the people are ruled by a council of elders it is thus possible for the really elderly men to carry no weight. (1963 : 13)

The scarcity of 'old' people in societies like this is thought to follow logically from the knowledge that expectation of life is very low. But expectation of life is a somewhat misleading expression, being instead a record of the average age of death of those who die, in which the high mortality of infants skews the

average. The 'ageing' of world populations has been brought about by saving infants from death, by reducing infant and child mortality (predominantly) and by corresponding reductions in human fertility, rather than by extending the life-span; and ageing is, anyway, culturally relative. However, it would be a mistake to suppose that – in any society – elderly people are accorded power simply because they have rarity value.

Where we find examples of older people enjoying power and status in simple societies, this is more likely to be associated with the slow accumulation of wealth and the possibilities of patronage this gives. Advancement for younger people in these societies may then depend on ingratiating themselves with their elders, but the deference is a forced and institutionalized one, like class deference in our society. We might mention two geographically spaced examples, the Tiwi and the Lele.

Among the Tiwi of Northern Australia, the status of males is as nothing until they acquire first a wife (a wife is not only a status symbol, but also has practical value as a gardener, food gatherer and producer) and then additional wives (wives produce not only foodstuffs, but also daughters, who can be promised in marriage to younger male clients). Hence, we might suppose the life of an elderly Tiwi man, surrounded by his wives, to be an enviable one. However, we are told that this is not the case. Instead, such a man may well be plagued with insecurity: he has constantly to be on the alert to snuff out conspiracies and adulterous liaisons between his working wives in the gardens and footloose young men (Hart and Pilling 1960). [The woman's perspective on Tiwi society is, as so commonly, 'invisible' to us (Rowbotham 1974).]

Douglas paints a sombre picture of the life of old men among the Lele of the Congo:

> In Lele society, under the veneer of good manners, it is evident that the younger men resent the old and the old men fear the young. The old know that their privileged position is precarious; they suspect their wives of infidelity, they feel frustrated that the courteous manners of their juniors do not go with willing service, and, finally, they are afraid of being accused of sorcery – with possible disastrous consequences for (themselves). So old men watch their step. (1963 : 13–14)

And this is a society unusual in that 'everything is arranged for the benefit of the old'. So let us not cloud our vision of today's society by reference to a romanticized vision of arcadia: old age in simple societies is a subject of study in its own right and students wishing to examine it further might be referred to Simmons (1945, 1960), Amoss and Harrell (1981) and Stearns (1982).

Old age in Britain today

After issuing these cautions about avoiding stereotypes and over-generalization, to advance towards any statement about even one society at any moment in time is of course problematic. The age range separating centen-arians – whose numbers have 'spectacularly increased' (Thatcher 1981) – and those approaching retirement is so wide and the social circumstances of people so various that, in striving for general statements, particular exceptions constantly spring to mind (Fennell *et al.* 1983). Should we begin by stressing the poverty of elderly people [as Walker (1981) implies we always should], when some of the wealthiest members of our society are elderly (Townsend 1979)? Should we stress the loneliness and isolation of elderly people, when so many suffer no such thing (Shanas *et al.* 1968; Wenger 1984)? Should we stress how many are frail and housebound, or how many are hale and hearty (Hunt 1978)?

Here we are guided by the scientific principle of *parsimony*: that is, to try to *focus* our enquiries as far as is possible. First, we refer to just three *social trends* which help us to put into context the evidence supplied by three *studies* of old people carried out in different places and at different times in Britain since the Second World War. Within the studies we focus particularly on family relationships and the question of isolation, since these issues crop up so often in general discussions about old age and the evidence of the studies is at such variance from the commonsense opinions received on these subjects.

Three social trends

The trends selected are *segregation, rising living standards* and *widening social cleavages*. In considering either studies or trends, there are many other candidates for inclusion, but the parsimony principle also encourages us to draw out as much as we can from as little as we need, so the list is deliberately kept short.

Many trends, of course, produce immediate or slightly delayed counter-trends as the limitations of newly embraced behaviour patterns come to be exposed or new factors enter people's balance of judgement. Hence, for example, the move out of cities is followed in due course by a reverse migration as the limitations of services and the time and opportunity costs of travel to and from outlying areas make themselves felt. But often the counter-trend is slighter than the main trend and over time a real change can be said to have occurred in society.

Segregation
The dominant trend in British society has been for greater physical segregation to arise between age groups, between social classes and between consumption groups within classes (Burns 1966). For instance, with the decline of privately-rented housing, a combination of planning and market forces has led to housing areas increasingly occupied by people sharing common characteristics which distinguish them from other consumption groups in the area.

Thus, on particular parts of the southern and eastern coastal strips, there may be miles of small bungalows, inhabited predominantly by retired people. On other estates, whole blocks of 'detached executive houses' are inhabited by couples at a certain stage of the life-cycle, all having a broadly similar standard of living, all having about the same size of family at about the same stage, committed to similar goals of improving their material position, doing the best they can for their children, and hoping to move onwards and upwards whenever the opportunity arises. Other residential areas become similarly dominated by particular groups through the operation of criteria for council letting and waiting lists.

Hence people come to occupy grouped dwellings for elderly people only if they are elderly; they only graduate to 'respectable' estates if they are respectable – which means they have a similar age and set of standards as the residents already there. In inner-city areas, complex forces create other patterns of residential segregation such as ghettoes, squats, slums and islands of affluence, whether we go back to Zorbaugh's classic, *The Gold Coast and the Slum* (1929), or to a later study like Harrison's *Inside the Inner City* (1985).

In the three studies we review, segregation was already occurring through the effects of bomb damage, slum clearance, the creation of new, 'desirable' suburban housing and (later) urban redevelopment. The elderly respondents shared their children's rising aspirations with them and for them, but the strains on family networks are clearly depicted. To improve living standards, many of the younger generation moved out to where there was better housing, new schools and fresh air for the children.

Much as they applauded and took pride in this progress, some of the grandparents became that much more impoverished in consequence. Contact within the family became more difficult to maintain: not impossible, but more difficult. Many still had adjacent children, but relatives who were separated by greater geographical distances could no longer operate on a 'popping in' basis. Perhaps the younger ones had cars and could call, perhaps telephones began to be used to bridge the gap, but these tend to change the nature of the interaction and reduce subtly the autonomy of the older person. In future, one might have to wait to be called upon, have to wait for the grandchildren to be brought to visit, instead of being in a position to call oneself, or for the grandchildren themselves to drop in on the way home from school.

Changes like this are partly the outcome of people having the resources to make positive choices: among the retired population, moves to the seaside or the purchase of a flat in a sheltered housing scheme are clear examples. They are also the outcome of decisions made by others – whether planners and other urban managers who decide about land use and redevelopment, industrialists who decide to relocate industry from an inner city to a green field site, or government giving positive or negative sanctions to various forms of economic expansion, contraction or change of location. Older people who lack resources can appear to be the passive victims of these relocation decisions which aggravate the segregation trend. However, we must remember that people have some scope for manoeuvre within these wider social trends and some elderly people have been shown to have enhanced opportunities for social interaction in what Rosow (1967) calls 'dense' age-segregated settlements, whether they arise by voluntary or involuntary selection processes (Jerrome 1981).

Rising living standards
Many indicators of improvements in living standards could be used. The Engels' coefficient is one (Rein 1970 : 50), i.e. the ratio of real disposable income left over in relation to what is spent purchasing basic necessities of food, housing, warmth and clothing. The poorer people are, the higher the proportion of their income they have to spend on food. As income rises, there is more scope for luxury expenditure. The fact that many elderly people today can contemplate a holiday abroad is one example.

Living standards may rise, not only in the sense of individuals having money to spend, but also through harnessing the wealth of the whole society to the common good: today's elderly people have witnessed in their lifetimes the dramatic enhancement of security made possible by pooling social resources in the National Health Service. They would recognize this type of situation, described by Mrs Lena Jeger in a letter to the *Guardian*, a situation of humiliation and anxiety from which they are now spared:

> I can remember nothing less dignified than when my mother used to sit in a misery of embarrassment on the edge of a chair in the consulting room on the rare and desperate days when one of us had to be taken to the doctor – opening and shutting her purse, waiting for the right moment to extract the careful, unspareable half-crown. . . . Sometimes we dropped the money and that was the least dignified of all, especially if the fat doctor let my mother pick it up.
>
> Sometimes he would shout at my mother for not having come before, like the time we had to wait for my sister's sore throat to turn unmistakeably into diphtheria before she was pushed off in a pram to his surgery. 'Good God woman, why didn't you bring this child days ago?' And then even he read the silence as the half-crown came out. 'Damn the money,' he said, as he slipped it in his pocket. (Quoted in Forsyth 1966 : 26–27)

Widening social cleavages
Sociologists have a traditional preoccupation with social inequality, a pre-occupation which seems old-fashioned to those who believe that rising living standards are inevitably diffused throughout the population. More commonly, what seems to happen is that wealth-holders increase their wealth first and, while average standards of living may certainly rise, particular categories [Townsend (1973) calls them 'social minority goups', such as elderly people or people who are unemployed, one-parent families or families containing a physically or mentally handicapped member] do not participate in these improvements. Relative to rising general standards, their position worsens, not only financially but also in wider social participation. For instance, as car ownership becomes more common and public transport declines, those without a car become actually and relatively worse off in terms of accessibility and in what they have to pay for transport.

The conundrum of rising standards and widening gaps is concisely described by Halsey in a newspaper article:

We are twice as well off in real income terms per capita as we were then [in 1953]. We work shorter hours with longer holidays. More than one in four Britons think of themselves as having moved into a higher social class and less than one in ten as having come down in the world compared with their parents. From the slump years of the 1930s the British have lived with better todays than yesterdays and the expectation of still better tomorrows. . . .

[But] the class structure of industrial societies is developing an under-class of those who cannot be placed in the stable workforce of the formerly employed. . . . They suffer from a cumulation of social pathologies – education failure, illiteracy, broken families, high crime rates, poor housing and spatial concentration in the inner city. . . . They tend to adopt a ghetto existence outside the normal social contract of citizenship and with little or no stake in official society.

They are the extreme social manifestation of a class structure tending towards a richer rich and a poorer poor. . . . Majority affluence in privatised security is possibly stable at the price of public squalor, unsafe streets, endemic crime and spasmodic riot. (1987 : 9)

Halsey goes on to discuss the different resource distribution systems which operate in society, particularly contrasting the market and welfare institutions and the varying shares of the product taken by contrasted types of household. Typically, high-income households receive the lion's share of income generated by the market, while the reverse is true of low-income households in respect of welfare benefits. However, as Halsey points out, the market distribution system accounts for about three-quarters of all income generated, so the amount received in welfare benefits by low-income households is steadily dwindling in relation to the prizes won by those who compete successfully in the market:

The class problem thus goes beyond the creation of an under-class to include the fears and insecurities of the old, the sick, the insecurely employed, and indeed everyone who depends on welfare rather than market distribution. (1987 : 9)

Townsend, in his numerous writings on poverty, has drawn attention to the relationship between income and social participation. It is not only that poor people are 'ghettoized', as Halsey suggests, but also that poor people participate less *in general* in societies where conspicuous consumption is the norm. However, because of increasing social segregation these cleavages are often quite invisible to us until briefly exposed by accident, scandal, media probe or other unusual event. Bornat *et al.*, for example, quote an instance which revealed how, for most of the time, older people are priced out of railway travel. But for the special offer, this pent-up demand remains invisible:

British Rail introduced a special 'day return to anywhere' concession to pensioners (in 1980 and 1984). The 1980 scheme prompted the biggest wave of mass travel since the evacuee trains of the Second World War.

Nearly one million pensioners bought tickets, some travelling from Scotland to Cornwall and back. (1985 : 103)

It is possible in a complex society, as Townsend argues, for deprivation to be so specialized in such a different variety of social categories that the total volume of it may strike us far less forcibly than the glittering displays of goods and conspicuous consumption in the high streets and places of public resort. We think, as a society, that we are well-off and it seems to be true. We see the evidence all round us whereas the less well-off participate less and are less visible to us.

Three studies of elderly people

The first of the three studies selected is Sheldon's *The Social Medicine of Old Age* (1948), based on a survey in Wolverhampton in the immediate aftermath of the Second World War. Then we jump a decade, to Townsend's classic study in Bethnal Green – *The Family Life of Old People* (1957) – when reconstruction after bomb damage along with slum clearance programmes and rising living standards were beginning to make an impact on the traditional working class community. Then we move to Glasgow, a decade later, to the work of Isaacs *et al.* (*Survival of the Unfittest*, 1972). These three studies were chosen because they are all examples of personal-involvement research in which the investigators met samples of elderly people at home. Each study has been important in its own right and together they help us examine two general themes: family relationships and the question of social isolation.

The social medicine of old age: report of an inquiry in Wolverhampton

The fieldwork for this study was undertaken by Sheldon alone. Four hundred and forty seven interviews, which included a medical examination, were carried out during a 21-month period beginning in May 1945. The sampling frame used was the register of ration cards, old people being defined as 65 years of age or over if male, or 60 and over if female.

The focus of Sheldon's investigation was the health of his subjects, though he ranged over many other topics. He found, as subsequent reports have confirmed, that many elderly women were in poor health, despite their 'tenacious hold on life'; whereas the men he saw were either very fit or very poorly. Overall, Sheldon estimated that up to 70% of old people were unrestricted in mobility on level ground but approximately 40% had difficulty with stairs.

He documents the extent to which elderly people have regular contact with their kin, even those who are bedfast, being cared for by untiring relatives. Far and away the largest group of old people [as the much bigger and later cross-national study (Shanas *et al.* 1968) has confirmed]: 'consists of (those) who are able to move about quietly in their immediate district and . . . do all their own shopping' (Sheldon 1948 : 32). Shopping began to get difficult after the age of 75 – not so much getting to the shops, as carrying the shopping back home. Most old women could manage their housework until aged 80 or so.

Commenting on family relations, Sheldon notes:

> to regard old people in their homes as a series of individual existences is to
> miss the whole point of their mode of life in the community. The family is
> clearly the unit in the majority of instances, and where such ties are
> absent they tend to be replaced by friendships formed earlier in life.
> (1948:142)

Sheldon emphasizes the importance of the family in the elderly person's daily
round and notes how often he or she has a relative living close by, defining this
ingeniously as five minutes' walk away or less, being 'a measure of distance a
hot meal can be carried without reheating'. He writes:

> A perusal of . . . case reports illustrates not merely the weight of the
> burden that family affection will sustain; it demonstrates the easement to
> the younger generation that would be achieved could these parents and
> children have had houses close to each other. (1948:155)

This early plea, echoed by other commentators on old age and family
relations, carries little weight against the strength of the segregation trend.
Bomb damage and neglect of property maintenance during the Second World
War was accompanied by unprecedented population movements: 60 million
changes of address in a population of only 38 million were recorded in a 5-year
period, to say nothing of unrecorded temporary moves (Ferguson and Fitzgerald 1954:4). Evacuation, conscription into the armed services and
mobilization of women's labour power made it seem, to the young Jonathan
Miller, as if the whole country was on the move:

> There was a huge convection current and nothing seemed to be anchored
> any more, but drifted instead in slow perpetual motion. . . . It was called
> total mobilization. And that's just what it was. The cutting of everyone's
> local attachments so that everything and everyone became chronically
> mobile – as if the whole of English society had turned into plankton.
> (1968:201)

It would be surprising, after this tremendous upheaval, if everyone who
survived the war simply settled back down where they started. Slum clearance,
post-war reconstruction, the drive to create new towns and 'garden suburbs', as
well as new economic opportunities meant that different styles of working-
class life were to be found concurrently in the traditional urban communities
and the new estates to which young families were moving. Sheldon found a
noticeable difference in styles of neighbouring with the more dispersed
housing in the open spaces of the new estates symbolizing a greater detachment
of people from one another. In the older urban areas, with terraced houses
having shared back entries, 'people live[d] in constant touch with one another'
and neighbours were a potential source of help for elderly people, 'accounting
for slightly more than one third of (all) help that would be available if needed'
(1948:177).
Despite their kin relations and despite neighbouring, one-fifth of Sheldon's

sample were affected in some degree by loneliness, 'a well-known calamity of old age . . . which attracts universal sympathy' (1948 : 127). He showed clearly that simply 'living alone' did not produce loneliness, for living alone is simply a statistical category which usually means that an elderly person is successfully maintaining an independent lifestyle, whilst having a family perhaps next door or within a few minutes' walk.

Nor was social isolation a clear predictor of loneliness. Some solitary men had what Sheldon thought was a demand for independence that verged on the paranoic and showed no wish for social interaction. Many women, he thought, were 'more able than men to endure a lonely life without being actually lonely'. Sheldon's conclusion was:

> loneliness cannot be regarded as the simple direct result of social circumstances, but is rather an individual response to an external situation to which other old people may react quite differently. (1948 : 130)

The sort of external situation he has in mind is recent bereavement or loss of physical mobility, the impact of disabling disease as we might now put it. Of the two, thought Sheldon, 'grief transcends physical movement' and this explains why, today, we talk increasingly not so much about loneliness as about depression in old age (Murphy 1982) and think carefully about the impact of serious life events involving grief, loss or threat of loss (Brown and Harris 1978).

The family life of old people: an inquiry in east London

Townsend's study explored directly many of the matters which arose incidentally in the course of Sheldon's medical survey. The fieldwork was carried out in a 13-month period starting in October 1954. A sample of 203 people, selected from GP registers and defined in the same way as Sheldon's, was interviewed: 160 by Townsend and 43 by Peter Marris, both of the Institute of Community Studies in Bethnal Green. The main interview, without any prior negotiation or arrangement, generally lasted 2 hours. Each subject was seen at least twice and often several more times. The first thing the researchers did was sit down and draw up a kinship diagram with the help of their subjects: this helped to break the ice and acted as a useful map to guide them through the dense network of family relationships in which many elderly residents in Bethnal Green were embedded.

However, a decade after the Second World War, the effects of social segregation were already causing stress in these traditional networks. Where families still lived together in Bethnal Green (and 45% of Townsend's sample shared a household with a relative), reciprocated and repeated exchanges of services were observed between young and old, prompting Townsend to observe: 'The fact that old people perform services for others has had less attention than the fact that others perform services for them' (1957 : 48).

These services – particularly those involving child-minding, doing shopping and preparing meals for workers returning home, helping round the house – are easy to exchange when people live within a short 'functional distance' of one another. [By 'functional distance' is meant, not so much the measured geographical distance, as how easy it is to get from one place to another. For anyone – but especially for an elderly person – gradients or distances involving the use of private or public transport are functionally more remote than those involved in moving quietly about on the level in the immediate district.]

Two factors might be identified in Townsend's study which were making it more difficult – particularly for very elderly people – to reciprocate family services. One involves changes in the generation span, the relative age gap between children, their parents and grandparents. All the work associated with the care of the young is most likely to be performed by young elderly people, those whom Isaacs (1974) has termed the 'silver-aged'. If more people live to advanced age and the generation span is reduced, a four-generation family can emerge. This may mean that grandparents are still at work when their grandchildren are small but are very elderly when great-grandchildren are tiny. With this structure, the generation to whom very elderly people may look for support are themselves retired or approaching retirement age.

Another factor was physical distance, which made elderly working-class people in Bethnal Green less able to *initiate* visits and more passively dependent upon being visited:

> Many children were obliged to make their homes elsewhere and could not find a home there for the parents. . . . The children had their own homes and families to look after and were not able to visit Bethnal Green as often as they wished. Their parents visited them, but found they had to limit their visits because fares were so high and because they were becoming more infirm. (Townsend 1957 : 94)

The crucial importance of Townsend's study was in demonstrating the vigorous existence of what he calls the extended family. That is:

> A group of relatives, comprising more than an immediate family, who live in one, two or more households, usually in a single locality, *and who see each other every day or nearly every day*. (1957 : 108)

This network of kin was of tremendous importance to elderly people as a unit in which routine services of shopping, cooking, housework and child-minding could be pooled, and also as the main arena for recreation and participation in the affairs of the wider community. Townsend writes:

> Even in extreme old age a person who had had children was rarely short of company, help and affection . . . [whereas] those with no available relatives were in the worst position. They were acutely conscious of what they considered to be a misfortune. (1957 : 96, 46)

Four out of five of Townsend's sample had had at least one child and 97% of the sample reported regular contact with relatives (once a month or more), whereas only 66% reported regular contact with non-relatives. Moreover:

> Few people had regular contacts as much as once or twice a week with

more than one or two persons unrelated to them, whereas most saw several relatives every day or nearly every day. (1957 : 121)

Townsend discusses the way in which processes he calls substitution and compensation take place within the family: if a spouse dies, other relatives increase their interaction with the survivor. A married daughter may act as a substitute cleaner, cook and general help for a man who has lost his wife. Nieces and nephews might substitute and compensate for the absence of children, performing similar services for their childless aunts and uncles. If a strategic family member emigrates, becomes incapacitated, dies or is otherwise lost to the network (a 'significant relative' or 'principal carer', as he or she might now be called), the network adjusts: another kin member moves up and takes on the support role.

Reinforcing Sheldon's comment about 'the easement . . . that would be achieved, could these parents and children have had houses close to each other', Townsend devotes a whole chapter on housing to the theme of 'keeping the family together':

> Again and again . . . in discussing the family system of care, the stresses of infirmity and the problems of retirement, poverty and institutional care, we have seen the value to old people of relatives, particularly daughters, living close at hand. People made repeated references to housing problems during the interviews. This was even more of a preoccupation than income. . . . Their main concern was to live near members of their families. (1957 : 194)

His main recommendation was that more attention should be given to the possibility of repairing and adapting old houses in city centres rather than clearing the population to new estates on the periphery and decanting elderly Londoners into seaside bungalows and other special accommodation. But the fashion of the times was for physical rather than social planning, and the wisdom of Townsend's recommendation did not receive official recognition until long after slum clearance programmes had destroyed urban dwellings on a scale equivalent to five cities the size of Manchester.

Survival of the unfittest: a study of geriatric patients in Glasgow

Isaacs *et al.* studied elderly people referred for admission to the geriatric unit of the Glasgow Royal Infirmary group of hospitals over a 15-month period beginning in October 1966. Isaacs, as the Consultant Geriatrician responsible for whether or not to admit, visited all the patients at home. The sample is not, therefore, a statistically-randomized community one like those of Sheldon and Townsend, instead it is a sample of crisis situations.

The study illuminates a paradox in studies of older people: why is it that so many health and social services practitioners complain about neglect of elderly people by their families, when the picture painted by social investigators is so much at variance with this idea? Could it be a methodological artefact? Could it be that in all social surveys there is an 'excluded twenty per cent' (Streib 1983) – the people who refuse to be interviewed because they are sick, dying, depressed or distressed – and it is precisely this twenty per cent whom practitioners see in crisis situations? Each category – the social researchers on the one side, the practitioners on the other – might suffer from selective vision, the one tending to an overly optimistic view, the other to an overly pessimistic one.

The great advantage of the study by Isaacs *et al.* is that it examines exactly those crisis situations from which doorstep callers could be excluded. The results do not conflict with other types of investigation but help us understand the importance of family support for those who have it, the significance of its lack (for those who do not have access to it) and the limits to family support where the demands or the distances involved are too great for it to be sustained.

Isaacs *et al.* categorize the reasons for which 280 elderly people were admitted to geriatric care from their own homes. There were two 'medical reasons', of which 'medical urgency' accounted for only 7% of admissions. The second was 'therapeutic optimism': 36% were admitted because the doctor diagnosed a medical condition which hospital care could cure or improve.

However, more than half of the admissions turned on social factors such as the existence or non-existence of the old person's kin or the physical or emotional strain kin were experiencing: strain sufficient, in Isaacs' judgement, to put their own health in jeopardy. Thirty one per cent were admitted 'to relieve strain' on carers (usually spouses or younger relatives of the elderly person) and 26% because they had what Isaacs *et al.* call 'insufficient basic care'. By this they mean a lack of at least one of the following: food, warmth, cleanliness and safety. The importance of the family as a resource system is highlighted here by its absence.

We have heard from Townsend that 'those with no available relatives were in the worst position . . . (and) were acutely conscious of . . . (their) misfortune'. Isaacs *et al.* show that those lacking basic care, compared with other groups, are particularly unfortunate in this respect. They were less likely than others to have a living spouse, more likely to live alone, to be poorly housed, to have few surviving relatives and to be drawn from the lower social strata. They were 'severely incapacitated, socially disadvantaged, very old people' (1972 : 20).

A special analysis was made by the researchers of those patients lacking adequate basic care who did in some sense 'have a family available'. There were 39 patients 'living in conditions of filth, hunger, cold and danger' who had children in Glasgow, and Isaacs *et al.* set out to discover if these children were 'shirking their responsibilities and leaving it to the state to look after the old people, or were there other reasons for the apparent neglect?' (1972 : 34).

Isaacs *et al.* divide these 'other reasons' into four, using terminology which can be traced back to Sheldon's study 20 years earlier. First there is a reason dubbed 'preoccupation' (17 instances):

Where relatives provided as much care as they could, and were anxious to give even more help, but were prevented from doing so by a prior commitment from which they were quite unable to free themselves, or by an impediment which they could not overcome. (1972 : 35)

This reason is found particularly where the elderly person in need of care is very old. The term 'children' miscues us: we tend to think of young people but these 'children' are in their late 50s and early 60s – in that very group (as we discuss in Chapter 5) who may be having to give up work because they themselves already suffer chronic ill-health. Another 'preoccupied' group of 'children' are *parents* whose own children are ill or disabled. A second, rather similar reason, is labelled 'dilemma' and this applied in four instances. Here:

> Care was withheld because relatives, although capable and desirous of giving more help than they did, were forced to adopt a different course in the interests of their own families. (1972 : 40)

The factors mainly influencing preoccupation and dilemma were the demands of employment, cramped accommodation, ill-health, commitment to another invalid, considerations of the demands of the younger generation and, in some cases, personality clashes. In a further seven instances, the care that relatives might have offered was 'refused' by the elderly person, again largely because of personality characteristics (we recall Sheldon's reference to 'desire for independence verging on the paranoic') and past events in the family's history, such as a disputed divorce or remarriage.

This left 11 instances in the authors' final category of 'rejection', where 'children in the Glasgow area who were capable of extending help . . . refused to do so' (1972 : 45). Isaacs *et al.* go through these instances one by one to establish whether, in common judgement, this rejection would be deemed 'reasonable' or 'unreasonable'. Few instances of 'unreasonable' rejection are identified:

> Seven . . . who received no help from their families were recruited from amongst the drunks, prostitutes and criminals of society, and had effectively cut themselves off from their children long before they reached old age. (1972 : 48)

Two others had broken with their families long before, over a disputed second marriage. Of perhaps only two cases (or less than 1% of all admissions):

> Might it justifiably be said that [the patients] had to enter hospital because their families were not prepared to do anything to help them. . . . Neglect of parents by children was rare: failure of children to accept their responsibilities played only a negligible role in the demand for geriatric hospital accommodation. (1972 : 48)

Indeed, what is most likely to impress the reader of this vividly written and carefully researched report of the background to crisis intervention is the poignancy of many of the accounts, the tremendous labour and self-sacrifice undertaken by family carers and the length of time over which this support is offered. One brief glimpse at problems arising from incontinence must be taken to symbolize many other examples recounted in the book or underlying the statistics:

The daughter of one patient and the home help of another wrapped each day's store of fouled linen in brown paper and gingerly carried it through the streets to their own homes, where they washed it. . . . One daughter who lived too far away for this last expedient, brought a large suitcase with her each day, loaded it up with the urine-soaked sheets and boarded the bus back home. She was acutely embarrassed by the bus conductor's witticisms on the lines of 'Going your holidays again, hen?', and by the subsequent strange glances as the pervasive odours escaped from the suitcase and wafted their way through the vehicle. But not one of these (twenty) patients was seen by a health visitor or . . . offered the services of the Local Authority laundries; not one received practical advice or help from the general practitioner . . . and not one received financial recompense for the cost of laundering. (1972 : 82)

What of help from 'the community' or, more specifically, neighbours: was that forthcoming? Twenty nine of the 280 received into the geriatric unit were almost exclusively supported by neighbours and another 18 received regular assistance. The care given by the first group:

Extended far beyond the ordinary neighbourly service to include such necessary activities as cleaning up incontinence, giving and emptying bed-pans, stripping beds, laundering sheets and helping in the toilet. . . . Regular assistance of a less arduous nature [included] house-work, shopping and the preparation of meals for the patient, while neighbourly social visits and sporadic assistance were given in countless other cases. (1972 : 89)

However, this was taking place in the vanishing world of 'the classic slum' (Roberts 1971). The findings by Isaacs *et al.* about the break-up of the traditional community mirror Sheldon's and confirm our discussion of the social costs of the segregation trend:

Neighbourly help was related to the patient's environment. Of the patients who lived in old tenement houses with outside toilets, twice as many were helped by neighbours as was the case with patients in more modern houses. Neighbourly help, unlike the formal social services, was a twenty-four-hour service to the patient. It was flexible and could be fitted in with the neighbour's own daily activities. It was acceptable because it was based on a similarity of social background and on an unwritten code of reciprocity. (Isaacs *et al.* 1972 : 90)

The extent to which substitute forms of 'community care' can arise spontaneously in other less traditional settings or be fostered by the authorities through devices like street wardens or community alarm systems remains a research question of continuing interest (Abrams 1978; Butler 1981; Power and Kelly 1981; Bulmer 1986).

Conclusion

Many lessons can be learned from a consideration of these three studies and we hope our readers are stimulated sufficiently by the extracts to read the originals and make their own reflections. We offer the following points.

The first concerns fallibility and the need to set on one side the ideas and preconceptions we carry with us. From the discussion of segregation, widening social cleavages and of the relationship between income and social participation, we draw the conclusion that it is easy to be wrong in making generalizations about the social circumstances of elderly people outside our own 'social fraction'. We may think we know, but a variety of social processes insulate us from contact with or knowledge of people very different from ourselves. If we are professionals, such as doctors or social workers, we may have role-specific interactions with different types of people but they are narrowly and specially selected through the professional connection and expose only a narrow facet of themselves in it. The great strength of the random community sample is that it brings us directly (if we are social investigators) or vicariously (if we read their reports) into representative situations in all their diversity.

The second point is about variability. Even when we focus on samples in which the writers have studied predominantly working-class people, there are several sources of differentiation, some of which change over time and some of which co-exist contemporaneously. There is, for instance, a line of differentiation between those who in old age have access to what Qureshi and Walker (1988) call the 'normatively preferred' family structure: put most bluntly, those who have a nearby female caring relative and those ('acutely aware of their misfortune') who do not. The fact this arrangement is normatively preferred does not mean it is the norm. Wider social trends, such as the tendency (among those who have children) to have fewer children than in the early twentieth century and to have their children much earlier in life (as we analyse in Chapter 2) means that there may be no such caring relative within immediate call; or the relative may be prevented (by reason of dilemma or preoccupation) from offering all the help which may on occasion be necessary.

A distinction can be drawn, therefore, between those who live in a more traditional community and those whose kinship networks have been spread out by the segregation trend. Even these traditional communities do not remain stable, as we note in Chapter 5, when we consider the differing retirement experiences of men in different sorts of areas. What once might have been the classic slum or supportive local environment may not be a 'zone of transition', a sort of limbo in which elderly indigenous residents are 'trapped' (Gans 1962) alongside inhabitants with whom they do not share 'a similarity of social background and an unwritten code of reciprocity'. In Chapter 7, where we consider old age and ethnicity, we note the very varied circumstances and backgrounds of 'ethnic elders', many of whom live in such areas. Differential access to resources and consequential differences in life chances are an important component of the 'political economy' perspective on ageing, which we examine in Chapter 3.

Finally, we return to images of old age. In reviewing the study by Isaacs *et al.*, we perhaps run the risk of reaffirming the 'pathology model' of old age – which we have no wish to do. However, a balanced picture must have something to say about ill-health, death, dying and terminal care: we return to these subjects in Chapters 8 and 9. While we do not subcribe to the 'old age as misery' approach to the subject it would be irresponsible to brush the problems aside in favour of the 'nudist beach' approach.

The great majority of elderly people get on quietly with their lives, hidden from history: we must beware of 'welfarization', discussing 'them' only in terms of needs and problems. Where people have *resources*, they actively create and recreate their own lives: we know, for example, that Scandinavian pensioners are increasingly over-wintering in the Canaries and other warmer climes and see the beginnings of such a trend in the United Kingdom. Voluntary retirement migration (Karn 1977) to the coastal strips and some rural areas contributes to the segregation already structured by planned relocation of population through the post-war urban reconstruction programmes.

Examples like these reflect people making active choices in old age, just as they do at other times in their lives, but their range of choices is restricted, as always, by the resources to which they have access (Fennell 1986b). There are many different types of resources and resource distribution systems in society and people have differential access to them. Wealth creates choices and close kin create other sorts of opportunities which are unavailable to those who lack access to either or both. As Sykes (1985) urges, we should think not only about the problems which arise because of lack of resources, but the social processes in the first place which give rise to the lack.

Should we '*above all*', as Townsend suggests, study 'very carefully the life of the poorest and most handicapped?' Our conclusion is that this may be a mistaken focus, a potentially welfarizing course which might reinforce the pathology model of old age. We should strive for a balanced view: to concentrate on one group 'above all' runs the risk of becoming an exclusive focus which marginalizes sociological writing from everyday experience. However, because of the widening social cleavages described by Halsey, we must also guard against the risk that the poorest and most handicapped become socially invisible and their existence denied through an assumption that the benefits of rising living standards are evenly distributed.

2

The history of old age

Introduction

Ideas and perspectives about old age have been challenged in recent years by important historical research on ageing. In Britain, some of the most influential work has been produced by the Cambridge Group for the History of Population and Social Structure, led by Peter Laslett (Laslett 1965, 1977, 1984; Laslett and Wall 1972). In America, significant contributions have been provided by Achenbaum (1978), Graebner (1980) and Haber (1983). For the continent, Stearns (1977) and Kohli (1986) have added significant commentaries on the emergence of retirement.

Much of this historical research has undermined a traditional view about the role and status of older people. A common assumption in post-war American sociology, for instance, was that older people had been marginalized in the move from pre-industrial to industrial society (Parsons 1942; Burgess 1960). This supposed change was attributed to three factors: the break-up of the extended family, the loss of veneration and respect for older people and the imposition of retirement. This chapter will provide a critical analysis, from the standpoint of historical research, of this assessment. Research has challenged these commonsense views about the role of the family and attitudes towards older people. Moreover, we shall suggest that this alternative perspective on old age has practical implications for how we see the problems faced by older people today.

Rather than present a narrative about old age from a particular historical starting-point, this chapter will be organized around three distinct themes: *demography*, *economics* and *retirement*. These elements have been highly influential in determining the social construction of old age. A history of each will also tell us much about the characteristics of ageing in contemporary society.

Old age and demographic change

A popular notion in contemporary culture is that of old people being 'abandoned' by their families today: this historical image or myth has also exercised a powerful hold on students of old age. The pre-industrial family is seen to 'care for' its ageing and dependent relations in a way which is no longer thought characteristic of the contemporary nuclear family. 'In the past', it is argued, people looked after their own, not only but *especially* in those emergencies and crises which punctuate daily life. This view was popular in functionalist sociology of the 1950s and 1960s (see, e.g., Parsons 1942; Burgess 1960).

The argument was extended in the 1970s by contributions from modernization theory (Cowgill and Holmes 1972; Cowgill 1974). The argument here was that the modernization of societies was accompanied by a demographic transition which led to an ageing of populations. At the same time, the forces associated with modernization also resulted in a lower status for older people. The key features of modernization producing this effect were held to be: (i) the introduction of new technology, (ii) the impact of urbanization and (iii) the importance attached to education. These factors, according to Cowgill (1974), set up a chain reaction which undermined the status of older people. Age itself was no longer held in the same regard as in traditional society: new technology undermined the skills of older workers; migration and urbanization disrupted family life, leading to the break-up of the extended family; and the growth of education undermined the traditional role of older people as teachers of skills and knowledge.

Historical demography raises serious doubts about many of these arguments. In particular, it has presented a different interpretation of the development of the family over the past 400 years and the relationship of older people to younger kin.

Family structure and old age

A major theme of modernization theory was that older people are deprived of family relationships in a modern, industrial society. From the standpoint of demographic research, however, we can see a number of confusions which lie at the heart of this argument. In one important sense a 'full family life', with older people having a child or children still at home, did last for proportionately longer in pre-industrial society (Laslett 1977). However, the reasons for this cannot be attributed to differences in customs and sentiment; instead, issues of demography and patterns of marriage and family-building are of greater significance.

In seventeenth-century England, for example, children were typically born at a later stage in the childbearing years of men and women than today, to a large extent reflecting the effect of delayed marriage, particularly among the middle and lower classes. With women marrying between the ages of 23 and 27, many would still be having children in their late 30s or early 40s (Stone 1982). In consequence, there was a strong possibility of having children still at home when parents (or, more likely, one parent) entered old age (Laslett 1977).

The role of unmarried children in maintaining care is an important theme in demographic research, one that is illustrated in a study of family relationships in a nineteenth-century Devon parish by Robin (1984). More than a third of elderly people aged 70–79 still had unmarried children at home and they played a major role in the care of their parents. The study by Fischer (1977) of elderly people in seventeenth- and eighteenth-century America also notes the effect of high fertility, with the youngest child often not marrying until the parents were in their 60s. Many older people, suggests Fischer, continued to live with unmarried children until the end of their lives. After the marriage of children, a solitary old age did become more common but, as Laslett argues, there were at least two factors which ensured that this was confined to a minority: first, the tendency of surviving grandparents to enter the homes of married descendants and, secondly, the lower expectation of life of older people in pre-industrial society (Laslett 1977).

When we see arguments about old people being 'abandoned' by their families this must, then, be related to the different demographic realities of pre-industrial and contemporary society. The key factors changing the family life of older people today include the general reduction in fertility, the clustering of births in the early years of marriage, the comparative rarity of spinsters and bachelors, and changes (although these are less dramatic than commonly thought) in life expectancy. As a consequence of these factors, older people are more likely to live on their own: two-thirds of couples age 65 and over do so, as do half of the women aged 75 and over (Wall 1984). However, in contrast to the past, they are much more likely to experience extensive contact with grand-children. Anderson summarizes this in the following way:

> The average woman in the 1970s finished childbearing at age 28 and her last grandchild was born when she was 56; a similar eighteenth-century woman finished childbearing at 39 and her last grandchild would have been born 77 years after his or her grandmother's birth; the contorted phraseology is made necessary because, while an average woman of the 1970s could expect to live 25 years after the birth of her last grandchild, a woman of the mid-eighteenth century could expect to die 12 years before her last grandchild was born. (1985 : 70)

Residential patterns and relations

Historical demography has also provided new answers to the question of where older people lived. Typically, the conventional answer has been in a three-generation, extended-family household. This is contrasted with the two-generational nuclear family common today, which is seen to lead to greater isolation for older people. Yet the conclusions from research suggest a different picture. There has been a decline in the last four centuries in the frequency with which both married and non-married elderly people reside with their children (Wall 1984) but there are also important continuities in residential behaviour. For example, the proportion of elderly people living in institutions has remained surprisingly constant over the same period (fluctuating between 3 and 6%). Again, there has always been a significant proportion of older

Table 2.1. Household position of elderly persons in Britain since the seventeenth century.

Co-residents	England 1684–1796		Great Britain 1962		Great Britain 1980–81	
	Males (%)	Females (%)	Males (%)	Females (%)	Males (%)	Females (%)
With spouse						
Spouse alone	27	14	47	23	60	32
Spouse and others	40	15	23	11	14	5
Sub-total	66	29	70	34	74	38
Without spouse						
Child (in law)	18	39	12	24	4	10
Other relatives	9	17	4	9	3	5
Non-relatives			2	3	2	2
Sub-total	27	56	19	36	9	17
Alone	7	15	11	30	17	45
All	100	100	100	100	100	100
n	116	149	1003	1496	3698	5425

Source: Wall (1984).

people who live alone (see Table 2.1): studies of English communities in the period 1684–1796 show 15% of women aged 65 and over doing so. This contrasts, perhaps, with the 45% of our own day, but Wall suggests that the comparison is not so straightforward:

> Although the percentage of elderly women who were solitary house-holders . . . was 15 per cent higher in 1962 than had been the case in pre-industrial times, between 1962 and 1981 it increased by a further 15 per cent. Indeed, the modification of residence patterns of the elderly since 1962 is in most cases equivalent to, or even slightly in excess of, the difference between the patterns of pre-industrial times and 1962. This applies to the proportion of men as well as women who are solitary householders, to the proportion of men and women who live with someone other than a spouse and to the proportion who live with a spouse, with or without others. Only in regard to men living with a spouse and no other person would major change appear to have occurred before 1962. (1984:488)

Wall concludes from his data that it is difficult to maintain the notion of a linear progression 'from pre-industrial times, when the elderly generally lived with their children or other persons, to modern times, when they live on their own' (Wall 1984:491). Indeed, in pre-industrial society, 44% of elderly couples lived alone. Even with the death of a partner, evidence is available to suggest that widows or (more rarely) widowers were, as now, more in favour of an independent household ['intimacy at a distance' to use the revealing phrase of Rosenmayr and Kockeis (1963)]. Thomas (1976) suggests that, in the seventeenth century, conventional wisdom followed that of Ecclesiasticus: 'As long as thou livest and has breath in thee, give not thyself over to any. For better it is that thy children should seek to thee, than that thou shouldest stand to their courtesy' (1976:239). Thomas cites the view of the elderly Daniel Rogers in 1642, describing the difficult position of parents in their children's house:

> for a time the old people might justify their keep by acting as servants and household drudges. But 'when all strength and ability is gone, then they are no longer set by, but . . . despised, counted as burdens'. 'Be wise, you parents', he warned, 'yield not yourselves captives and prisoners to your children; no prison can be more irksome to a parent than a son or daughter's house.' (1976:239)

The likelihood of older people entering the homes of offspring was limited for reasons other than custom or sentiment. Thus, at least one in three of those entering old age would have no surviving children with whom they might have lived (Thomson 1986). For those with children still alive, migration (particularly for those in rural areas) would further reduce the opportunities for co-residence.

As for family care itself, it must also be acknowledged that there existed no 'binding cultural norm' (Robin 1984; Hanawalt 1986) that care would be received. Indeed, the very existence of, for instance, elaborate retirement contracts, whereby retirees exchanged their land and buildings in return for specific services and support, indicates the tensions between generations; the contract itself often leaving very little to chance in respect of the provision of food, clothing and shelter (Hanawalt 1986).

Care, in other words, was no more or less complex as a social relationship in medieval England than it is today. To be sure, it involved different dynamics, resources and, perhaps, sentiments, but its negotiated nature was an important aspect. Older people did not invariably reside in the houses of their children and where they did, it was through the force of specific events (loss of a partner and/or loss of their own home), rather than through deliberate choice. As Laslett remarks:

> The conclusion might be that then, as now, a place of your own, with help in the house, with access to your children, within reach of support might have been what the elderly and aged most wanted for themselves in the pre-industrial world. (1977:213)

Expectation and experiences of life

A final confusion concerns the experience and texture of everyday life – particularly for the very young and very old. The myth of the extended family invites us to see childhood and old age as comfortable and secure, supported by the existence of numerous kin. But death stalked the pre-industrial village and people lived out their lives in circumstances which were fraught with painful events. Stone observes that 'death was a normal occurrence in persons of all ages, and was not something that happened mainly to the old' (1982:54): childhood was particularly risky, with between a quarter and a third of all children of English peers and peasants dying before they reached the age of 15 (Stone 1982). Plague epidemics could lead to enormous loss of life: the Norwich plague of 1579, for example, decimated the parishes by a third (Wrigley 1969). Epidemics could kill off all the older people within a community in a very short period as in one Oxfordshire village in 1643 where, after one epidemic, 'there scarce remained alive any for upholding the customs and privileges of the parish' (cited in Thomas 1976:234).

Children suffered very high mortality from infection and malnutrition and just how tenuous the hold on life could be is summed up by McManners in his account of attitudes towards death in eighteenth-century France:

> Of every 1,000 infants, only 200 would go on to the age of fifty, and only 100 to the age of seventy. A man who had beaten the odds and reached his half-century would, we may imagine, have seen both his parents die, have buried half his children and, like as not, his wife as well, together with numerous uncles, aunts, cousins, nephews, nieces, and friends. If he got to seventy, he would have no relations and friends of his own generation left to share his memories. If this is a description of the average, what can we say of the unfortunates whose sombre ill luck weights down the figures to this mean? (1985:5)

Faced with this environment, people often expressed a 'disinterest [or] disbelief in ageing' (Stearns 1977:22). If, none the less, they grew old it was likely to be a difficult and often unpleasant experience. Fischer comments that, 'to be old in early America was to be wracked by illness. It was to live in physical misery, with pain as a constant companion' (1977:67). In seventeenth-century England, old age was viewed as 'itself a disease', 'a perpetual sickness', 'the dreg's of a man's life' (cited in Thomas 1976:244).

Finally, lest it be thought that there were very few elderly people around to experience such indignities, there is research evidence which suggests otherwise. Hanawalt (1986) cites the analysis of bones from medieval English burials which indicate that 10% of the people were over 50. She also notes that late-sixteenth and seventeenth-century parish registers suggest that between 8 and 16% of the population were 60 years of age or more.

With this last point in mind we now turn to issues of economics and survival: how have resources been distributed to older people, in both pre-industrial and industrial society?

The economics of old age

Central to any history of old age must be the question of how communities give material support to elderly people. In this area we again find a powerful consensus operating within popular culture. The argument is a familiar one: history, it is argued, has been the onward march toward citizenship, culminating in the mid-twentieth-century foundation of the welfare state. In our time, if elderly people have 'lost' their families, they have at least found a benevolent state to support them. We have moved, in this account, from welfare provided by the family to collectivist provision from state and society as a whole (Marshall 1965; Robson 1976).

The perspective contains two distinct elements, one that the state has become more supportive, the other that the family has become less so. Both these suppositions are subject to challenge. In one sense, it is possible to find an important continuity in the economic position of elderly people over the past 400 years. At different times, and invariably when communities face hardship (through famine, war or mass unemployment), the legitimacy of help to older people has been questioned. Such support has always been conditional on a plentiful supply of food, adequate housing or secure work (Phillipson 1982). Where communities lack one or more of these elements, groups such as older people can be pushed to the margin with their relief being perceived as a 'burden on the community' and regarded as a 'low priority' (Thomas 1976).

Sometimes this tension has been expressed through relationships between elderly and younger kin. The study by Hanawalt of peasant families in medieval England found:

> A persistent tension existed between the possessors of land, goods and power and their heirs. Once the old person retired and passed on these accoutrements of adult life, he or she could be left at the mercy of the younger generation. From the younger generation's viewpoint, the aged pose problems. They no longer worked equivalent to the amount they consumed; they stood in the way of the young adult's advancement; their appearance offended the aesthetics of their juniors. A young man might have to wait until his father died or retired before he could marry and set up his own household. If old men married younger women, then they were taking potential wives of young men in the community. A young man might marry an older widow to get her rights in dower and thereby deprive a village girl of a desirable marriage partner. The young, therefore, had ample reason for not regarding old people as benign, and their prudent elders sought legal safeguards for retirement rather than relying on cultural precepts about honouring father and mother and respecting the aged. (1986:228)

Thomas, writing about the position of elderly people in the seventeenth century, argues that the voluntary nature of retirement in this period should not be taken as a sign of respect of older people or evidence of a desire to give them freedom of choice:

> On the contrary, what it suggests is an underlying hostility towards those who opted out of the economic process and a reluctance to devote much of society's limited resources to their maintenance. It shows the weakness of old age not its strength. (1976:237)

Such hostility has surfaced on numerous occasions in the twentieth century, particularly in periods of high unemployment or when concern has been expressed about a rise in the proportion of people of pensionable age (see, e.g., Rowntree 1947; Royal Commission on Population 1949).

The ambivalence about giving help to older people can be seen in other ways. For example, historians such as Thomson (1984) suggest that in the 1840s and 1850s around two-thirds of women aged 70 or more were in regular receipt of a Poor Law pension. Further, they have challenged our ideas about the generosity of provision today in comparison to the past. Here, a crucial distinction is made between absolute and relative incomes. In terms of the former, pensions today can indeed provide a more prosperous standard of living. However, in a relative sense, payments in the last part of the twentieth century are inferior to both the mid-nineteenth century and to Edwardian times. Drawing on a range of historical and contemporary social surveys, Thomson argues:

> Elderly dependants from the 1830s to the 1870s received from their communities cash allowances with value equivalent to two-thirds or more of the incomes of non-aged working-class adults. It has been accepted in the present century [by contrast] that the elderly [in Britain] should be given little more than one-third of the resources of other adults. (1984:453)

Finally, any analysis of the economics of old age must conclude with the recognition that it is older women who have suffered most from the ambivalence towards older people (Walker 1987). Widowhood (though not all widows were elderly) could often lead 'to the most grinding of poverty' (Anderson 1974:144) although wealthier widows (particularly of a younger age) might re-enter social life through marriage. Alternatively, Thomas (1976) suggests that middle-class widows often gained a new independence when they took over their husband's businesses and ran them in their own name (though, in a patriarchal society they could and still can expect opposition to their ambitions).

Social and economic changes in the sixteenth and seventeenth centuries were to increase the problems faced by women. In his study *Religion and the Decline of Magic*, Thomas argues that the decay of the manorial system undermined many traditional patterns of support:

> Population pressure eroded many of the old customary tenancies, and led to the taking in of the commons and the rise of competitive rents. These changes were disadvantageous to the widow. So were the enclosures and engrossing which broke up many of the old cooperative village communities. This deterioration in the position of the dependent and elderly helps to explain why witches were primarily women, and probably old ones, many of them widowed, 'They are usually such as are destitute of friends, bowed down with years, laden with infirmities', said a contemporary. Their names appear among the witchcraft indictments, just as they do among the recipients of parochial relief. For they were the persons most dependent upon neighbourly support. (1978:671)

The extent of witchcraft accusations against older women is revealing of attitudes in early modern England. In addition to the general reasons Thomas outlines, older women were also targeted because their eccentric behaviour might be taken as a 'sign' of witchcraft and because prejudice and bad-feeling could arise from the mere sight of elderly women. For example, their bodies might be marked by growths and blemishes which could indicate witches' magic. Nor should it be supposed that all such accusations were groundless: older women were among the least powerful individuals in the community and sorcery could provide them with a useful means of protection (McFarlane 1970; Held 1987; Levack 1987).

The fate of some older women must remain completely lost. Despised by traditional culture, the death of a husband could mean abandonment by the village, for widowed women might be driven away by their neighbours who feared an increase in the poor rates. Where children lived nearby, however, a happier prospect might be in store. With the rise of the factory-system, grandmothers could be a valuable help in taking care of the youngest children (Anderson 1974), a role they have maintained to the present day. Nor must we forget important cultural variations. Thus, Mediterranean wives, even if oppressed and abused by their husbands, might at least look forward to an old age when they were 'venerated and respected by male children' (Ladurie 1980). But what leaves a more lasting impression is the experience of the majority: 'the old women' or 'old crones' of popular culture, those with neither status nor independent means in their community. In Edwardian Britain, nearly one in ten elderly women could expect to end their days in the workhouse; for those in their 80s, around one in three would be paupers. The crisis of old age was thus endured principally by women, a fact which continues to be the case in the present-day (Walker 1987).

Historical perspectives on retirement

Retirement is an essential part of the history of old age and this is so for at least three reasons. It has been used as a marker for the onset of old age – 60 or 65 being a common starting-point – and it has had a decisive influence on the financial position of older people; loss of work invariably being accompanied by a drastic reduction in income (Walker 1981). In addition, as Graebner (1980) and Phillipson (1982) suggest, retirement has played an important role in periods of mass unemployment. The idea of older workers being surplus to labour requirements has been crucial to the development of pensions both in Britain (the 1925 pensions legislation) and America (the Social Security Act of 1935). Similarly, the growth of unemployment in the 1970s and 1980s stimulated early retirement policies in a number of European countries (Laczko and Walker 1985).

Retirement on a mass scale is, of course, characteristic of the mid- to late twentieth century, although the practice of retirement has always been part of economic and social custom: it may be seen as a functional necessity in economies where work is in short or fluctuating supply (Thomson 1986). On the other hand, for the more prosperous, such as middle-class businessmen, there has been a desire to leave work once the raising of a family has been completed (Davidoff and Hall 1987).

Modern retirement policy is a product of the last quarter of the nineteenth century as large private companies and branches of the civil service adopted pension policies. Subsequently, at key periods in the twentieth century (usually in periods of economic slump or through the impetus of war), pension coverage has been extended to cover virtually all sections of the population (Hannah 1986).

Behind this development in social policy can be traced some important industrial, economic and political influences. Thus, as a number of studies have shown, retirement and the spread of pensions were stimulated by demands for greater efficiency and productivity in the workforce (Phillipson 1982; Thane 1978). Fischer (1977) suggests that the growth of the factory system accelerated the process of retirement, with the development of assembly-line production hastening the displacement of older workers. However, as Quadango (1982) and others note, the issue is not simply one of technological change creating the right climate for the emergence of retirement. For one thing, older people probably entered the new industries at a slower rate than younger workers. Thus technology may have been less important than the fact that older people were clustered in industries subject to historical decline. For another, retirement has to be seen in more global terms. According to Graebner (1980), retirement provided for industrial capitalism a means of challenging security of tenure or jobs for life. It was a reaction against the persistence of personal modes of behaviour [*gemeinschaft* vs *gesellschaft* in the classic terms of Tonnies (1955)], providing a mechanism for discharging loyal workers. As a bonus, it also assisted the stabilization of corporate hierarchies, creating a permanent flow of employees and guaranteeing promotion through the ranks.

An additional perspective introduced by historians concerns the differential impact of retirement on working-class and middle-class life. Stearns (1977), for instance, argues that retirement created considerable difficulties for working-class people. On the one hand, it was a policy imposed on workers from without (albeit with the support of trade unions and labour organizations); on the other, workers themselves often expressed a desire to leave what was often arduous physical employment (with long hours of overtime). The unskilled and semi-skilled understood, better than anybody, that to grow old in manual labour was a fate to be avoided. But what was the alternative? In Britain at the turn of the century, 5% of workers had an occupational pension. The introduction of the 1908 Pensions Act was scarcely a help. Hannah comments:

> As a measure to facilitate a secure retirement, the [Act] was very limited, given that the majority of adults could not expect to live to 70 and that the money was below subsistence level for those living in urban areas. (1986 : 16)

Inadequate (or non-existent pensions) invariably forced people to continue in low-paid work on the fringes of the labour market (Stearns 1977; M. L. Johnson 1986). Such workers had been noted by Booth in his London survey (1892–7): they increasingly attracted comment in reports on the problem of unemployment (Chapman and Hallsworth 1909; Rowntree and Lasker 1911).

In policy terms, until at least the economic slump of the 1920s and 1930s, the general view was that most people wanted to stay in some kind of occupation – until decline or exhaustion overtook them. This aspect emerges clearly in the parliamentary debate on the Old Age Pensions Bill in 1908. Lloyd George, answering suggestions that the age limit should be 65 instead of 70, argued:

> The expenditure would be too great to begin with and in my own judgement I do not think that is the best way of dealing with the period between 65 and 70. I am not sure that the German method is not better here as it deals with infirmity rather than with age. That is the test under 70. I can well understand a man of 70 saying, 'I am willing to retire, I have earned my pension'. There are many men of 65, 66 and 67 who are much more effective and vigorous and capable of doing good work than many men of 57. I think when we come to deal, as I hope we will in the near future, with the problem of infirmity, that will be the time to consider the question of the broken down old man of 67 and 68 who is left to charity. (House of Commons 1908 : 575)

In the period when Lloyd George was speaking, 606 out of every 1000 men over 65 were still working, so his argument had a strong foundation in the existing pattern of employment; but the use of the term 'broken down old men' is revealing. True, its accuracy for elderly men, after a lifetime of labour in a harsh industrial and social environment and with varying standards of nutrition, cannot be underestimated. However, it is significant that the problem is put just in terms of men, ignoring the fact that it is women who live longest and who are most likely to experience old age directly. Moreover, the choice of phrase is itself important, reflecting as it does a historical tradition of identifying the retired working-class elderly as useless, worn-out and unemployable – to be grouped with the infirm and feeble-minded as a category in social policy (Phillipson 1982). The possibility or the potential of old age being experienced some other way is hardly countenanced, for if elderly people are not ready to be included among the infirm and the feeble-minded, then it is work which is put forward as the obvious alternative. Seemingly, there is nothing in between.

The limits to state involvement in supporting elderly people were brought out graphically in the second reading of the Conservative's Contributory Pension Bill in 1925. The Bill provided for a pension of 10s 0d per week which the Minister (Neville Chamberlain) moving the Bill admitted was, 'obviously insufficient by itself to provide a grown man or woman with the necessities for life'. Two reasons were given for this: the first was financial, that a larger pension would inflict an excessive burden both on industry and the state; the second was that by fixing the pension at such a level this would encourage the virtue of thrift:

We believe that there are many people who today feel that it is perfectly hopeless for them to try and provide completely for their needs in old age, but that when they see this scheme they will feel they have a foundation upon which it is worth their while to try and build something more. In that way we shall be encouraging those virtues of thrift which have done so much for the country in the past. (House of Commons 1924:79)

In general, we can see that retirement has been viewed with great ambivalence throughout the twentieth century. In the 1950s, with 'panics' about an ageing population, shortage of labour and the priority of post-war reconstruction, pressure was placed on people to delay leaving work. Older workers were eulogized for their 'steadiness' and 'reliability', in contrast to the 1930s when politicians were praising older people's ability to withstand 'idleness' and their willingness to be 'pensioned-off'. By the 1980s, retirement was once again in vogue as a means of redistributing jobs to the young (for example, through policies such as the job-release scheme) and was the target of a powerful leisure and consumer industry (Dex and Phillipson 1986a).

Within this history of retirement, however, we find very little being expressed by retirees themselves – with the exception perhaps of some members of the middle and upper classes. In part this is because, as Stearns (1977) suggests, retirement has been imposed on working-class people from the outside. Writing of the inter-war period in France, Stearns argues:

Retirement increased, rapidly becoming a common phenomenon for the first time in the history of the class. But with this, and admitting an immense variety of individual reactions, we return to the potential tragedies prepared by working-class culture (and expressed widely in the labour movement). First, of course, inadequate material preparation, so that retirement was a time of immense physical hardship, quite apart from deterioration of health. But second, the lack of any active concept of what retirement should be: it represented stopping something, work, but did it represent starting or continuing anything of interest? Without pretending to fathom the fate of retirees as a whole, for even in old age, and perhaps particularly then, individual variations are immense, we can suggest that a rapidly changing behaviour pattern found no correspondence in public policy or collective activities. (1977:65)

However, working-class retirees were not left entirely to their own fate. In the inter-war period, and to a much greater extent in the 1950s and 1960s, an army of professional workers emerged to interpret and service the needs of an ageing population. Their activities provide a final strand to the history of old age and it is to a consideration of them that we now turn.

Conclusion: old age and the professions

So far we have argued that old age can be viewed as a social construction formed out of demographic, economic and work processes. However, old age has been given a distinctive shape by the ideas and beliefs of, first, older people themselves (and those about to reach old age) and, secondly, of those who work on their behalf – doctors, social workers, health visitors, district nurses and many others. The views of older people have been explored through the work of oral historians and can also be gleaned from the writings and autobiographies of working people (Burnett *et al.* 1986). Arguably, however, and especially for working-class people, beliefs about ageing have been controlled and manipulated in the welfarization process of those working on their behalf: those who are part of what Estes (1979) describes as the 'Ageing Enterprise'.

Of central importance (if only because they took the first step in conceptualizing old age) has been the medical profession, although even here the intervention of doctors has been relatively recent. As late as the nineteenth century, few elderly people would have regular contact with a doctor, those who were very rich or very ill being the main exceptions (Stearns 1977). For the physician, there were few guidelines regarding the care of elderly patients. Most doctors prescribed – if they prescribed at all – the same as they would for younger people. In general, though, there was much pessimism about the value of medical intervention. According to the American historian Carol Haber:

> The weakness of the old was not considered a state amenable to cure. Instead, physicians believed that this was the essential irremediable quality of growing old. (1983 : 50)

Haber argues that nineteenth- and early twentieth-century physicians medicalized ageing by defining it as a pathological process. The word 'senile', to take one example, was transformed during the nineteenth century from a general term indicating 'the state of being old' to a medical term suggesting the inevitable deterioration accompanying old age. Emerging from this model was a professional ideology which saw old age as necessitating specific forms of surveillance and therapeutic intervention (Armstrong 1983).

The term 'geriatrics' was coined in 1909 by Nascher, an American physician. In the sphere of gerontological research important developments took place in the 1920s and 1930s, with the establishment of journals, the founding of gerontological institutes, and an increasing variety of scientific books and monographs. In Britain, the late 1940s saw the emergence of geriatric medicine, along with a number of surveys discussing the health implications of an ageing population (Blaikie and Macnicol 1986; Burns and Phillipson 1986). There was also an extensive discussion in medical and related journals on a range of issues associated with retirement and old age.

By the 1950s, then, a body of knowledge was available to respond to the needs of an ageing population. Crucially, however, much of this knowledge was medically-inspired and orientated. In some respects this was understandable given the limited help available for chronically sick elderly people (highlighted by the Emergency Medical Service during the Second World War). But the influence of the medical perspective was adopted by other professions in the post-war period as they struggled to find an effective role with older people. Thus, for example, neither social work nor health visiting have built an independent knowledge base for work with this client group. Both their training (Phillipson and Strang 1986) and their practice (Day 1981; Marshall 1983; Bowl 1986) followed a medicalized approach to ageing which gave secondary consideration to economic and social issues.

The professions have also played an important role in reinforcing ideas within popular culture about the way in which older people are 'abandoned' by their families. Indeed, paid staff often see their own involvement as proof of the way families are rejecting elderly kin, relying instead upon the services of the welfare state.

The above discussion of demographic and economic factors and retirement has illustrated the value of a historical perspective. We see, first of all, that research does not provide support for notions that we care less now than in the past. The capacity and willingness of individuals and communities to provide help is a complex phenomenon, one which is perceived very differently in times of hardship as opposed to prosperity. Moreover, the historical record shows that there are no convenient models which can guide our current activities. On the contrary, the conclusion to be drawn from demographic research is that the position of older people has as many differences as similarities in comparison with the past (Laslett 1977). In practical terms, therefore, we are faced with the need to innovate rather than to attempt to repeat previous patterns of care and support.

3

Social theory and old age

Introduction

This chapter reviews how social theory has been applied to the field of old age and analyses the main ways in which sociologists have tried to explain and theorize about older people's place in the social structure and considers the implications of the various theories for policy and practice.

An initial observation must be that in the field of social gerontology at least social theory has had a somewhat chequered history. Marion Crawford (1971) has noted the tendency to treat ageing largely in terms of social welfare policies, a perspective which, focusing as it does on the consequences of social arrangements and ad hoc responses to discovered 'needs', tends to discourage systematic theorizing. Moreover, as Malcolm Johnson (1982) points out, even those theories which have been produced have been insulated from mainstream sociological, political and psychological theory. In general, we can say that gerontologists have been happier to describe the activities and lifestyles of older people, rather than consider causal linkages between ageing and the social, political and economic structure (Estes 1979).

Our view is that such characteristics have created many problems and dilemmas for researchers, the failure to apply theory allowing a number of important issues to be ignored. As Craib argues, theorizing must be seen to have a serious intent and should not, therefore, be seen as marginal to research on old age. He observes:

> The problems that force people to theory do not solely belong to sociological research; they are problems we all face in our every day lives, problems of making sense of what happens to us and the people around us, the problems involved in making moral and political choices. (1984:3)

A characteristic feature of social gerontology, however, has been that theory has been brought in 'through the back door'. Thus research has invariably made certain decisions about the difficulties facing older people; it has also been *normative* in character, with implicit or explicit judgements being made about the lives of older people. The danger is not that these assumptions exist, but that they have rarely been examined systematically in research (or, indeed, put to any kind of test).

Some exceptions to this can be found. Amongst British research, for example, the work on institutional and family life by Townsend (1957, 1962) was firmly rooted in a wider, sociological and social anthropological discourse. This was also the case with Tunstall's (1966) study of loneliness in old age. Crawford's (1971) study of retirement is one of the few British attempts to test a particular theory (the disengagement hypothesis), though Fennell (1966) tested disengagement against activity theory on a Swedish sample. More recently, Malcolm Johnson's team used a biographical or life-history approach in their attempt to understand consumer perceptions about meals on wheels (Johnson *et al.* 1980; see also di Gregorio 1986a, b).

Much more characteristic of British research is the lack of attention to theory of any kind. The descriptive (and prescriptive) focus of research is brought out most obviously in studies such as *Retiring to the Seaside* (Karn 1977), *Beyond Three-Score Years and Ten* (Abrams 1978b, 1980), Booth's *Home Truths* (1985) and Wenger's *The Supportive Network* (1984). Influential though these studies have been, they largely ignore theoretical issues about their subject matter; or, to be more accurate, they tend to assume a theoretical position, without testing it to make it clear to the reader.

This failing has been a feature of the social gerontological tradition. It is equally characteristic of American research, although the sheer volume of work produced in the United States makes it easier to cite examples of studies where theory is taken seriously (see, especially, the work of Rosow 1967; Estes 1979; Riley *et al.* 1972, and forthcoming).

The failure to make theory explicit is only one side of the problem; another difficulty has been the dominance of a particular kind of theorizing about the relationship between older people and the social structure. As we observed in Chapter 2, theory has contributed to the mood of cultural pessimism about the role and status of older people. The elderly are seen as cut-off from their family and trapped in a 'roleless role' (Burgess 1960), perceiving society as 'distant, alien and oppressive' (Dowd 1980).

Another feature of sociological theorizing has been its focus on *individual adjustment* to old age. Social arrangements are typically viewed as non-problematic. This is a theme which we touched on in Chapter 1 and return to particularly in Chapters 6 and 7 where the supposedly 'natural' disadvantages suffered by elderly women in general and elderly black people in particular are shown to be socially constructed. As Estes remarks: '[the] focus [is] on what people do rather than the social conditions and policies that cause them to act as they do' (1979:11). This tendency must be attributed as much to the dominance of the functionalist perspective in social gerontology, examined below, as to its welfarist proclivities discussed in Chapter 1. In contrast, the challenge to functionalism from the 1960s onwards – for instance with the development of the political economy perspective – made a concern with structural issues more evident.

In our review of social gerontological theory, we shall examine some of the assumptions made within existing theories. Our survey must necessarily be selective but we shall try to cover the main themes that have influenced research since the 1940s. At the end of the chapter we shall explore some policy issues arising from the various theories that have been described.

The 'problem' of old age: functionalist perspectives

The early 1950s was a crucial period for research in social gerontology. In this period many social scientists (mostly American) contributed monographs and scholarly articles on the implications of an ageing population and we refer below to some of the key works by, for example, Burgess, Cavan, Havighurst and Neugarten. Influential figures from mainstream sociology such as Parsons were also prominent in some of the debates.

For American (and British) commentators old age was seen as representing a major social problem. The causal factors were attributed to the impact of compulsory retirement, the rise of the nuclear family, the impact of industrialization and urbanization and increased rates of social and geographical mobility. These trends were interpreted within the dominant functionalist perspective. In consequence, old age was essentially viewed as a problem of adult socialization: how could older people be re-integrated within a social order which was undergoing rapid change? As indicated earlier, the problem was viewed largely in terms of individual adjustment. One such example is the influential study by Pollak, *Social Adjustment in Old Age*, as illustrated in this discussion on the role changes accompanying retirement:

> The individual who is able to make these changes quickly and effectively adjusts well to his problem of aging. The individual who cannot do so becomes the socially ineffective and unhappy old person whose problems challenge the research worker to determine their causes and their solution. (1948 : 40)

Role theory

The functionalist perspective in gerontology had two main variants: (i) role and activity theory and (ii) the disengagement hypothesis which will be discussed in the next sub-section. In respect of the former, functionalism gave particular emphasis to the impact of social roles in determining individual behaviour. In this context, the loss of the work role for men was seen to create a major crisis of identity. Parsons describes the problem in the following way:

> In view of the very great significance of occupational status and its psychological correlates, retirement leaves the older man in a peculiarly functionless situation, cut off from participation in the most important interests and activities of the society. . . . Retirement not only cuts the ties to the job itself but also greatly loosens those to the community of residence. It may be surmised that this structural isolation from kinship,

occupational and community ties is the fundamental basis of the recent political agitation for help to the old. It is suggested that it is far less the financial hardship of the position of elderly people than their 'social isolation' which makes old age a 'problem'. (1942 : 616)

Finding new roles was seen to be fraught with problems. Michelon, for example, spoke of:

the rare individual who can look ahead to the golden years, make the needed changes in values, and substitute new vital activities for the meaning of work. (1954: 371)

Role theorists saw loss of work as producing demoralization and reduced self-esteem – especially as there were no substitutes with the same cultural value in American society (for statements supporting this view see Cavan *et al.* 1949; Miller 1965; Blau 1973). This view was combined with a sense of pessimism about people's ability actually to use leisure, as is explicit, for example, in Loether's suggestion that: 'One of the serious problems facing our society is the problem of teaching the average working man how to use his leisure' (1967 : 76). It also underlay Zena Blau's view that:

Ordinary men and women have relied on cultural scripts throughout their earlier lives, and when these no longer exist they often lack resources and the experience to improvise new ones. Instead, many older people just cling to life as they wait to be relieved of a lonely and useless existence. (1973 : 177)

The counterpart to this concern with the absence of roles for the elderly, was a theoretical argument that psychological and social well-being was enhanced through involvement in new social roles and activities. Through the work of researchers such as Cavan *et al.* (1949) and Havighurst and Albrecht (1953), activity theory emerged as an attempt to integrate accumulated knowledge and to explain empirically-based findings (Bell 1976). Havighurst, for instance, argued:

Research has established the fact that activity in a wide variety of social roles is positively related to happiness and good social adjustment in old age and also that a high degree of activity in a given social role is positively related to happiness and good social adjustment. (1954 : 309)

He linked this view with the notion of 'role flexibility':

From about 50–70 the individual is deprived of several roles. At the same time he grows discontented unless he is able to compensate for this by increasing activity in other roles or by the developing of new ones; that is, by role flexibility. The latter defined as the capacity of 'personal quality' to change roles easily and increase or reduce activity. (1954 : 309)

One of the results of this approach was a considerable amount of data produced by researchers on the activities pursued by older people. Much of this data was purely descriptive, with often only tenuous linkages to any explanatory theory or set of hypotheses. For example, Havighurst, in a major American textbook, contributed a lengthy chapter on the various roles played by the elderly in America and seven European countries. On Switzerland he noted:

It might seem that older people in Switzerland lead a dreary life compared with those in England or Sweden, for example. But this is probably not true of those in the villages and country, where they retain the functions of the elderly in an agricultural society. In the cities their life probably is somewhat dreary. (1960:316)

On the elderly in Britain he reported that:

While the British rather expect a man to retire from his work at about 65, there is no clearly defined role for the older person as a user of leisure time. The upper-class person has been more or less leisured all his adult life and is expected to go on fairly much as in the past. The working class man is expected to be tired and to be happy with little or nothing to do. For the middle-class man in the expectations are even less clear. Women of the working class or the middle class are expected to go on keeping house much as usual. (1960:333)

At the same time, some research in this period did go beyond these rather unsatisfactory generalizations. A notable example was Friedmann and Havighurst's (1954) *The Meaning of Work and Retirement*. This research was influential in initiating a debate (which is still being developed) on the likely relationship between attitudes toward retirement, and attachments to, and perceptions about work. Among the hypotheses examined in the study were:

work has recognised meanings in addition to that of earning a living;

those who regard work as primarily a way of earning a living will prefer to retire at age 65 (or normal retirement age);

those who stress values of work other than that of earning a living will prefer to continue working past 65. (1954:7)

The results suggested that those most reluctant to retire were often the people who gained the most satisfaction from work; conversely, those who looked upon their employment merely as a means of financial support tended to look forward to retirement. But there were some important exceptions to these findings. For example, a majority of the skilled craftsmen who were studied and who stressed that work had a value other than that of simply learning a living indicated that they welcomed retirement. The authors note here:

We cannot categorically assume that, because a man's life may have become intimately bound up with the performance of his job, retirement may not hold a set of appeals for him which is capable of superseding or even replacing the satisfaction he got from his job. Instead we have to contrast the nature of the satisfactions obtained from work with the type of substitutes present in retirement. (1954:185)

In the long-term, this research was to lead to a more balanced assessment of retirement, with a recognition that occupational and other social variables will determine the individual's attitudes to leaving work (see chapter 5). Activity theory was also to be modified, with research indicating that rather than focus on activity *per se*, we should consider the *type* of relationships and activities which are important to older people (Maddox 1970; Lemmon *et al*. 1976). In the short-term, however, gerontological theory was affected by a different kind of discussion, with the disengagement hypothesis raising fundamental questions about the nature of older people's involvement in society.

Disengagement theory

Disengagement theory was developed in the late 1950s by a group of social gerontologists associated with the Committee on Human Development at the University of Chicago. The group included Havighurst, Neugarten, Cumming and Henry. The research group considered that to understand old age, older people had to be studied within their own environments as opposed to institutions such as hospitals and nursing homes. Furthermore, understanding old age meant studying people at different time periods in order to discover and evaluate the changes taking place within the individual as he or she became older. The environment selected was Kansas City, Missouri, a large metropolitan centre. Here, a panel of healthy persons aged 50 and over were chosen as subjects and interviewed over a number of years. The theory of disengagement was derived subsequently from analyses of these interviews.

The central postulate of the theory has been summarized by Cumming and Henry as follows:

> Aging is an inevitable mutual withdrawal or disengagement resulting in decreased interaction between the aging person and others in the social system he belongs to. The process may be initiated by the individual or by others in the situation. The aged person may withdraw more markedly from some classes of people while remaining relatively close to others. His withdrawal may be accompanied from the outset by an increased preoccupation with himself; certain institutions in society may make the withdrawal easy for him. When the aging process is complete the equilibrium which existed in middle life between the individual and his society has given way to a new equilibrium characterized by a greater distance and an altered type of relationship. (1961 : 14)

A key assumption made in the theory is that 'ego energy' declines with age and that as the ageing process develops, individuals become increasingly self-preoccupied and less and less responsive to normative controls. The theory is predominantly a psychological one, though references to social components locate it within functionalism in theory and conservatism in political ideology. The sociological premise, taken as self-evident, is that, since death occurs unpredictably and would be socially disruptive if people 'died in harness', there is a functional necessity to expel from work roles any older person with a statistically higher risk of death.

This illustrates a common criticism of functionalist theories, that they simply provide a convenient rationalization for unequal power relationships, presenting as 'natural and inevitable' something which is merely expedient. The theory may be on stronger ground when discussing changes occurring within the individual. According to the theory, either the individual or society may initiate the process of disengagement. When done by the individual it is the result of ego changes; when done by society it is the result of organizational imperatives.

As in the case of role theory, the central task for men is considered to be their work. Retirement – or the giving up of work – means that a man's central life-task is finished and it is from this point that disengagement begins. The process is made easier for the individual by the setting of fixed retirement ages and pension schemes, developments which undercut individual dilemmas about when to disengage. Retirement is seen, in fact, as a form of permission for men to disengage from demanding social roles; for women, widowhood is considered to be the formal marker of disengagement.

In addition, it is also argued that disengagement or withdrawal from social relationships will lead to the individual maintaining a higher morale in old age – higher, that is, than if he or she attempted to keep involved in a range of social affairs and activities. Thus, disengagement is seen as both a natural and desirable outcome, one which also produces a stronger sense of psychological well-being. Finally, this feature of ageing is suggested to be a universal phenomenon, associated with ageing in all cultures.

From its inception, disengagement theory attracted a highly critical response, both from gerontologists and those involved in working with older people. The concept itself was seen as legitimating a form of social redundancy among the old, a product of structural changes in the economy and the labour market. This view was expressed by Zena Blau, when she remarked that:

> The disengagement theory deserves to be publicly attacked, because it can so easily be used as a rationale by the non-old, who constitute the 'normals' in society, to avoid confronting and dealing with the issue of old people's marginality and rolelessness in American society. (1973:152)

Disengagement theory was further attacked because it challenged a traditional view about the importance of maintaining a high level of activity and interaction in old age. Townsend, for example, argued that there was little evidence of old people taking the initiative to 'disengage' or withdraw and a good deal to suggest that they are distressed by the loss of roles and relationships. He went on to suggest that:

> Insufficient attention has . . . been given to forms of compensation, replacement and substitution when there are losses of roles and of relationships in old age. Widowed people remarry or rejoin their married children, or develop more intensive relationships with one or more of their children. They may see more of their neighbours. *Extensive* social interaction may be gradually replaced by *intensive* local interaction, involving many fewer people. (1973:230)

The variety of responses to ageing and retirement was also a point made by Shanas in an article questioning the identification made by Cumming and Henry between retirement and disengagement. Some men, she argues, want to re-engage in new activities and interests after retirement, others simply want to enjoy the sense of freedom and relaxation which retirement brings. Shanas comments:

> The evidence that retired people from various countries say that they miss nothing about their work or that they miss primarily the income, the diverse ways in which retirement is accepted in various countries and by different individuals, the fact that industrial workers in many countries are asking for earlier retirement ages, should serve to alert us that there is not necessarily a decrease in social activity or engagement with retirement. (1971 : 114)

Atchley (1972), while conceding that disengagement did indeed take place, saw it as a product of the opportunities for continued engagement in the social world. Thus, he suggested that much voluntary disengagement has resulted from the fact that people saw disengagement as inevitable because of the rules of the institutions they participate in: 'That is, it is really the result of societal disengagement.' This view was subsequently to receive some support via the work of Crawford (1972) in Britain and Hochschild in America, who argued:

> It is not ageing per se which determines disengagement, but a combination of factors associated with ageing (e.g. poor health, widowhood) and other factors associated with the nature of society and one's location in it which together influence engagement or disengagement. (1975 : 563)

Most of the above writers, while disputing the position which takes disengagement as a natural correlate of ageing and retirement, still admitted its reality as a consequence of given physical and social conditions. Other writers, however, in their speed to bury the theory, have often tended to dispute the reality of disengagement under *any* conditions. Reichard *et al.* (1962) suggested that there was little evidence from their sample of ageing or retirement leading to any extensive decline in social or leisure activities; and Blau, while conceding that disengagement might be found among some elderly people, argued that this was the exception rather than the rule. She went on to attack strongly the idea that disengagement was a healthy or desirable response to ageing:

> Empirical evidence shows that *as a rule* just exactly the opposite is the case. Numerous studies in a variety of communities and in institutions for old people report that activity, whether in the form of a single, intimate relationship or more extensive social relationships of a less intimate character, are the most stable and consistent correlates of high morale in old age. (1973 : 151)

As well as criticisms on substantive issues there have also been questions about the logic of the theory. Hochschild (1975) has attacked the theory on three grounds. She argues that it is so constructed as to make it unfalsifiable, that the major variables are composed of sub-parts which do not vary in a unitary way and that the theory ignores the meanings which actors attach to experiences in old age.

All the above criticisms cast some doubt on the extent to which disengagement can be regarded as a unitary and universal phenomenon. Yet, caution is necessary before exercising a blanket condemnation of the theory. Certainly, the universality of withdrawal either within or across cultures must be rejected (for the relevant critiques see Rose 1964; Crawford 1971), as must the view that withdrawal is an intrinsic feature of the ageing process (as opposed to it being just one of a number of styles of ageing). While acknowledging these points, however, important questions remain still to be answered. Thus, the issues raised by Atchley (1972) regarding the likely conditions precipitating disengagement clearly need to be developed further; and the view should also be noted of researchers such as Loether (1967), who suggest that rather than see social activity and disengagement as opposites, the two may in fact complement each other. Once again, there may be a number of different types of adaptation to the ageing process.

On balance, then, while many elements of the theory must be discarded, subsequent research has suggested it has some heuristic value in understanding some aspects of growing old for some people. However, as functionalist perspectives such as role and disengagement theory came under increasing attack from the 1960s onwards, gerontologists became increasingly concerned with the meaning of old age and its biographical and sociological context. It is to an analysis of this perspective that we must now turn.

Growing old: the biographical context

The late 1960s and 1970s saw a marked change in theorizing about older people. On the one hand, there was the break-up of functionalism and the application of a range of other theoretical approaches to the study of ageing. Accompanying this was a fundamental change in the style of theorizing in social gerontology, with a rejection of the need to find a 'special or universal theory of ageing' (John 1984:10). On the other hand, critical perspectives were being introduced regarding older people's experience of welfare and the maintenance of inequalities in old age (Townsend 1981; Phillipson and Walker 1986).

From the late 1960s onwards we see, in fact, attempts to contexualize the ageing process, both in respect of life- and work-histories and political and economic processes. In addition, greater attention was attached to understanding the meaning of old age and retirement, this being particularly prominent in the writings of those influenced by interactionist perspectives in sociology (Marshall 1986). Also, where role and disengagement theory had emphasized *discontinuities* between old age and earlier life-cycle stages, later theoretical approaches laid stress on *continuities*. These continuities are seen to arise through having a particular biography which gives meaning to old age (M. L.

Johnson 1986), through membership of a particular class, gender or ethnic group and through being a member of a cohort (a group of people born within a specified time period) which may influence certain characteristics of ageing.

Two examples of this type may be quoted. The heavy excess mortality of young adult men in the First World War in comparison with women led to an exaggerated imbalance in the sex ratio when those cohorts reached old age. Demographers have referred to the surviving women as 'the vanishing spinsters' (Benjamin 1968) because, after this period, sex ratios in the typical years of first marriage became more equal and marriage became a more universal experience. The Second World War was characterized by mass mobilization of women into industrial work and a sudden associated increase in smoking by women: the impact of this is now beginning to show, 40 years on, in their mortality statistics (Hagestad 1985).

There were a number of influences which coalesced to produce a stream of research utilizing biographical or life-history perspectives. The notion of work careers and work-histories was first used by British, American and French researchers as a means of explaining and understanding behaviour in retirement. The case for this was presented in the early 1960s by George Maddox:

Interpretations of retirement are (often) seriously marred by the inadequate attention to variations both in the social context within which retirement takes place and in the personal biographies of elderly individuals. Too often retirement is treated implicitly as a fact with a given social meaning, rather than as a sociological variable to be understood within the social life-space of an individual. (1966 : 163)

Subsequently, this theme was taken up by Johnson, when he argued for retrospective life-history studies which would see later life 'as an intricate pattern of life careers' rather than as a single event or stage. The biographical/life-history approach has also been influential in the work of European researchers (Kohli 1986). A notable example is Rosenmayr who uses the work of social philosophers such as Dilthey, Husserl and Mannheim (as well as sociologists of the life-course such as Thomas and Znaniecki and Daniel Bertaux), to generate hypotheses about links between biographical events and experiences in old age. In particular, Rosenmayr raises the idea of cumulative disadvantages which can affect specific groups of old people, becoming internalized and even leading to self-destructive behaviour:

The social devaluation (through the life course) not only generally reduces the chances of social participation and of access to resources. It also works as a multiplication of factors in terms of *cumulating disadvantages* of the economically weakest and socially most isolated groups [among older people]. Differences between socio-economic strata are thus greater among the elderly than among the younger and middle-aged cohorts. This is due to greater differences in their *initial* social situations and to biographically created conditions which lead to a progressive reduction of chances of the deprived of coping with [changes in old age]. (1981 : 46)

This argument found support in American research, conducted in the 1960s on work and retirement. In particular, studies by Wilensky (1961) and Simpson *et al*. (1966) showed the extent to which the social relations generated through work persist well into retirement. According to these studies, if social involvement and favourable self-evaluations (both of which are seen as being anchored in work) had not been built up before retirement they are unlikely to be established afterwards. In an important observation, Simpson *et al*. concluded:

> It is not retirement per se which is responsible (for some older workers') lack of self-anchorage, but their work histories which had not allowed them to develop ties with society. Support from other sources is needed if these individuals are to enjoy favourable self-evaluations. (1966:73)

The use of work and life-histories has since been broadened to cover a range of themes. Among these we might include Matthews' use of oral biographies in her study *Friendships Through the Life Course* (1986), the exploration by Marshall (1980) and Coleman (1986) of Butler's (1963) 'life review' and the analysis by Silvana di Gregorio (1986a) of the strategies adopted by men and women for managing old age.

One advantage of the use of the life-history method is that researchers cannot ignore so-called 'cohort effects'. In Chapter 7, for instance, we show that generalizations about 'ethnic elders' must be closely specified. The ageing experience of someone migrating to England from Pakistan after retirement age, being quite unfamiliar with the culture and environment and unable to speak the language, will obviously differ from that of a third-generation child who knows no other world; but cohort effects, even if less dramatic than this example, are important for all groups as Riley argues:

> Long-term social changes (in occupations, pension plans, etc.), com-bined with increases in longevity, have markedly altered the ageing process by extending the years spent in retirement. Cohort differences in retirement mean that a twenty-year-old man in 1900 could scarcely have looked ahead to retirement at all; today such a man can expect to spend nearly one quarter of his adult lifetime in retirement. These added retirement years have important consequences for income, social in-volvement, leisure, health, and indeed nearly all aspects of the process of ageing. (1987:4)

However, as she points out, these cohort changes affect social institutions as well as individuals:

> In response to social change, millions of individuals in a cohort begin to develop new age-typical patterns and regularities of behaviour (changes in ageing); these behaviour patterns then become defined as age-appropriate norms and rules, are reinforced by 'authorities' and thereby become institutionalised in the structure of society (social change); in turn, these changes in age norms and social structures redirect age-related behaviours (further changes in ageing). Through such a

dialectical sequence, the members of each cohort, responsive to social change, exert a collective force for further change as they move through the age-stratified society: they press for adjustments in social roles and social values, influence other people throughout the age strata, contribute to continuing alterations in both ageing and social structure. (1987 : 4)

Biographical and life-history approaches have provided an important corrective to the limitations of functionalist accounts of ageing, yet at the same time it is likely that these perspectives will themselves prove limited in the context of the crisis in public expenditure in the 1970s and 1980s. This crisis has seen the rise of a radical and highly political analysis of old age, one which draws its inspiration not from interpretative life-history approaches but from Marxist and neo-Marxist critiques of social and economic policy.

The social construction of old age

Biographical and symbolic interactionist perspectives raised the issue of the social construction of old age. This notion was to be extended with the political economy perspective which emerged in the late 1970s. The background to this theoretical development was the crisis affecting public spending from the mid-1970s.

The origins of the crisis lay in a rise in world old prices, the slow-down in economic growth and the simultaneous rise in unemployment and inflation (Walker 1985). Alongside this economic collapse came a political and ideological transformation, with cuts in public expenditure in general and welfare spending in particular. Given that half of Department of Health and Social Security (DHSS) expenditure was allocated to older people, they were inevitably subject to a sustained political attack – by right-wing governments in America and Britain (Estes 1986; Bornat et al. 1985). Older people came to be viewed as a burden on Western economies, with demographic change seen as causing intolerable pressure on public spending. Financial commitments to elderly people (for instance, the State Earnings Related Pension Scheme) were viewed as posing a long-term threat to Britain's economic recovery (Treasury 1984; DHSS 1985) and the living standards of working people (Bornat et al. 1985; Walker 1986).

The response to this attack has been a politicization of social gerontological theory (Phillipson and Walker 1987; Kart 1987). Critical perspectives on old age have been given particular prominence in the United States, Britain, France and Germany. The basic tenets of this approach have been defined in the following way:

The central challenge of a political economy of ageing is to move beyond a critique of conventional gerontology, to develop an understanding of the character and significance of variations in the treatment of the aged, and to relate these to polity, economy and society in advanced capitalism. This requires an examination of society's treatment of the aged in the context of the national and world economy, the role of the state, conditions of the labour market, and class, race, gender and age divisions in society. At base, this requires examination of the relationship of capitalism to ageing. It also begins with the proposition that the status and resources of the elderly, and even the experience of old age itself, are conditioned by one's location in the social structure and the local to global economic and social factors that shape that location. (Estes 1986 : 121)

Implicit in this definition is a view that old age is a social rather than a biologically constructed status. In the light of this, we need to see many of the experiences affecting older people as a product of a particular division of labour and structure of inequality rather than a natural concomitant of the ageing process. Townsend, for example, sees dependency in old age as structured by dominant economic and political forces. He writes:

Retirement, poverty, institutionalisation and restriction of domestic and community roles are the experiences which help to explain the structured dependency of the elderly. [In this analysis it is] society [that] creates the framework of institutions and rules within which the general problems of the elderly emerge or, indeed, are 'manufactured'. In the everyday management of the economy and the administration and development of social institutions the position of the elderly is subtly shaped and changed. The policies which determine the conditions and welfare of the elderly are not just the reactive policies represented by the statutory social services but the much more generalised and institutionalised policies of the state which maintain or change social structure. (1986 : 21)

The political economy perspective has been used in a variety of ways by social gerontologists. Graebner (1980), Phillipson (1982) and Guillemard (1986), for example, use this approach to examine the institutionalization of retirement. The retirement experience, its timing and eventual outcome is related to the supply and demand for labour and the production relations of capitalism. The evolution of pensions is itself related to economic factors; the experience of mass unemployment creating the environment for legislation in both Britain and America.

Political economy analysts have also developed a range of counter-arguments to perceptions of demographic change as a *cause* of the state's fiscal crisis. Blaming older people is seen as a means of obscuring 'the origins of problems [which stem] from the capitalist economic system and the subsequent political choices that are made' (Estes 1986 : 123). Attacks on the burden of the elderly population are seen to legitimize a transfer of responsibility from the state to individual older persons. At the same time, the class basis of old-age policies means that inequalities are not only maintained but may indeed be widened – through the encouragement of privatization in areas such as health care and financial support.

Thirdly, the political economy approach has also theorized about the relationship between age, race, gender and class. This has helped to produce a new range of questions for social gerontologists to tackle. For example: how does the individual's life-long class identity change (if at all) with retirement? Is 'being old' viewed as a classless experience? What implications might this carry for class consciousness and action in Western, capitalist societies? Are middle-class, as opposed to working-class older people, more or less resistant to processes which lead to the commodification of old age (see below)? How, in a patriarchal society, do older women experience growing old (see Minkler and Estes 1984 and Peace 1986 for reviews of these issues)?

Finally, political economy has also provided a critical analysis of the character of health and welfare services (Estes 1979; Townsend 1981; Phillipson and Walker 1987). These are seen to reinforce the dependency created through the wider social and economic system. Older people may find themselves treated and processed as commodities. Welfare services are criticized for stigmatizing older people, compounding their problems through the imposition of age-segregated policies. In practical terms, this analysis has raised issues about challenging older people's experience of being passive consumers of welfare and medical services (Bowl 1986). It has also raised questions about the relationship of professionals to older people: how far do they challenge the low expectations that elderly people sometimes have about services? To what extent do they contribute to the experience of old age as a period of dependency?

The idea of dependency being in many respects socially constructed has been a liberating perspective within gerontology. It has challenged professional workers to consider their own role in the creation of passivity and marginality; at the same time, it has offered a powerful critique of governmental policies which see the elderly both as a social problem and a cause of economic ills. The practical benefits of this approach are further explored in the final section below.

Conclusion: the uses of theory

In our opening remarks we suggested that theoretical issues have played a relatively small part in the history of gerontology, particularly in the case of Britain. At the same time, it is clear that theory has been used in very practical ways to understand and confront certain problems. First, role theory, with its stress on the psycho-social crisis caused by retirement, helped to influence the growth of courses in pre-retirement education (Phillipson and Strang 1983). Indeed, many of those social gerontologists active in formulating role theory perspectives, were also involved at a practical level in organizing pre-retirement programmes in industry.

Secondly, disengagement theory, although rejected as a theoretical model of social ageing, has been reintroduced in a different guise by psychologists. Here we might note the concept of 'terminal drop', an idea which refers to a characteristic decline in system function when a person is a few weeks or months away from death. In this perspective, disengagement has become separated from ageing itself, and is related to the process of dying. At the same time, important questions are raised about appropriate care for those facing death, as well as for those who are bereaved (see Chapter 9).

Thirdly, the life-history perspective has been influential in at least two areas. Researchers such as Johnson have used the biographical approach in consumer-based research, as in the study of the meals on wheels service in Leeds (Johnson *et al.* 1980). In this research, the analysis of attitudes towards meals on wheels, came towards the end of a lengthy interview reviewing significant events in the individual's life-history. In this way it was possible to achieve a better understanding of the relevance of the service to older people and gain a clearer understanding of their own perceptions as to its adequacy.

The biographical approach has also been used as a therapeutic measure. Robert Butler, for example, who first brought to the attention of gerontologists the importance of the life-review, writes:

> I have used the concept of the life review in my psychotherapeutic work with older persons. Life review therapy includes the taking of an extensive autobiography from the older person. . . . Use of family albums, scrapbooks and other memorabilia . . . evoke crucial memories, responses and understanding in patients. . . . Such life-review therapy can be conducted in a variety of settings from senior centers to nursing homes. Even relatively untrained persons can function as therapists by becoming 'listeners' as older people recount their lives. (1975 : 413)

The uses and value of this perspective have been explored in Britain by Coleman, particularly in his study *The Ageing Process and the Role of Reminiscence* (1986).

Finally, we have already indicated some practical benefits from the political economy perspective, in particular its attack on victim-blaming and scapegoating of older people. This critique has assisted the development of a more positive approach to old age, one which focusses on the strengths and potential of older people to improve the quality of their lives. At the same time, the political economy perspective has also contributed to a reassessment of the way professional care can, in the words of Kuhn (1986), 'demean and diminish older people'. This perception raises creative and challenging possibilities for new forms of health and social services work *with* older people, with the development of relations of care which foster interdependency rather than dependency and powerlessness in old age.

4

Researching old age

Introduction

The purpose of this chapter is to examine some of the ways in which sociologists generate the type of knowledge about old age which they believe is more satisfactory than what *passes* for knowledge (stereotypes, commonsense, implicit theories). Researchers also try to make visible what might otherwise be socially invisible and create data wherewith theoretical propositions can be tested and interpretive understanding advanced.

Our principal focus is on sociological research, although reference is made to the substantial body of information generated by social research more broadly defined. Examples here include the many cross-sectional surveys of elderly people undertaken by local health and social services authorities, the routine collection of statistical information by government departments made available in *Social Trends*, the *Census* and the *General Household Survey*, as well as research directly commissioned or undertaken by central government departments such as the Department of Health and Social Security (DHSS) or the Department of the Environment (DoE).

Research methodology can appear both as a 'dry as dust' textbook issue and also as a highly polemical one, as books such as *Knowledge from What? Abandoning Method* (Phillips 1971, 1973), *Beneath the Surface* (Fletcher 1974), *Realities of Social Research* (Platt 1976), *Doing Sociological Research* (Bell and Newby 1977) and *Doing Feminist Research* (Roberts 1981) all testify. The extent to which even statistics can be 'politicized' – manipulated, suppressed or misused by those with a vested interest in so doing – is apparent whether we go back to Huff's *How to Lie with Statistics* (1954) or forward to the many 'adjustments' to the unemployment statistics and Retail Price Index of the Thatcher governments and attempts to reveal the 'real facts' by, for instance, the Radical Statistics Health Group (1987) and Counter Information Services (1980).

The general position we adopt here is that all sources of data may have some use and should be used where appropriate: there is no one 'correct' method for doing research. (For instance, we would not agree with the following propositions either as they are stated or if each was stated the other way round: that large data sets are necessarily better than small ones; solo investigators are better than big teams; cross-sectional studies are better than longitudinal ones; government statistics are totally trustworthy.)

Secondly, a critical perspective has to be applied to the way data is created by researchers, just as a critical/interpretive perspective has to be applied to everything else we discuss. We do, however, have a certain prejudice in favour of methods which bring researchers into face-to-face contact with elderly people though other types of data (for example, the big statistical data sets created by government agencies and survey research firms) are invaluable for locating, contextualizing and triangulating the more personal studies.

Before entering the discussion of methods we touch on some professional discomforts of research and some arguments for overcoming them.

Fieldwork avoidance

Already I had talked to officials of the National Assistance Board and of the Ministries of Labour and National Insurance and . . . had done the round of borough councillors, trade union secretaries, personnel officers and welfare workers. . . . I could avoid the hardest job no longer. The first address I had chosen at random proved to be a dark, terraced house and I remember the whitened doorstep and the tall chimneys rising above the roofs in the distance. Twice my courage failed me and I walked past without knocking. My hands were thrust in my raincoat pockets and I can still remember fumbling with some scraps of paper and tearing them into minute pieces while I stood at the corner of the street and pretended to be looking for a bus. I knocked hesitantly and when the door opened explained myself rather abjectly. (Townsend 1958:106)

Townsend's account of his initiation into fieldwork reminds us that what pass for 'facts' about old age are at some stage of their manufacture the product of human interactions with all the characteristic frailties and strengths which the mind and body bring to bear on problems.

To undertake research is to engage in a somewhat unnatural activity, deliberately violating normal social conventions: we find ourselves approaching strangers and asking them intimate questions – we want something from them and apparently offer little in exchange. By contrast, the norms of our society permit us to accost strangers in very limited circumstances and to have only brief exchanges with them: otherwise, if we want something of value from strangers, we usually have to pay for it. These are the norms of 'balanced reciprocity' (Sahlins 1968) in a large-scale society where we have personal knowledge of only a fraction of the multitude of other citizens.

Good social researchers need to be sensitive to other people, to physical surroundings, nuances of meaning and to information offered and withheld. If they have this sensitivity, however, they may find good reasons for abstaining from fieldwork. To manage the intrusiveness into others' lives, to project a self-confidence in themselves and the value of their enquiries – perhaps quite the reverse of what they feel – they have to grow a thicker skin and find ways ('easing' techniques – Cain 1971 : 72) of coping with the work. However, if they grow too thick-skinned, they risk losing the very sensitivity which is their strongest asset. The most straightforward easing technique is simply fieldwork avoidance, finding *any* reason to postpone the evil hour when they have to steel themselves to knock on that door and confront the stranger within. This is one reason why we find few personal-involvement studies of elderly people of the type we extolled in Chapter 1 – few that is, relative to the number of surveys carried out by 'hired hands' (Roth 1966). Other reasons include the personal and financial costs of undertaking such projects and the difficulty of getting them funded, relative to the popularity of cross-sectional surveys with the people who commission research.

Arguments for doing research

In an analytical model of the research process Bateson (1984) points out that different sets of people have different sorts of necessary expertise. 'Ordinary' people – the subjects of research – are experts about themselves and their social worlds; researchers have research expertise and research sponsors know better than anyone else what it is they want to know. Researchers mediate the transmission of knowledge from the first group to the third and this can create a certain ambivalence about the professional role which has to be recognized and overcome. Let us follow Townsend into his first interview:

> My questions were bad, my manner worse, and I felt a complete charlatan – a bungling amateur with no right to scientific pretensions. Yet somehow [the respondent] patiently coached me through my interview, tactfully answering the really important questions which it had not occurred to me to ask. (1958 : 106)

Or let us consider this quotation from Bertaux:

> If given a chance to talk freely, people appear to know a lot about what is going on; a lot more, sometimes, than sociologists. (1981 : 38)

If it is the case that ordinary people are more expert about the subject (themselves) than the professionals, the case for research could be argued thus. First, there is some demand for research and only researchers satisfy it – better that knowledge is produced by those who have training in research method, who know something about sampling, bias, reliability, validity and sound statistical technique than simply by 'investigators' (journalists or other writers) who have no such training.

Secondly, if we all have the 'curiosity' which, as we said in Chapter 1, is a characteristic impetus in doing sociology, the researcher's job in satisfying this curiosity is to collect and filter information from a variety of sources and make it more widely accessible: dispersed informants may 'know all there is to know' about a topic but their knowledge is not necessarily available either to them or to others. Accessing this knowledge has various components – collecting the information (like deep-sea fishing), processing it in various ways (like gutting and filleting) and purveying it to the customer (packaging and marketing). This last aspect is often neglected – research is only complete when it is *read* and therefore it has to be written up and packaged in a readable format.

Thirdly, a lot of what ordinary people 'know' is not, for them, problematic, whereas for researchers it is. People know what they need to know as a guide to daily action, but they do not need to debate and review their knowledge systematically and draw out the implications so that others may learn. Bertaux-Wiame expresses these ideas well:

> It is essential for the researcher to first of all listen to those who have lived and who therefore know. Of course their knowledge is not presented in a theoretical and written form; quite often it does not emerge explicit in the oral form either. This is because their knowledge is entirely focussed on real life choices, on day to day activity. Social investigation is not a matter reserved to sociologists. *Everyone* is investigating, all the time. But the results of these 'investigations' are not construed into ideas, concepts or discussion; they materialise, as acts. Hence, it is necessary to listen, but this is not enough. The individual researcher has to put together bits of social and human knowledge: and beyond this also to find ways of making the results of social research more easily accessible to everybody. (1981 : 264)

Fourthly, there is a latent inconsistency in the writings of authors like Bertaux, who praise the accounts which 'ordinary' people give of their lives and actions: the implicit suggestion is that these accounts are 'true'. But clearly we can all make mistakes about ourselves, have imperfect information and embellish and distort the accounts which we give of our activities. Accounts given by different actors may be in conflict. So one thing the researcher can do is compare, corroborate and validate the accounts which different individuals give us.

Finally, although the current trend is to 'demystify' the research process – and there are very good reasons for minimizing the 'scientific' and 'professional' pretensions of the researcher – this minimalist position should not be taken too far. Researchers can 'add value' to everyday accounts. They bring to the research act either a mind which is informed by wide and scholarly reading about the subject or one which is deliberately blanked of preconceptions about it but schooled in scientific method. They are trained to try to avoid bias and – through the process of formulating, testing, discarding and reformulating hypotheses – to resist jumping to conclusions.

This is one set of arguments for social researchers doing research, but another set could equally well be deployed. Research aids self-knowledge: it is in demand as a guide to making informed social policy decisions; it can assist in identifying a need for reform and in improving social justice or efficiency; it satisfies an individual curiosity but also a collective one. In large-scale mass societies with high levels of 'invisibility' we need reports about how other people live constantly. We are not alone in laying this stress on visibility: Rowbotham's *Hidden from History* (1974) and Unruh's *Invisible Lives* (1983) are pleas, respectively, for more attention to be paid to women and to elderly people. In the next sections we consider some of the main methods whereby social researchers attempt to increase the visibility of old age.

Data collection methods and problems

Participant observation

Observation means trying to learn about society from the systematic use of our senses. While there are various types of observational study, including direct and covert observation, it is participant observation which is the most commonly used. This came to be regarded as *the* method in anthropology for finding out about people different from ourselves, though it was 'discovered' for the subject almost accidentally by Malinowski (1922, 1932), who found himself forced by the exigencies of the First World War to live and work for longer than he had intended in Melanesia. An example within the sociological tradition is that of Charles Booth on the *Life and Labour of the People in London* (1892–7): as well as collecting data by a variety of other methods, Booth was in the habit of 'exploring the East End of London, mingling with the people and becoming familiar with their lifestyles' (Kent 1981 : 53) and he took lodgings with poor families to gain experience at first hand.

The claim for the virtues of participant observation has several components. One aspect is that social life and the interconnections of different aspects are appreciated *in the round*, rather than artificially separated as is possible in questionnaire surveys, which have to compartmentalize topics and follow an artificial logic. The observer can sense and make explicit the interconnections between, for example, work and home, religious beliefs and ideas about health, personal morality and deviant behaviour. In the field of gerontology, the continuities and discontinuities between old age and previous life-history will be experienced more forcibly than can ever be conveyed by what Brown *et al.* (1975) call the 'meretricious fixed choice questionnaire'.

Apart from the richness and fullness of the knowledge gained by living and working not only *in* but *as a member of* a given environment, the participant observer is said to put this knowledge to direct test: if he or she did not know how to behave in a given place or situation, maintaining a presence there would be unviable. [One famous definition of participant observation is 'maintaining a presence in an environment in order to carry out research activity' (Schwartz and Schwartz 1955).]

Various problems confront those who want to use the participant observation technique in studies involving elderly people in British society. One is – as we know from general experience – that research is more generally done by younger people on elderly ones and by those with more social power on those with less. 'Passing' as an elderly person – perhaps the ultimate accolade on the successful participant observer – is unlikely to be achieved. Related to this is the spread of retirement among elderly people. Participant observers are recommended to adopt a role in which they feel comfortable. However, since full-time research is inherently a 'work'-type activity, usually carried out during daylight and working hours, the type of role in which an adult observer is likely to feel comfortable is almost bound to have some kind of 'work' connotation, which in turn can restrict contact with retired people.

Fennell, for instance, wanted to observe the social interactions of elderly people living in grouped dwellings. Here the repertoire of roles occupied by visitors to the group included relatives, friends and acquaintances, tradesmen, council employees such as rent and refuse collectors, social services personnel (particularly home-helps), health service workers, police, clergy or other church visitors. He comments:

> Most of these roles are not easily assumed. The contact with residents is either intensive with some and nil with others (relatives, friends, doctors) or involves contact with all or most but of a brief and superficial kind (rent collectors, tradesmen). (1982:181)

A second problem is the generally *privatized* nature of modern British society. Many anthropologists have experienced a strategic benefit from the sunnier climes in which they have worked and from the fact that there is generally little privacy in simpler societies: much of the life they wanted to observe has been 'public', taking place in the open and in full view (Barley 1983). In societies such as our own where more takes place indoors and a greater part of life is defined as private, observation is more difficult as Fennell found:

> Each old person's bungalow was self-contained. There were no communal facilities such as a common room, a laundry room or even a covered corridor. There was no staff or staffrooms, no cover of any kind – not even a bus shelter. In most of the groups there was little passing or through traffic. On foot I was a conspicuous loiterer and periodically got soaked. In a car I could only sit behind my windscreen looking out at old ladies who sat behind their windows looking out at me. (1982:177)

In such circumstances, 'participation' is negligible and 'observation' unfruitful.

Where observation comes into its own, therefore, is where people are gathered together, where they have little privacy – or the reason they are gathered together is for a non-private function – and where observers can sustain legitimate 'work'-type roles. Hence the use of this method in researching 'special settings' for elderly people, such as residential homes, geriatric wards, day centres or old people's clubs (see Chapter 8). Here people are gathered together, so the researcher can observe several people and their interactions simultaneously. The reason they are gathered together is either a legitimate public activity, as in a club or on an outing, and hence observable; or the subjects are relatively powerless to resist invasions of their privacy, as in the geriatric ward and old people's home. This idea is precisely captured by the title of a critique of residential life in local authority old people's homes (*Private Lives in Public Places*: Willcocks *et al.* 1987). Paradoxically, because what goes on in such settings is less visible to the outside world, they have a certain attraction to the 'penetrative' observer and even forbidding institutions like the old-fashioned psychiatric hospital or prison, once penetrated, can offer a rich field for observation and reportage.

Examples of such studies include *The Unexpected Community* by Hochschild (1973) and *Old People, New Lives: Community Creation in a Retirement Residence* by Ross (1977) – both studies of residential complexes of elderly people; studies of day centres such as *Number Our Days* (Myerhoff 1978) and *The Limbo People* (Hazan 1980), as well as numerous penetrations into the closed world of institutions of which perhaps the most famous are Goffman's *Asylums* (1961) and Townsend's *The Last Refuge* (1962).

A bonus of the technique is that, whether appreciative or critical in tone, the writings of observers have an appealing immediacy. Hochschild, describing her 'community of grandmothers', strikes a cheerful note:

> Merrill Court was a beehive of activity; meetings of a Service Club which was soon set up; bowling; morning workshop; Bible study classes twice a week; monthly birthday parties; and visits to four nearby nursing homes. Members donate cakes, pies and soft drinks to bring to the nursing home, and a five-piece band, including a washtub bass, played for the 'old folks' there. During afternoon band practice the women sewed and embroidered pillow cases, aprons and yarn dolls. They made wastebaskets out of discarded paper towel rolls, wove rugs from strips of old Wonder Bread wrappers, and Easter hats out of old Clorox bottles, all to be sold at the annual bazaar. They made placemats to be used at the nursing home, totebags to be donated to 'our boys in Vietnam', Christmas cards to be cut out for the Junior Women's Club, rag dolls to be sent to the orphanage. . . . There was a potluck luncheon every other week for residents only and on alternate weeks, luncheons for outsiders. There were post-potluck luncheons to use up leftovers. (1973 : 38–9)

Townsend, observing life in old people's homes, witnessed less pleasing episodes:

> A (newly arrived) woman . . . went over to the fire, which was burning low, and placed a few knobs of coal on the embers. . . . A female attendant standing a few yards away immediately started shouting at her, placing her hands on her hips in an aggressive manner. 'Who are you to touch the fire? There's been a roaring fire all morning. What are you complaining about?' The old woman answered quietly that she was not complaining but that she felt colder (at which a number of other residents silently nodded their heads). 'I won't do it again, I promise.' The attendant went on shouting at her in a loud and raucous voice and then stalked out of the room, returning a few moments later with a charge attendant. The latter took one look at a thermometer on a wall and then

went and opened the window over the old woman's chair. She then told the woman it was warm enough and that she was not allowed to touch the fire. (1962:79)

We respond strongly to this mode of writing because it is evocative. The observer has privileged access and can 'tell it like it is'. Because we can relate to the human motivations of the participants in the scenes described, we reflect and ponder and feel our knowledge deepen, experiencing what Matthews calls the 'quiet catharsis of comprehension' (1977 : 163).[1] Its advantages in terms of readability can be instantly appreciated if we contrast one of the passages above with the not untypical product of a large-scale survey:

15.8 per cent of those aged 75–84 and 27.3 per cent of those aged 85 and over receive home help. Other groups where the percentage is well above average are: widowed (15.2 per cent); bedfast and housebound (31.0 per cent: 19.0 per cent receive visits more than once a week); those living alone (18.9 per cent). Home help is received by only 4.4 per cent of those aged 65–74, only 3.1 per cent of those living in two-person households and 2.7 per cent of those in households with three or more persons. (Hunt 1978 : 89)

There is also the lurking attraction in the 'penetrating' observation study of the exposé. The precise role of a social researcher is always somewhat ambiguous and the image of the investigator fearlessly exposing abuse and corruption is a cultural model hard to resist. This is one variant of a problem which Titmuss identifies in his Foreword to Goldberg's *Helping the Aged*:

It is relatively easy . . . for academic social scientists to criticise the 'helping' professions'; many of the critics find satisfaction and certainty in self-defined entrepreneurial success goals. Industrious denigration can often spell academic promotion. (Titmuss 1970 : 13)

The risk in this case is that the observer/raconteur is drawn away from the ordinary, the commonplace, the everyday, the normal, towards the scandal, the exposure, the deviant and the untypical. We consider abuse more extensively in Chapter 8, arguing that scandal for its own sake is not illuminating but careful analysis of the seemingly endemic conditions under which scandals and deviant behaviour occur might help to explain why abuse may tend to increase. rather than diminish.

Advantages and disadvantages of participant observation

If the strengths of the participant observation method are the richness, fullness, vividness, readability and convincingness of the reportage, what are its disadvantages? Can it, indeed, have any disadvantages to set against these powerful advantages?

The first disadvantage we have noted by implication: it is a technique

[1] Quoted in Plummer (1983).

particularly applicable to situations where people are gathered together – it is very time-consuming, if not impossible, to operate where people are living dispersed lives, where observing one person (if this is socially permissible) precludes observing others. The second is the general issue of representativeness: observers can study only one place/group at a time, and anyone committed to the method is better advised to seize on the vividness and not worry unduly about 'typicality' or 'randomness'. Usually it is not possible to gain access to a range of settings and, therefore, it may be necessary to make use of a different style of research to discover how typical the chosen setting is (for instance, are there many other places which are similar in terms of age, size, location?).

A third disadvantage for participant observation is what is known as 'intra-observer reliability'. Researchers are unique human beings and each brings a personal dynamic into the situation: they are not simply identical pieces of litmus paper to be dipped into social situations to take on a predictable colouring as a result, from which the characteristics of those situations can be read. Would different observers see different things and bring back alternative reports?

The reliability problem can be confronted by the researcher, to some extent, by an honest self-examination on the subject of bias and distortion. However, this is perhaps as much the reader's problem as the researcher's – and readers solve it effectively by what is called 'triangulation': that is, different accounts are compared. Readers are also sensitive to cues of internal consistency and general plausibility. This is only one of a number of instances where the value of new research can be seen – for as long as a particular author is depended upon, the reader may be vulnerable to misinterpretations, even if it is a 'classic' study. The more accounts that are available (up to what might be regarded as saturation point), the more different sources can be compared and validated and also the better the reader can decide whether or not the presence of an observer has itself altered the situation being studied and whether he or she has concentrated on the 'wrong things'.

A further and final limitation of the participant observation technique is that, while it does permit the coverage of certain sorts of topics, the very intimacy of the observer precludes those which are not normally discussed among friends. This will vary from one social group to another, but an example was given at an Economic and Social Research Council symposium on *The Ageing Initiative*: an anthropologist present, who had rich data on friendships and interactions among older women in various village and club settings in England and France, noted that the English survey researchers could ask older people questions about a great range of things, including sexual behaviour. She herself would have found it impossible to do so and maintain her fieldwork, for this was not a permissible topic for her to broach and stay in role (Okely 1986).

Direct observation

There are relatively few studies in our field using direct observation without 'participatory' intent: the technique may anyway be unnecessarily limited for sociology. The subject is concerned with the meaning of social behaviour so there is every reason to talk with people and ask them questions, in addition to observing them. However, two examples of direct observation studies can be cited to illustrate the technique. Both, unsurprisingly, are observations of special settings and are quoted for their intrinsic interest. Simply to observe people continuously (unless done covertly, which raises ethical dilemmas for sociologists) is difficult both in human and scientific terms. It is socially difficult for the observer to manage and the obvious presence of the researcher might alter the behaviour of those under study. Hence both examples use 'time-sampled' observations: snapshots of what people are doing and where they are sitting at a given moment, but with these observations made at carefully controlled (sometimes randomized) times.

Lipman (1967) took up the theme in residential care which is sometimes called 'custodial seating': the phrase suggests that the new resident is allocated a chair in the main lounge (perhaps the chair of the previous resident) and is then 'fixed' there, regardless of the person's personal preferences. If the seating pattern is rigid, some chairs will be less desirable than others, inhibiting the view of what is going on, having their backs to the television or being adjacent to the draughts and traffic through the main door. Sometimes it is argued that people establish territoriality in chairs at home and, since the residential home is now 'home', it is only natural that residents become symbolically attached to their chairs. However, when Lipman conducted his study, the ideology of the home in question was that there was 'free seating', that territorial rights in chairs was not a good thing and that residents should group and regroup themselves for informal conversation.

The study examined how often a particular chair was occupied by the same individual at different observed times. A figure of 100% against a chair in Lipman's sketch of the lounge would indicate that it was always occupied by the same person. A low percentage figure would indicate a chair that did not 'belong' to anybody, one that was frequently occupied by different people. Lipman describes his method thus:

> After a period of getting to know the staff and the old people, I began to sit in on conversations in the sitting-rooms. When I felt that my presence had become accepted, I made daily recordings of seat positions for each resident on prepared plans of the rooms. I constructed 'logbooks' to show who was in the room, where he or she sat, what each was doing, who spoke to whom and what about. Over a period of 12 days I devoted a total of 18 hours to each room, with one-hour and two-hour sessions taking place on alternate days. (1967 : 564)

Figure 4.1 shows the results graphically. As an observer, Lipman also noted incidents such as this one in which possession of chairs was disputed:

> Once Mrs M, a small and frail woman of 90, found the contentious chair No. 25 occupied by Mrs A. . . . Mrs M demanded, on her return from the toilet, that the chair be vacated. Mrs A refused, claiming the chair

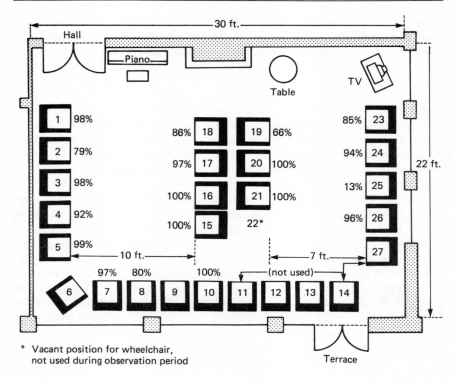

Fig. 4.1. Chair occupancy in an old people's home (after Lipman 1967).

was hers. After some argument, Mrs M lifted her walking stick and began beating Mrs A about the head and shoulders. In the uproar of weeping, cries and moans which followed, the opinions expressed by the other residents fell into two categories. Some saw Mrs M's behaviour as 'evil' and 'vicious'; the other attitude is epitomised in the comment: 'She's quite right. That one's always coming in here when she's got her own place in the chair by the other room. Serve her right it do.' (1967 : 566)

Lipman concludes that 'these claims on personal territory appear to reflect deeply felt needs' and expresses doubt that '"non-custodial" seating arrangements improve [either] the social lives of patients [or] their mental and physical health' (1967 : 566).

The study by Godlove *et al.* (1982) was more elaborate. Described as 'an observation study of elderly people in four different care environments', the object was to observe what given individuals were doing in day centres, day hospitals, local authority homes and hospital wards. Sixty five individuals were observed (approximately equal numbers in each environment), with observation time totalling 21 127 minutes:

Three observers worked in pairs (two observers on any one day), each observing the subject alternately for a period which was usually one hour. Handover times were pre-arranged. The subject's activities and the nature of his contacts with others were recorded on simple recording sheets. One sheet was used for each ten minute period of observation and recordings were made in each of sixty boxes constructed to represent intervals of ten seconds each. To avoid the necessity for observers to look at the subjects, the recording sheets and a watch at the same time, timing was done by means of (specially made) 'bleepers'. The convention was that as each 'bleep' indicated the end of a ten second interval, the observer would record the events of the preceding ten seconds in the relevant box, concentrating on the location and posture of the subject, the activities in which he was engaged and the nature of any contacts with others occurring during the interval. All this was recorded rapidly by using a symbol code as a form of shorthand. (1982 : 10)

Observation was not the only method of data collection in this interesting and careful work, which repays the effort required to locate and read it. Perhaps the best example of the yield of the enquiry is when the authors tabulate how much time individuals spent in 'isolated inactivity' in the different settings, as in Figure 4.2. Godlove *et al*. note that:

While some individuals in each environment spent a lot of their time doing nothing, this state of affairs was much more common in the residential settings. The average inactive time in hospital wards (63 per cent) was almost twice that in day centres (32 per cent). Expressed in terms of the percentage of subjects who spent more than half their time in isolated inactivity the difference is more striking – 23 per cent in day centres, 40 per cent in day hospitals, 53 per cent in local authority homes and 72 per cent in hospital wards. (1981 : 30)

Both of these studies indicate the power of the observation technique when thoughtfully applied, while also clearly indicating some of its costs, limitations and difficulties.

The small-scale survey

If participant observation has become *the* method associated with anthropological enquiry, so the social survey has, since the Second World War, become the typical hallmark of British sociological enquiry. Any discipline will be limited, however, by over-reliance on one method, and the late 1960s and early 1970s saw considerable 'restiveness among younger scholars' (Bruyn 1966: vii) about the domination of the survey technique. Townsend commented that:

The future of sociology may depend, more than anything else, on the question whether statistical and survey techniques can be married to the complex but often inexplicit techniques of personal observation and description. As yet there are relatively few signs of earnest courtship, let alone betrothal and consummation. (1962 : 15)

With respect to the general domination of the survey, the situation has changed little, though the expansion of social research in the next decade

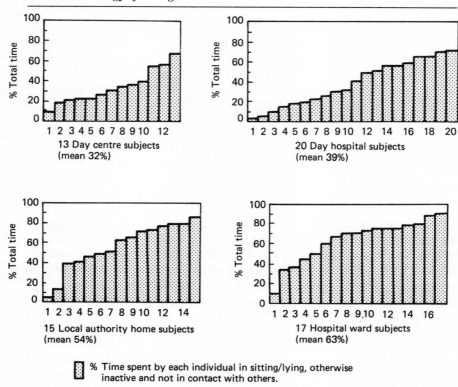

% Time spent by each individual in sitting/lying, otherwise inactive and not in contact with others.

Fig. 4.2. Percentage of time spent in isolated inactivity in various special settings (after Godlove et al. 1982 : 30).

naturally produced some diversification of technique. The review by Taylor (1980) suggests that, rather than substitute some other method completely, researchers may be more inclined to use subsidiary methods in addition. The reason the survey retains its dominance may perhaps be attributable to its proven efficiency; but another reason may simply be its familiarity to and popularity with research sponsors and funding agencies.

In Chapter 1 we examined three small surveys in some detail. Other examples include Snellgrove's *Elderly Housebound* (1963), in which 329 interviews were carried out by a solo investigator in Luton and Tunstall's *Old and Alone* (1966), in which the investigator carried out 'follow-up' interviews with 195 elderly people in 'at risk' categories in four urban areas. This was in the wake of the cross-national survey by Shanas *et al.* (1968), discussed below: a team of interviewers had previously screened 538 households which enabled Tunstall to select his sample. More recently, Wenger's *The Supportive Network* (1984) is based on 534 interviews of elderly people in Wales. Seventy four per cent of the sample were interviewed wholly in Welsh, so it is understandable that Wenger recruited a specialist team of interviewers for this study.

While the observer might be preoccupied with questions of the type, 'what shall I observe, what role should I adopt, how shall I gain entry, how shall I maintain access, how shall I record my observations, what, out of the mass of material I have, shall I select to write up?', the surveyor typically faces a different set of questions. These are more likely to be of the type, 'how shall I draw my sample, how big should it be, what form of interview shall I use, how shall I record my material, how shall I analyse my results, how can I make my report interesting?

One of the key differences is that the surveyor usually has only one opportunity to gather information. Each respondent/subject/interviewee is met only once: this is almost one of the rules of the game and legitimizes some of the frank enquiries people are prepared to tolerate from interviewers. The knowledge gained by the interviewer cannot be 'used against one' in daily life: questions can be put and answers given at a level of intimacy which derives support from the fact that the parties will probably never meet again.

The risks of muffing the survey interview are correspondingly greater than with participant observation – if the batteries on the tape recorder run out, if the interview is interrupted at a critical moment, if a key question or topic is forgotten, or if an interview schedule is lost in transit, the data are irretrievable. It is virtually impossible to turn up on the doorstep subsequently, saying, 'I'm sorry, but I've lost your interview, do you mind doing it again?' The surveyor takes partial refuge in numbers – some wastage is almost inevitable, although this tends to show up more in the statistics, whereas the participant observer can 'cover' for losses and mistakes by drawing on a wealth of other material.

Advantages and limitations of the small survey

There are many different types of survey, but we restrict ourselves here to the type discussed in Chapter 1, where elderly people were interviewed at home. One of the great strengths of the random sample survey is that – so long as the researchers overcome any tendency they may have to avoid fieldwork or devolve it to others – they are brought into contact with a wide range of people, people whose existence they might otherwise never suspect or be able to imagine. Sheldon makes the point for illness and medical practitioners, but what he says is of wide applicability:

> The necessity of using a true random sample of the population in a survey of this nature is well known [but] . . . contact with such a sample provided a new experience. The actual practice of medicine is virtually confined to those members of the population who either are ill, or think they are ill, or are thought by somebody else to be ill, and these so amply fill up the working day that in the course of time one comes unconsciously to believe that they are typical of the whole. This is not the case. The use

of a random sample brings to light those individuals who are ill and know they are ill, but have no intention of doing anything about it, as well as those who never have been ill, and probably never will be till their final illness. These would have been inaccessible to any method of approach but that of the random sample. Perhaps one of the deepest impressions left in my mind after conducting the survey is the fundamental import- ance of the random sample – unusual as it is in most medical work. It does not make for ease of working: all sorts of inaccessible personalities may be encountered, and it is more time-consuming; but the degree of self-selection imposed by the population on itself in regard to its approach to doctors inevitably gives anything other than a random sample a considerable bias. (1948 : 8)

The discipline of the random sample then, brings us into contact with people and lifestyles we might otherwise not know about; and people whom we might otherwise deliberately or subconsciously avoid.

Another major advantage of the survey (compared with observation) is that it permits firmer identification of sub-groups within the population. An observer (like Jerrome 1981) who studied friendship in middle-class women (see Chapter 6) can surmise that patterns for working-class women might be different, but has no means (within the study) of establishing the point. By contrast, all three of our survey authors (Sheldon, Townsend and Isaacs) could note and test for differences in family life (even within the working class) according to whether or not adult children had moved from the traditional inner-city centres to suburbia and examine the effect of sex, age, marital status or other variables.

A third main benefit of the survey method is to provide estimates of typicality. The study by Isaacs *et al.* (1972) is a good example. Accusations of neglect of older people by their families is commonplace. A small observation study which argued against this stereotype could easily be dismissed as unrepresentative, whereas the reader who follows through the documentation of the 255 examples whom these researchers studied is more likely to be convinced that the cases of 'neglect' are genuinely a small minority.

A fourth advantage of the sample survey method is the collection of standardized data, which is invaluable for making comparisons between individuals and groups within the population. Our society values a degree of individualism, so we readily agree with statements of the type that 'everyone is different' and that 'we must avoid stereotypes'. The suggestion that there are patterns, rhythms and typicalities which can be identified (in people or human behaviour) is less readily acknowledged. In innumerable ways we accept standardization – we know it is helpful to make clothes and shoes in stock sizes, we happily accept standardization in the heights of door frames or the size of baths, we buy 'package' holidays – but we sometimes resist sociological generalization about people. None the less, like it or not, even the small survey shows up patterns and these can be confirmed by increasing sample size. As an example we might refer back to the demonstration by Isaacs *et al.* (1972)

discussed in Chapter 1 that most of the cases of 'rejection' by children of their elderly parents can be traced back to a previous history of parental neglect or rejection of the children earlier in life.

The disadvantages of small surveys can be considered in relation to the problems of smallness, such as potential untypicality and lack of representativeness (which they generally share with observation studies) and the problems of the survey method itself, which they often share with large surveys considered below. The main criticism of the survey method, in a nutshell, is that it is a powerful engine for producing results, but what do the results *mean*? A single example must suffice to indicate the many variants of this problem.

If surveyors ask elderly users of day centres if they are satisfied with them (interviewing them in the staff office, perhaps within earshot of other people) and 98% reply in the affirmative (Carter 1981), does this mean that day centres are doing a splendid job, or that the respondents hesitate to reveal their 'true' opinions? They might be mistrustful of possible repercussions if they express criticisms, they might have a greater sense of loyalty to the staff than to the interviewers and think it was churlish to seem ungrateful, or they might simply want to get the interview over quickly. (Most people answering survey questions know that negative answers to evaluative questions lead to further questions, of the type 'now, why are you dissatisfied . . . ?') The figure of 98%, then, is a datum, a fact: it is what 98% of elderly day centre users said in reply to a particular question and it could only be produced by doing a survey: we learn *something* from it, but perhaps the main conclusion we draw is that, to find out what people 'really' think, we need a more subtle approach.

The large survey

By a large survey we mean the type of study which requires a team of interviewers to be put into the field following a standardized research design. *The Elderly at Home* (Hunt 1978) is a well known example. It was carried out by the Social Survey Division of the Office of Population Censuses and Surveys (OPCS) on behalf of the DHSS. Approximately 2600 people were interviewed, a response rate of 83% of the target sample – people aged 65 and over living in the community in England in 1976. Another large community survey is that by Abrams for Age Concern (1978b, 1980): 1646 people were interviewed in four locations (Hove, Merton, Moss Side and Northampton) by Research Services Ltd in 1977. The object of the sample was to achieve approximately 800 interviews with people of 75 years of age or more and 800 with those between 65 and 74.

Large numbers of elderly people figure in surveys designed to explore welfare issues. The study by Harris (1968), *Social Welfare for the Elderly*, carried out in 13 local authority areas in England, Wales and Scotland, is inexplicit about the numbers interviewed in different samples, though a figure well above 7000 seems probable. In Hunt's (1970) study of *The Home Help Service in England and Wales*, 1112 elderly people were interviewed as well as relatively small numbers of younger 'chronic sick and other' recipients of the home help service. We refer in Chapter 6 to *Handicapped and Impaired in*

Great Britain (Harris 1971): of the 12 700 'impaired people' of 16 years or above interviewed in that survey, 7393 were aged 65 and over. These three studies were carried out by the Government Social Survey.

Recurrent analyses are carried out within the General Household Survey, which is a continuous survey of the adult population, reporting every year but with special sections at less frequent intervals. Elderly people were a special group in the 1980 survey, published in 1982. The fieldwork for the 1985 update has been completed, but the analyses were not publicly available at the time of writing this book (mid-1987), nor will the data be available for secondary analysis for many years. The General Household Survey is a portmanteau survey incorporating areas of interest to different government departments. Questions about elderly people were included at the request of the DHSS:

> About their circumstances in general and, more specifically, about the extent to which they had difficulty in getting about and looking after themselves, their social contacts and their use of health and welfare services. (OPCS 1982:168)

Information was obtained for 4516 people aged 65 and over living in private households, of whom most were interviewed directly and proxy information gathered from another household member for just under 5% of the total.

These are all general population surveys, even if candidates for inclusion in the sample have some special characteristic, such as being in receipt of home help or having some form of impairment. More narrowly within what we call 'special settings', other large surveys can be identified: in a survey of old people's homes under Townsend's direction, 489 'new residents' were interviewed and 'simple statistical information' compiled in addition for 7689 elderly residents of 173 institutions (1962:13). Several studies of sheltered housing tenants have used large samples – Butler *et al.* (1983) analysed interviews with 608 tenants in 51 sheltered housing schemes: interviews were carried out by Public Attitude Surveys. Fennell (1986a, 1987) has studied 1664 tenants in 240 schemes throughout England and Scotland: interviewing was conducted by Social and Community Planning Research. Another survey with a specific focus is Tinker's (1984) *Staying at Home: Helping Elderly People*, in which 1310 elderly people were interviewed by Public Attitude Surveys Research in 'innovatory housing schemes'.

Many of these surveys reflect large-scale social research but they are not generally informed by any sociological or theoretical perspective: the main aim is to 'establish the facts' by enumerating the distribution of certain characteristics in the population – those living alone, those having difficulty opening screwtop jars or those having a certain number of hours of home help and so on – and publishing this data in statistical form with concise commentary. Most of the statistics are simple frequency counts, giving estimates for a larger population, with some cross-tabulations in which, for instance, males and females are contrasted, or those living alone with those in shared households, or those aged 75 and over with those in the younger age group.

To find a really large, sociologically purposive survey, we have to track back to fieldwork carried out in 1962 and published most extensively as *Old People in Three Industrial Societies* (Shanas *et al.* 1968). Collaborative teams in England, Denmark and the United States worked on this cross-national study, which also involved interdisciplinary collaboration. The target appears to have been to interview 7500 people living in the community (2500 in each country) and these targets were largely met. In Britain the services of the Government Social Survey were put at the team's disposal and the contribution of Amelia Harris (the officer responsible for two of the other large studies we have cited) in questionnaire design and analysis is acknowledged.

What distinguishes this study from the others is the scholarly and theoretically informed background of the authors. This means that although much space has to be given to the simple presentation of results – inevitable in a large survey – the results are contextualized and sociologically interesting. To select just two areas, the chapters by Shanas on health, in which 'self-perceived' health status is related to more 'objective' illnesses and disabilities, and by Townsend and Tunstall on loneliness, isolation and desolation, explore the interconnections between variables and seek intellectually satisfying meanings to the findings. The interpretive flavour of the writing can be seen in this summary about social isolation:

> The great majority of those living alone have a number of daily social activities and relationships and, although there is some falling off with increasing age, the fall is not marked and most of it is attributable to the higher prevalence of infirmity. . . . The data . . . do not suggest that, independent of growing infirmity, social disengagement is a widespread phenomenon. Bereavement is perhaps the most important isolating experience in old age and yet even this, as at other ages, draws a chain of 'reintegrating' responses from family and community. (Shanas *et al.* 1968:286)

Advantages and disadvantages of large surveys

To put a team of interviewers into the field is expensive, so, whereas we may find ourselves from time to time in the position of weighing up the pros and cons of one or another small-scale research method, we seldom realistically need to contemplate whether or not it is a good idea to conduct a large survey: the option is ruled out by funding considerations. Even if funds were unlimited, however, a large survey would not necessarily be the 'best buy' every time.

The great virtue of the large survey is that, properly designed and conducted, it can lay authoritatively to rest the accusations of bias, unrepresentativeness and unreliability which are sometimes levelled at smaller studies. If we study a handful of people in one seaside resort, or spend a year in one day centre – even if we draw a random sample from one particular town – queries are always raised about how 'typical' the reported findings are. Such questions were certainly raised in the wake of Townsend's *The Family Life of Old People* (1957), but the cross-national study (Shanas *et al.* 1968) showed that family relations in old age in Bethnal Green were not so untypical, either of the British Isles as a whole, or even of the three Western nations studied.

Similarly, anxieties about the supposed 'burden of dependency' can be examined more authoritatively when nationwide samples in Britain, Denmark and the United States reveal that, respectively, 89%, 93% and 95% of elderly people are 'ambulatory', with approximately 80% in each of the three societies able to 'go outdoors without difficulty' (Shanas *et al*. 1968 : 23). Moreover, the large survey allows estimates of specific needs to be assessed more accurately. In Abrams' survey of the 75 years and over age group, 35% reported difficulty in taking a bath (only 7% saying they had help from someone else), 12% reported difficulty having an overall wash and 25% reported difficulty in 'getting round the house' (1978b : 58).

Findings like these highlight both the strengths and limitations of the large survey: we are given the figures but their explanatory power as they stand is limited and much is left open to conjecture. How big is the group who have difficulty both having a bath and having an overall wash, yet have no help? Unless the authors have specifically reported the findings in this form, this type of detail is buried in the data and can be elicited from it only by direct access to the computer tape (if available) or by correspondence with the authors.

This is perhaps an inevitable frustration with large surveys: they produce so many raw facts, and their statistical potential for generating even more facts by sub-analysis is so vast, that it is hard for authors to judge what to report. Surveys are notoriously difficult to write up in an interesting way. Masses of statistical tables create indigestible reports and, while they can be quarried for information (researchers use the *Census*, which has little or no commentary), writers do not want to be accused of producing unreadable books. Hence a balance has to be struck between what to include and exclude in reporting results and some dissatisfaction is bound to result: each set of facts reported tending inevitably to suggest another set of questions. The reader's 'quiet catharsis of comprehension' is usually conspicuously absent and we can generally only conjecture about how to explain the findings, unless the authors are unusually skilful.

Standardization is inherent in the large survey: there are so many critiques of this problem (e.g. Bruyn 1966; Bechhofer 1967; Phillips 1971, 1973) that we need not enlarge upon it. The whole point of the survey is to plane away individuality and idiosyncrasy, to show up patterns and trends. Hence, while it lends itself to certain purposes and to certain research questions and analytical perspectives, it is quite unsuited to others. As an example, we can refer again to the authoritative statements by Shanas *et al*. (1968) about the limited evidence for greater disengagement with age (as opposed to infirmity – which the original disengagement theorists excluded). A comprehensive review of a large range of data is excellent for testing a well-established theoretical position.

However, if the state of knowledge requires exploratory work and it is necessary for the subjects to 'coach' the researchers – like Townsend's respondent quoted earlier – it will be clear that the large survey is unsuitable. If the questions are wrong, the subjects cannot 'answer back' and communicate with the researchers. Contact with the subject matter is mediated through the research agency, whose role is simply to execute the task given. The large survey is also unsuited to the theoretical perspectives which urge an under-standing of how people respond to particular events and contruct their lives in continuity with previous lifestyles and solutions. These demand a smaller-scale and more interactive method of research.

We make one final observation about the large survey as a double-edged sword. While the large numbers interviewed give it the convincing strength of numbers, processing the huge mass of data is inevitably time-consuming: the fieldwork for *Old People in Three Industrial Societies*, for instance, was conducted in 1962 but potential readers had to wait until 1968 for the comparative analyses. The fieldwork for Townsend's massive study on *Poverty in the United Kingdom* (1979) was carried out in 1968–9. Hence, in any but the most superficial form (like the 'how will you vote tomorrow?' polls) the large survey is not likely to be a suitable vehicle for producing sociologically interesting analyses fast.

However, a corresponding advantage for the future is that today such surveys invariably involve computerized analysis and, so long as the data tape is accessible to other researchers (e.g. through being lodged in the ESRC Data Archive), the material can be accessed and reanalysed by different contempor-ary researchers and by future ones interested to explore 'how we lived then'. The likelihood of these large data sets being stored in a retrievable and reusable form is much greater than with any of the other methods we discuss in this chapter.

Documents of life

A reading of Chapter 3 suggests that certain types of theoretical perspectives enjoy more of a vogue at one time than another: we suggested that the collapse of the central consensus about functionalism was replaced by a diversity of theoretical perspectives, including the biographical one. Within the more specialized field of research methods, the same broad trend can be seen in the development of critiques of the positivist survey methodology and the advo-cacy of a range of other methods, including those generically described as 'documents of life' (Plummer 1983). These include diaries, letters, the pur-posive collection of life-histories, oral history and photographic records. These 'softer' methods are so diverse that we cannot possibly do justice to their range, or to their respective strengths and weaknesses: readers whose appetite is whetted can be referred to sources such as Plummer (1983), Bertaux (1981) and Hareven and Adams (1982).

That there is no necessary association between the twin developments in theory and method mentioned above we see from the fact that one of the chief advocates of the biographical approach (Johnson 1976) – as we noted in Chapter 3 – could apparently harness it to a straightforward survey of meals on wheels consumers funded by the DHSS (Johnson *et al*. 1980). Contrariwise, it would be perfectly possible to apply positivistic methods to analyses of life-histories. Hence there is no inevitable association, but there is a strong correlation between functionalist theory, pragmatic empiricism and positivistic survey methodology on the one hand and, on the other, the advocates of a whole range of different theoretical perspectives and 'softer' research methodologies.

Plummer's review notes a paradox. A staple part of many sociologists' working lives is straightforward survey design, sampling, interviewing and statistical analysis and, as we have noted, this has become almost synonymous in the public mind with respectable research activity. Yet the use of life-history documents was part of the classical inheritance in sociology and many of its products were so appealing, readable and vivid that many researchers would prefer to work in that tradition.

Certainly this is true of research on old age. The Centre for Policy on Ageing has regularly produced a register of research in progress and, in recent years, provided an analysis of the balance of topics being researched and the type of methods used. This took up and extended an analysis by Abrams for Age Concern. Abrams noted that:

> two-thirds of all the projects are based on interview surveys . . . and in
> nearly one fifth of the studies the researcher collected all the information
> . . . from administrative records [etc.]. (1978a : 7)

Only 6% of the studies could be regarded as participant observation and 5% as 'experimental'.

Examination of table 4 in Abrams (1978a) suggests a maximum of 3% of studies could have involved such exotic methods as diary keeping and 'qualitative work'. However, analysis by Taylor (1979, 1980) of later projects revealed that the use of more than one technique was not unusual. In the 1980 analysis, 70% of projects used the interview survey and 34% used administrative records, while 8% are recorded as involving diaries, 24% case studies and 7% listed as 'qualitative'. (Since more than one method could be listed, these figures total more than 100%.)

Advocacy of the use of documents of life is really a plea for methodological pluralism: there are many different types of potential life-history documents and they can be put to a multiplicity of research ends. However, proven experience of their fruitfulness is still too limited to warrant extended discussion: what can be surmised is that, following the interest displayed in these methods, more examples will be published in the next decade.

The most notable 'document of life' in social gerontology in recent years is Newton's *This Bed My Centre* (1980). This lady, in hospital recovering from an attack of angina, found herself unexpectedly debarred from returning home by the complicity of what Goffman (1961) calls the 'circuit of agents'. These 'agents' (in Newton's case, her sister and the hospital doctor) conspire to structure the options in such a way that the person has no realistic alternative but to accept the fate which has been mapped out on his or her behalf. This is the doctor:

'Your sister feels she can't stand the strain of your long illness.' Then another of his Grand Pauses. 'We've decided it will be best for you to live in a nursing home where you will get the expert care you need.' *We've decided*. Angels would have trodden more warily. So would Matron. And clever, downright Sister Mead could have told this highly qualified young doctor that they might at least have given me a small voice in their decision to wrap up my life forever. There were things I might have said, too, if I hadn't suddenly felt tired, and as cold as buried stone. . . . As quickly as that, he had stripped all brightness from the day. (Newton 1980 : 4–5)

Newton's book is a gift to posterity, an unsolicited document of life : it would be the lucky researcher or publisher who discovered such a treasure, ready-made. She describes it as a diary, begun in despair, which became her 'close companion and gradually grew into a book':

Nothing in the diary is invented. . . . Incidents and conversations are set down exactly as they happened, sometimes while they were actually happening. Gaps here and there, sometimes of days, sometimes of months, are due to illness, intrusive curiosity as to what I was writing about, and some editing at a later stage to improve the narrative. Very often I wrote in the small hours, and in the morning, in pencil, mostly, on salvaged spare pages of notebooks and the backs of used envelopes. These bits and pieces were scattered in bags and boxes for want of a desk to hold them. There was no thought whatever of publication. (1980 : 1)

Can such documents be solicited? Here our main consideration is the life-history interview and readers planning to do life-history work might refer to Thompson (1978) and to the chapter on 'The doing of life histories' in Plummer (1983). Two areas are of particular interest. One is what Plummer calls the technical questions, 'the nuts and bolts, nitty-gritty of doing the actual research'; the other he calls the personal questions, dealing with 'the dual impact of the research on the researcher's personal life and of the researcher's personal life upon the research'.

Under the first, Plummer considers the question of who should be invited to contribute a life-history, schematically counterposing 'the great person' and 'the ordinary person'. Great people, of course, often contribute their own version of events spontaneously and Plummer notes anyway that sociologists have preferred 'to seek out the marginal or the commonplace':

The ordinary person seems to come closest to providing a source for generalisations to a wider population, but in effect it is notoriously difficult to locate such a person. Almost everyone stands 'out of the ordinary' on some dimension or the other. . . . Nevertheless, with due caution, researchers have often focused upon samples of 'ordinary people' as a source (this is particularly true of oral history), or have sought a few people about whom initially there appeared little that was extraordinary – not too marginal, not too great. (1983 : 89)

Under the second have to be considered some of the real difficulties of the work. These go beyond the question of selecting the appropriate 'lives' to examine, and to the problem of living in harmony with them, sometimes over a period of years. The research enterprise is constantly in jeopardy, as much from the researcher's loss of heart as the intractability of the subject. If tape recording is involved, the labour of transcription is enormous, as quality control on an early American study revealed:

> Every hour of recording required 6.3 hours of skilled typing and 2.8 hours of checking. . . . Attempts to analyse even brief interviews or non-directive interviews directly from the tape are subject to very great expenditures of time. . . . Most research projects will require that sound recording be transcribed. The *tremendous cost* is frequently overlooked. (Bucher *et al*. 1956 : 363; emphasis added)

Once the material is collected, it cannot be relied upon to 'speak for itself': it has to be edited, often drastically. This involves discarding masses of material which has been so laboriously collected: this does not come easily. Further, there has to be analysis and commentary for the work to have some sociological significance. Readers sense the interactive process in data collection and want to know, not only how the subject interprets events, but what interpretation the researcher places on these interpretations. Simple packages of verbatim talk – interesting though they can be to read for their novelty value – are ultimately only a stepping stone towards improved knowledge, but they are insufficiently worked to constitute knowledge in itself. Examples include *Working* (Terkel 1977) and *The People of Providence* (T. Parker 1985).

The contemporary use of documents of life has hitherto been longer on advocacy than on the production of results: the great length of time involved in producing the material, the personal and professional isolation of the researchers involved in it and the lack of institutional support compared to the funding poured into routine surveys have doubtless contributed to this state of affairs. Within our field of study, recent writing by Ford and Sinclair (1987) and di Gregorio (1986a, b, 1987) begin to advance the frontiers of understanding and demonstrate the harvest which can be reaped from the use of these methods. The fact that they have received so little support in the way of public funding affords at least the hope that such methods will be less vulnerable to the remorseless cut-backs in university and research funding which have so blighted more conventional research on old age in the 1980s.

Conclusion

Bertaux-Wiame's comment, quoted earlier, that 'everyone is investigating, all the time' is perhaps over-optimistic. Human beings are investigative and evaluative creatures but there are times when they prefer to rely on received wisdom and popular prejudice than risk the uncertainty of putting knowledge to the test. Also, as we discussed under the heading of fieldwork avoidance, there are physical, financial and social considerations which deter people from doing research – it can be laborious, uncomfortable, costly and embarrassing, the rewards uncertain.

None the less, we advocate more research, not simply because that is what researchers always say, but for three main reasons. The first is that there is a genuine lack of high-quality sociological research in our field and we have a duty – to elderly people, to ourselves and to the wider democratic interest – to remedy it. Secondly, times are changing and so also is research methodology: we need new studies to keep abreast of developments in society and studies of ageing should be fertilized by new ideas and techniques, just like other areas of inquiry. Thirdly, a persistent battle has to be waged against the tendency to marginalize elderly people and let issues of importance to them slip off research agendas.

This chapter has reviewed some of the main strategies whereby knowledge about ageing and older people is created by sociologists, arguing not in favour of one method rather than another but for a catholicism of method appropriate to the particular research topic. We have a preference for studies which bring researchers into direct contact with their field but the real criteria for research studies are that they should be systematic, open-minded and openly reported. If these criteria are met, readers can decide safely for themselves how to interpret the results.

PART II

5

Men and retirement

Introduction

Retirement has now become a period of considerable significance in the lives of older men, with the experience of permanent withdrawal from the labour force affecting them at an increasingly earlier age. By the 1990s, it is likely that half the men in the 55–59 age group and two-thirds of the 60–64 age group will either be registered as unemployed or otherwise out of the workforce. This shift in employment must also be related to a historical decline in the percentage of older men who remain economically active. In Britain, for example, nearly three-quarters of the male population in 1881 were in work but by 1981 the number had shrunk to less than 11%.

During the twentieth century, then, retirement in Western industrial nations has become a 'universal social institution' (Townsend 1986 : 22). The reasons for the emergence of retirement are outlined in Chapter 2, where we identify factors such as the desire to increase 'efficiency' and 'productivity' in the workplace, together with the pressure created by the recurring problem of mass unemployment. We also note, however, different approaches to retirement among working-class and middle-class men and women. For the former, there appears to be the absence of an 'active concept of retirement' (Stearns 1977); instead, leaving work has been interpreted more in terms of providing an opportunity for rest and relaxation within the framework of limited financial resources. For middle-class people, on the other hand, there has developed a leisure-orientated lifestyle in retirement, built around an expanding consumer market and culture and supported, in some cases, by a substantial occupational pension (Featherstone 1987).

Many questions need to be asked about this stage in the life-cycle: how far is retirement still a problem in a culture which values work as opposed to non-work and leisure; what is the impact of retirement on men's lives; does it still create tension and stress for individuals; how far does it affect their relationships within the family and community?

These are some of the questions to be discussed in this chapter. In exploring them we shall draw upon the substantial literature written on the subject over the past 20 years. However, we begin with some illustrative examples of lives of men in retirement, drawn from our research, to indicate both the choices and constraints which they face.

Men in retirement: four pen portraits

The men described below were interviewed during the course of a study on the experience of retirement (Phillipson 1978). The focus of the research was analysis of the way in which particular class, community and occupational contexts affected retirement. These were seen to have a major impact on the individual's life, setting significant boundaries and creating different opportunities. As a result, it was argued that there is not one retirement experience but many, each reflecting the divisions and diversity within British society.

Frank White

Frank White is in his late 60s and lives in an inner-city part of Newcastle-upon-Tyne. He worked as an unskilled labourer at a freight depot until he was 51, when the physical demands of the job forced him to find a different one. His work career ended when he was made redundant at the age of 59, after which he found jobs almost impossible to get:

> Jobs were getting bad because I was getting older . . . and it was a bugger when you were used to the big wages and then you had to drop onto the dole.

His problems were reflected in the social environment around him, an environment which added to his difficulties in adjusting to retirement. He was living in a group of flats which were generally regarded to be some of the worst in Newcastle. His own block was half-empty, with smashed windows and peeling paintwork much in evidence. He lived on his own after being divorced from his wife and was completely dependent on the single person's old age pension, plus a supplementary pension which paid the rent and also occasional necessities such as blankets and shoes. Here is his account of an ordinary day in retirement:

> I generally get up about eight . . . eight to nine . . . you have a cup of tea . . . have a look round . . . have a bit of breakfast . . . perhaps tidy up a bit. So time rolls on to about eleven. What I generally do . . . I generally go out about eleven and go and get me rations and sit in the bar with the lads and have a yap. You don't have to drink a lot of beer. So I just sit with the lads and have a couple of pints. I then go and get some groceries perhaps and then land in here [home] about three o'clock . . . after just sitting there killing time [in the bar]. After this I generally have a cup of tea and a lie down, not that I'm drunk or anything like that, I just have to lie down to kill the monotony. I generally get up about 7 pm and have another cup of tea, and then I put the telly on and maybe have some dinner. Then it's about 9 pm and I listen to the news and then again at ten.

Frank White saw the problem in terms of finding friendships and contacts. He had not built up many of these when he was working and since coming to his present home 8 years ago he has not found many there either – apart from a circle of friends in a local bar. The bar was important in providing a regular source of contacts – often people in the same position who would be sympathetic to the difficulties encountered through living alone on a low income. Outside of this situation, however, for instance in the street and other public places, hostility and rejection were seen as the likely outcome of overtures of friendship:

> If I go and sit on a seat and try to talk to a bloke he would want to know who the hell I am. He would ask me what did I want, might think I was a dip [mad] or something. See, when I go into the bar the lad knows. That's how I break my loneliness. But I'm frightened if they move us away from here I will be back in the desert again, that is what I'm frightened of. If they put me away where I don't know anybody and I've got to make a fresh start . . . go into a new bar . . . I would be lost . . . that's what worries me now. The bar is my second home but it's not for the drink . . . it cannot be on this money . . . it's just a second home where I can go over and kill the strain of this because if I stop here like any other man or woman of my age . . . I would just fade away, without anybody at all to talk to.

John Keithley

John Keithley lives in a Durham mining village. In contrast to the men like Mr White interviewed in an inner-city area – where the personal disorganization of their lives was reflected in the social disorganization and physical decline of the local environment – Mr Keithley displays considerable continuity from the pre-retirement to post-retirement period. Part of this was provided through solidarity with and neighbourhood support from a traditional working-class community where many of the older miners had chosen to accept retirement together, when the pit closed. This community solidarity was reflected in the self-confident and relaxed attitude of the miners to being interviewed on the subject. Mr Keithley had spent all his working life in mining, apart from 3 years in the steel industry after the local pit closed. Retirement for him did not lead to a separation from valued friends and workmates, for many remained in the immediate vicinity of his village. He comments:

> I think at the finish I was looking forward to it 'coz I knew I would be alright here working on the garden . . . having me mates when I wanted to see them.

With his network of friends, Mr Keithley had taken a positive approach to retirement:

> It's a day to day thing with me . . . can you understand that? To me . . . 'coz sometimes if it's a nasty morning you know . . . it depends . . . you've got to find something to do, it's no good just sitting about looking

at the rain . . . you've got to be doing something . . . you've got to be looking for something and trying to enjoy what you're doing . . . without doing something that you didn't want to do . . . forced to do like sometimes was the case in the pit.

This attitude was further supported by a close relationship with his wife. As Mr Keithley put it: 'Retirement makes you closer . . . it seems as though you need each other more I think.'

Peter McLean

Peter McLean had worked at the Longbridge car plant in Birmingham since the 1930s. His recollections about factory life are particularly vivid:

There was nothing to like about it at all. There was the din . . . the smoke . . . the hard work itself . . . and you was chained to your vice practically . . . everybody used to fight for the good little jobs that was about. You'd not only got to work but to fight for it as well . . . any of the good jobs that was going . . . if you was slow about it . . . if you was a ninny then you'd be a ninny . . . and your wife and kids would – because you was one . . . they'd suffer. You'd got to be prepared to stand up to them [other workers] and tell them . . . 'Hey . . . you've had your corner I'm having mine.' And you've got to be prepared to be ready for them . . . you'd got to fight for the decent jobs . . . so you would get some money out of it as well.

Despite these pressures and conflicts at work, retirement was still experienced as an emotional and disturbing event. According to Mr McLean:

When I retired I had a ruddy great lump come in me throat. I couldn't help it . . . you can't help it, when you get lads like that . . . that you've been with for a long time.

Four years later he still suffered a sense of loss and, like many of these formerly 'affluent workers' (Goldthorpe *et al*. 1968–9) he was acutely aware of the decline in his standard of living. Retirement undermined many relationships and worthwhile activities – those based at work and those maintained because of work and the income it provided:

I've had to leave my Trade Union . . . to me that was part of my life . . . it was part of my life's blood . . . I had to leave that . . . in fact I was a member of the Trades Council . . . I was a shop steward . . . nothing used to be better for me than to put a kid's case forward . . . that was taken away . . . With me being involved as I was . . . being a shop steward and all the rest . . . you was more involved with the boys. I knew more about every individual one down there than perhaps he knew himself. You see I would be the one blokes would unburden themselves to . . . every shop steward respected by his blokes is in the same position.

On the other hand, Mr McLean says of retirement:

To me . . . to retire all men at 65 is wrong and no-one will know about it until they've been retired 2 or 3 years . . . then it begins to get to them just what retirement really does . . . it means nothing else but bloody boredom, worse than you had at work . . . especially with the weather getting like it is now. There ain't no old person . . . there's one or two old people in this road here . . . and I've seen them down at the hall there . . . what day is it . . . Wednesday . . . I'll bet you they're there now . . . I've seen the old people going there . . . and I've seen them walk about and I've felt heartily sorry for them and I dread the day when I ever get like that. But when you retire from work you feel like that . . . people look on you as that.

Mr White, Mr McLean and Mr Keithley illustrate different retirement experiences within the working class. Mr Kendrick supplies a contrasting middle-class example.

Richard Kendrick

Richard Kendrick had been a senior partner in a large architectural practice based in the Midlands and recalled the way that architecture had seemed to become an all-consuming part of his life:

I'm afraid I always seemed to be working on it. I did a lot of work for charitable people like schools – Quaker schools; a lot of that I did in my spare-time. So that I was working in my spare-time in architecture . . . so it did take up a great deal of time and I found it very difficult to get my mind off it. Then when I went on my holidays we went looking at buildings . . . part of the time.

Arising out of this work experience was a view that retirement must also be 'worthwhile' and that useful tasks must be found. In Mr Kendrick's case this involved sharing his wife's interest in botany and researching the flora in the area of their second-home in Spain:

I think this is what has been, until recently, . . . a sort of worry . . . that I was becoming useless. But now I think I've got myself all weighed up and I've got something which – I mean – photographing a lot of flowers and cataloguing them may not be very much, but there's something to show for it when you've finished . . . which I think is why I've taken that sort of line . . . that if I was playing golf or something . . . I wouldn't be likely to win any championships or anything. There would be nothing to show for it . . . if one just went on playing. We've made a number of friends in the botanical line and this research we may do in this area – which has not been very well covered in a botanical way – could be a contribution. Whether it is or not, the thought that it might be makes it very acceptable.

Resources – financial, social and cultural – were significant in this approach to retirement. Mr Kendrick and his wife had been fortunate enough to buy a second home on the Costa del Sol, where they spent half the year and were developing their botanical interests. In this context, the freedom of retirement could be made to mean something tangible for the individual rather than a burden as it became for those without money or significant friendships:

> It's the sort of freedom from responsibility . . . the feeling that . . . when you wake up in the morning that . . . only occasionally do you have to jump to it . . . get up . . . and rush off somewhere . . . I think it's just that . . . being fairly active . . . I think it's the freedom to do what I want . . . and not to have a programme set for me . . .

The growth of early retirement

Retirement must be seen from the outset as a constantly changing institution; for instance, in terms of the numbers of people involved, as well as in respect of individual and social attitudes to retirement and the age at which people decide to retire from their full-time career. In this last respect, there has been a significant shift in the 1980s towards earlier retirement ages for men (and women) in the labour force. Table 5.1 indicates older men retaining their hold in the labour market in the boom years of the 1950s, although even here the trend for those aged 65 and over was clearly downward. Between 1971 and 1981 all age groups aged 45 and above show a downward trend, this being particularly marked for the 60–64 age group.

Table 5.1.   Male economic activity rates, Britain: 1951–91.

Age	Percentage of each age group economically active				
	1951	1961	1971	1981	1991
45–54	97.8	98.6	97.6	94.8	91.7
55–59	95.0	97.1	95.3	89.4	80.1
60–64	87.7	91.0	86.6	69.3	50.8
65–69	47.7	39.9	30.6	16.3	9.3
70+	20.3	15.2	11.0	6.5	3.6

Source: Social Trends, **6**, 84, 1975. London, HMSO. *Employment Gazette*, May 1987.

In Table 5.2, the shifts in the position of older workers are examined in more detail, focussing on the period 1971–91. This confirms the steep fall in economic activity for men aged 60–64, especially in the 10 years from 1976 to 1986 (a drop of 27%). The change for men aged 55–59 was also significant, showing a decline of 12%.

The one slightly contrary trend is the levelling out of the decline in the economic activity rate for men aged 65–69. The estimates suggest a slight increase from 1983 to 1985, with the resumption of the downward trend thereafter. However, in global terms, male part-time employment (histori- cally, an important area of work for men over pensionable age) is taking an increasing proportion of total employment in Britain; hence we might expect

Table 5.2.   Male economic activity rates, Britain: 1971–91.

Age	Percentage of each age group economically active										
	1971	1972	1973	1974	1975	1976	1977	1978	1979	1980	1981
45–54	97.6	95.8	96.0	96.1	96.2	96.1	96.0	95.7	95.4	95.1	94.8
55–59	95.3	93.0	93.0	93.0	93.0	92.4	91.8	91.3	90.8	90.1	89.4
60–64	86.6	82.7	82.6	82.4	82.3	80.4	78.5	75.8	73.0	71.2	69.3
65–69	30.6	29.3	28.2	27.0	25.9	23.9	22.0	19.4	16.8	16.6	16.3
70+	11.0	10.3	9.6	9.0	8.3	8.0	7.6	6.8	6.1	6.3	6.5

	Estimates					Projections				
	1982	1983	1984	1985	1986	1987	1988	1989	1990	1991
45–54	94.0	93.1	92.6	92.3	91.7	91.6	91.6	91.7	91.7	91.7
55–59	86.8	84.1	82.1	82.0	80.3	80.1	80.1	80.1	80.1	80.1
60–64	64.3	59.4	56.7	54.4	53.4	53.2	52.6	52.0	51.4	50.8
65–69	14.8	13.3	13.6	13.9	12.5	11.8	11.1	10.5	9.9	9.3
70+	5.9	5.3	5.5	5.2	4.7	4.5	4.3	4.0	3.8	3.6

Source: Employment Gazette, May 1987.

to see a small but significant number of older men remaining active in service-type jobs such as portering, caretaking and cleaning.

The overall trend of withdrawal from the labour market is unmistakable. Moreover, the trend is highlighted if we distinguish among the economically active those who are actually in employment and those who are unemployed. To analyse this, Table 5.3 summarizes information from the *British Labour Force Survey*. This is an annual survey of the employment experiences of 0.5% of the population, reviewing hours worked, how jobs are found, the amount of training people receive and so on. Once again, the table shows the general deterioration in the labour market position of older workers. However, the data show more clearly the way in which, during the 1980s, exit from the labour force spread downwards to embrace a substantial proportion of the 55+ age group. Indeed, while in 1979 the critical division was still between the 55–59 and 60–64 age groups by 1986 a significant gap had opened between those in their mid- to late 50s and the younger age groups.

It is important to recognize the complexity of the trends under discussion. What has emerged in the 1980s is an increase both in the range of pre-retirement categories and statuses and the numbers of older men in them. Some will include those who opt for early retirement voluntarily with a substantial occupational pension to support them. Others will be 'discouraged workers' who fail to register as unemployed in the belief that there are no jobs available (Laczko 1987). A substantial number will comprise long-term sick and disabled people. Inevitably, expansion in the routes by which people can enter retirement carries implications for the retirement experience itself – producing greater variety and diversity in both attitudes and financial circumstances.

Table 5.3.   Male economic activity and inactivity rates, Britain: 1979–86.

Age		1979	1981	1983	1984	1985	1986
40–44	Economically active	98	97	96	96	96	95
	In employment	94	91	89	88	88	88
	Unemployed	3	6	8	8	7	7
	Economically inactive	2	3	4	4	4	5
45–49	Economically active	97	96	95	94	95	94
	In employment	94	90	87	87	87	87
	Unemployed	3	6	8	7	8	7
	Economically inactive	3	4	5	6	5	6
50–54	Economically active	95	95	93	92	92	90
	In employment	92	88	85	85	85	83
	Unemployed	3	7	7	7	7	7
	Economically inactive	5	5	7	8	8	10
55–59	Economically active	91	90	85	82	82	81
	In employment	88	83	76	74	75	73
	Unemployed	3	7	8	8	8	7
	Economically inactive	9	10	15	18	18	19
60–64	Economically active	73	70	59	57	54	53
	In employment	69	62	53	51	50	48
	Unemployed	4	8	7	5	4	5
	Economically inactive	27	30	41	43	46	47
65+	Economically active	10	10	8	8	8	8
	In employment	9	10	8	8	8	7
	Unemployed	1	0	0	0	0	0
	Economically inactive	90	90	92	92	92	92

Source: British Labour Force Survey. Special tabulations supplied by the Department of Employment.

Men in retirement: challenging the stereotype

The retired male has been the subject of a number of negative and misleading stereotypes. He is viewed as poor, depressed, unhappy at being deprived of work and in conflict with his wife and family. Sociological theory has, in a number of ways, reinforced this view. As we saw in Chapter 3, role theory emphasized the extent to which retirement created a sense of crisis and loss – for men in particular. Paradoxically, disengagement theory presented a more optimistic view, but couched in an inherently pessimistic framework, suggesting that the best-adjusted were those who bowed to the ineluctable dictates of biology and social imperatives by voluntary withdrawal from social life.

Later work has emphasized the diversity of experiences in retirement, a feature illustrated by the case studies which opened this chapter. Yet the stereotype of the inactive retiree still persists. In part this has been maintained because of deficiencies in the studies about retirement. In Britain the majority of such studies employ a cross-sectional design (see, e.g., Parker 1980; McGoldrick and Cooper 1980). With this method it is virtually impossible to distinguish between the causes and consequences of leaving work. Thus, many studies in the 1950s and 1960s reported increased rates of sickness as a result of retiring from work (Logan 1953; Anderson and Cowan 1956; Crawford 1972). Unfortunately, on closer inspection of the study design it is impossible to say whether this sickness is caused by the poor health which people bring into retirement or whether it is an outcome of being deprived of work.

One solution to this problem is the longitudinal design which follows people's lives prospectively from an earlier point in the life-cycle. Longitudinal studies are, however, expensive and require considerable organizational commitment, as well as taking many years to complete. Fortunately, the findings from American surveys of this kind are now available and they have added considerably to our own understanding of the retirement period (see below).

There is, though, a second issue that has to be confronted in studies of retirement. When people are asked about how they feel about leaving work, we have to remember that their replies are framed within a political and social context. In the 1950s, when people were urged to remain at work and retired people were seen as a 'burden', it is hardly surprising to find negative views expressed about retirement (Phillipson 1982). In the late 1980s, when there is pressure on people to leave work to create jobs for the young, positive views about retirement are perhaps more likely to be expressed (Bytheway 1986).

There is a final reason for the persistence of negative stereotypes about retirement: the fact that poor health *is* a problem for many older men. However, the evidence suggests that this is not *because* of retirement, but is, instead, connected with factors associated with work, the physical environment and ageing itself (Haynes *et al.* 1978; Palmore *et al.* 1979; Cribier 1979; Vallery-Masson 1981). We must remember that there are high levels of sickness and death which occur prior to leaving work. For example, one in four men who reach 35 will not survive to retirement age (Bosanquet 1987). Of those who do, among manual workers, one in three may already have a chronic illness when they enter retirement (Shephard 1978). Recent work on the political economy of health and disability has begun to make more visible to us the health hazards of work (Doyal 1979; Walker 1980), but in the popular imagination these are less salient that the association of poor health with retirement. This association does, therefore, have a grounding in everyday experience, although the causal relationship is almost certainly indirect. Confusion on this has, however, greatly contributed to popular conceptions of retirement as a time of crisis and decline. How far has sociological research justified or affirmed such views?

The experience of retirement

The historical analysis of retirement in Chapter 2 suggests that leaving work has rarely been open to influence by individuals – especially those from working-class backgrounds. There has, it is true, been a strong body of opinion stressing the virtues of flexible retirement (Bosanquet 1987) but in reality most people find that the timing of retirement is largely beyond their control. It may arise through ill-health (as with many people who retire early); it may come through extended unemployment (as with the 130 000 men aged 60–64 who in 1986 received long-term supplementary benefit without having to register as unemployed); or it may be the result of compulsory termination of employment at the age of 65. Retirement, in short, rarely comes as a result of people choosing when *they* would like to leave work, in line with their priorities and time-scale as opposed to that of their employer. Added to this is the fact that few employees receive formal preparation to assist them through the transition (Coleman 1982), even though a high proportion of workers enter retirement with no clear idea of what they are intending to do with this period in their lives (Phillipson and Strang 1983; Long 1987).

If the lead-up to retirement appears stressful, however, it is less clear that the same can be said for retirement itself. Indeed, the general conclusion from research points in a more optimistic direction. The French study by Cribier (1981) confirmed both a 'marked increase in the proportion of people who view retirement as a desirable goal, and early retirement as particularly desirable'. The retirees in the British study by Parker (1980), while more cautious in their views, had still, in the majority of cases, 'settled down' some 12 months after leaving work. The analysis by Palmore *et al.* of a number of American longitudinal data sets concluded:

> Retirement at the normal age has little or no adverse effects on health for the average retiree. Some have health declines, but these are balanced by those who enjoy health improvement.
>
> Retirement at the normal age has few substantial effects on activities, except for the obvious reduction in work and some compensating increase in solitary activities.
>
> Retirement at the normal age has little or no effect on most attitudes for the average retiree. Some become more dissatisfied, but these are balanced by those who become more satisfied. (1985 : 167)

Beyond these general findings, however, some qualifications must be expressed. The research also tells us that biographies and work histories remain important in influencing retirement outcomes. We can see this in very obvious ways: people in retirement are survivors and this in itself is class-determined – those in social class five are two-and-a-half times more likely to die before reaching retirement than those in social class one (Townsend and Davidson 1982). Working-class people are also more likely to enter retirement with a chronic health problem and, in consequence, to have some limitation placed on their retirement activities.

Class variations in income were highlighted in the study by Taylor and Ford of Aberdeen men (1983). Here, it is striking to observe that nearly one-quarter of working-class men aged 60–74 had savings of less than £250 compared with 4% of middle-class men. Conversely, very nearly 60% of middle-class men had savings of £5000 or more, compared with less than a third of working-class men. This study also reported class differences in health, with middle-class men reporting fewer difficulties than working-class men of the same age.

Such variations confirm Featherstone's view that we need to talk about a number of retirements, these arising through the 'different resources groups possess in terms of economic, cultural and symbolic capital' (1987:128). These different resources are ultimately highly influential on daily living. In general terms, the striking finding from research is the continuity of lifestyles for many retired people, with most involved in activities they had pursued before their retirement. Long's (1987) study confirms earlier British research by Richardson (1956) and Crawford (1972) in this respect, noting, as well, the re-engagement in family life:

> Apart from watching television, reading, social activities (principally visits to or from friends and relatives), walking, DIY/decorating and trips/sightseeing/holidays were among the already popular activities mentioned even more frequently after retirement. Of the activities rarely mentioned prior to retirement but now cited more frequently, several suggested a greater emphasis on interaction with others (e.g. helping family and friends, chatting, playing with children). These were almost certainly not new activities, but now had a different value. (Long 1987:63)

The single biggest advantage of retirement, reported by numerous studies (see, e.g., Crawford 1972; Age Concern 1974), is invariably that of 'more freedom' or 'to be able to do what you want to do, when you want to do it' (Long 1987:62). Yet even here, as Phillipson (1987) suggests, the language spoken about retirement remains contradictory. Cribier (1981) notes that in her survey the proportion of people 'genuinely' satisfied with retirement (40% overall), varied from 34% of male employees and blue-collar workers to 59% of middle- and upper-level executives. Similarly, Guillemard (1982) has shown how different types of retirement lifestyles are related to class position. Thus for working-class retirees social withdrawal may be a typical mode of response. because their exploited position presents them with few resources to consume and convert into meaningful leisure during retirement. Middle-class retirees, on the other hand, are seen to have the economic and cultural capital to assist the conversion of free time into leisure.

Such research suggests that we need to see the retirement transition as an area where the social ties an individual has developed with society and the type of skills he or she has been allowed to accumulate assume a new importance. In short, it is in the retirement transition that the individual calls upon the resources he or she has developed during the early and middle phases of the life-cycle. In this sense the transition is not a movement from an old to a completely new life (as disengagement and role theories would suggest); rather it is the final confirmation of the advantages and disadvantages attached to given social and class positions: once the advantages accruing to a particular position are consolidated they are likely to be sustained even into very old age.

Similarly, where there are disadvantages, retirement and old age may simply add to the individual's sense of powerlessness and loss of control and the period of time involved may itself be shortened by aggravated mortality (Phillipson 1987).

Domestic and social relationships in retirement

An important area to consider is the effect of retirement on marital and social relationships. Once again, there is a stereotyped view to be considered. This suggests that retirement is a source of tension because of conflict between husband and wife. The husband is supposed to feel frustrated at home, deprived of a central role and purpose; the wife feels threatened, with her own routine and daily activities facing disruption. Such a view did find support in sociological research in the 1950s and 1960s. Peter Townsend, in *The Family Life of Old People*, certainly found evidence of strained relationships between husbands and wives:

> Retirement produced frustrations in men, because they could not fill their time and because they felt they were useless, and it also produced frustrations in women, because they had been used to a larger income and to a daily routine without interference from the husband. (1957 : 89)

Such findings have tended to be taken as typical of retired couples. But even if this was the case in the 1950s (and one suspects there were many variations even then), does it still hold for domestic and family life in the 1980s, given both earlier retirement and changing attitudes towards work and leisure?

A consistent observation from both American and British research is that retirement produces more intensive involvement within the family, for example in parenting (Crawford 1972) and grandparenting activities (Crawford 1981; Cunningham-Burley 1986). This is part of a broader finding that family life – for both men and women – remains crucially important in old age, even if 'intimacy at a distance' has tended to replace (in many communities) everyday face-to-face contact between elderly parents and their children. Even here, the survey by Abrams (1980) of older people in four socially different urban areas indicated extensive visiting by children of men aged 65–74 and those aged 75 and over, particularly at weekends. Moreover, numerous studies have reported intensive involvement (especially from daughters) in support of older people with health problems (Nissel and Bonnerjea 1982; Peace 1986).

One reason for the importance of marital and family relationships for retired men is the problematic nature of friendship in old age. Taylor and Ford (1983) demonstrate this in their Aberdeen study, where they report high proportions of men aged 60–74 with no close friends (31% of middle-class men and 41% of working-class men). This finding was repeated among very elderly men, with those from the working-class being at a particular disadvantage. These class differences probably reflect the impact of poverty and ill-health in causing the networks of working-class men to shrink at a faster rate in comparison to those from the middle-class. This may be especially marked in declining inner-city areas, as we saw with Mr White. A related point is that cross-gender friendships remain comparatively rare (Matthews 1986; Willmott 1987). This creates problems for older men, who find themselves heavily outnumbered by women in settings such as clubs for old people. Men, in fact, are less likely to join these clubs (Wenger 1984) and where they do join tend to remain 'socially invisible' (Jerrome 1986 : 350).

By contrast, neighbours may assume greater importance for men in retirement, particularly in the context of their extensive involvement in outside tasks such as gardening (Wenger 1984; Long 1987). A study by Willmott (1987) found that among men aged 60 and over, one-third of their last-seen friends were in fact neighbours. The research by Abrams (Bulmer 1986) also points to the same general finding about the salience of neighbours for older people.

There is much, unfortunately, we have yet to discover about the conflicts and contradictions of domestic and family life. There appears, as we have observed, to be regular visiting and support from children (and grandchildren) to elderly relatives. Yet we should also note the finding in the study by Abrams, where 45% of parents aged 65–74 said that they would like to see their children more often; among parents aged 75 or more the figure was 39%.

There is impressive documentation of wives acting both as confidants (Wenger 1984) and carers to sick husbands (and vice versa; see Bytheway 1986; Sidell 1986; Phillipson 1987). But we have only limited understanding of the texture of relationships between husband and wife, between son/daughter and retiree or between (and this is increasingly common) stepson/step-daughter and retiree.

American research suggests that for most couples retirement brings very little change in the organization of domestic tasks (Keating and Cole 1980; Dobson 1983). In general, if husbands increase their participation in household activities, the increase tends to be in masculine-orientated activities (Brubaker 1983). At the same time, we know less about how couples readjust their lives and routines in the face of diminished mobility, poverty, or a serious illness. The pressures among elderly men and women and their informal carers have been documented (see, e.g., Parker 1985; Peace 1986; Sidell 1986). We also have some evidence of couples using their relationship successfully to negotiate the retirement transition (Phillipson 1987) or movement to a new home (Karn 1977). In general, as with many other aspects of retirement, the character of domestic life will depend upon a pattern set during the early and middle years of marriage. The extent to which retirement changes or can change this pattern (if it is desirable), remains a matter for further research.

Conclusion

From a sociological perspective, we have moved some distance from the interpretation of retirement prevalent in the 1950s and 1960s. This focussed upon retirement as a time of crisis and disorientation, reinforced by the poverty characteristic of the majority of older people (Townsend and Wedderburn 1965). Given the contradictory trends we have noted in Chapter 1, in which we counterposed the widening gaps between those who do or do not participate in generally improved standards of living, it is now more accurate to highlight the contrasts emerging within this major social institution of retirement. On the one hand, there is the growth of new patterns of consumption, built around access to occupational pensions and the growth of leisure industries aimed at people aged 50 and above. The sociological evidence here is considerable: specialist magazines, holiday companies, the second home industry, retirement communities, private sheltered housing schemes. These are the outward trappings of a substantial group of people concerned to develop a positive lifestyle in the years following departure from full-time work.

On the other hand, old age remains a period when poverty can be expected – by most women and most working-class men (Walker 1986, 1987). In 1983, 5 700 000 elderly people were living in poverty or on its margins – 64% compared with 24% under pensionable age (DHSS 1986). In addition, while a minority of older people enjoy access to a second home, the current generation of older people represent a majority of the worst housed in the population. Although they are roughly one-fifth of the population, they occupy one-third of all the dwellings built before 1919, almost one-half of all dwellings in need of rehabilitation and at least half of the dwellings lacking a basic amenity. These figures need to be seen in the context of retired people spending a substantial proportion of their lives indoors, in conditions none the less of substantial deprivation (Wheeler 1986).

These divisions in old age are likely to grow with the development of earlier retirement, with working-class men especially drawing-upon their savings in the period leading up to state retirement age. At the same time, we shall also have an increasing number of men and women constructing a more ambitious lifestyle in retirement. This development must be seen as part of a significant social and cultural trend, whereby full-time work is seen as a necessity for a limited period in the life-cycle, to be replaced by a different set of values and relationships thereafter. If we recall the vignettes of Mr White, a retired unskilled labourer in a declining inner-city area, eking out his time on a restricted income and suffering ill-health and Mr Kendrick, developing his botanical research on the Costa del Sol, it is clear that the extent to which individuals will be able to make the most of retirement will depend upon their access to various forms of financial, physical, social and cultural capital. Without radical socio-political changes, this access will largely be determined by the extent to which they have accumulated such resources earlier in life.

6

Women and old age

Introduction

It is well known that women generally outlive men and that the gap between men and women in expectation of life has widened during the twentieth century. In 1901, expectation of life at birth was 48 years for males, 51.6 years for females. By 1983, the corresponding figures were 71.4 and 77.2 years, respectively. As a result, women outnumber men in old age – by more than 2:1 over the age of 75 (CSO 1987) – so clearly retirement and old age are very much issues for and about women. A chapter on women in retirement and old age is therefore necessary, not simply as a complement to the previous one with its focus on men, but because the experience of ageing for women warrants particular analysis. None the less, little more than a decade ago older women remained virtually invisible in gerontological and feminist literature (Beeson 1975), although recently the subject has begun to receive attention in scholarly and popular literature (Pym 1977; Matthews 1979; Phillipson 1981; Bailey 1982; Markson 1983; Macdonald and Rich 1984; Evers 1985; Peace 1986).

The reasons for this invisibility derive from a combination of ageism and sexism. Ageism means unwarranted application of negative stereotypes to older people. For example, it is common to assume that old age inevitably brings ill-health. Thus Mrs Jeavons, a subject in the study by Evers (1984), reported that she avoided going to the doctor, because when she did so, he often responded only by saying, 'Well, what can you expect at your age?' Mrs Jeavons observed that she was well aware of her age – she was in her 80s – and took exception to her complaints being dismissed like this.

Sexism means unwarranted application of negative stereotypes to women, which, as with ageist stereotypes, serve to legitimize institutional and individual discrimination against women simply on the basis of their sex. For feminists, sexism means 'that people count sex as relevant in contexts where it is not' (Radcliffe Richards 1982:29). 'Sex' becomes transformed into 'gender' through socialization processes by which males and females 'learn' roles and behaviours commonly associated with their sex. The socialization process is so pervasive that the mistaken assumption is often advanced that gender roles – such as women's role of nurturing family members – are not only natural and normal, but above all, innate. It is but a small step from there to justify discrimination against women which leads, for example, to their over-representation in low-paid, part-time work, as part of the 'natural' order of things between the sexes. (Regarding social processes as 'natural' has been discussed as 'mystification' in Chapter 1.)

Our gender-ordered society features a division of labour between the sexes such that women tend to be ascribed roles in the 'private domain' of the home and family and to be subordinated to men, whose interests dominate the 'public domain' of the workplace and other social institutions. Women's position and experiences have been addressed in sociology in only a limited way, since sociological concepts, methods and problems have featured male-dominated definitions of the issues (see Stacey 1981; Dex 1985).

Suffering from the double burden of ageism and sexism, older women have for too long been marginalized by society at large and by the literature stemming from sociology, gerontology and feminism: their visibility invari-ably restricted to portrayal of negative stereotypes, as 'old hags', 'mutton dressed as lamb', 'crones' and so forth. Sontag writes:

> Getting older is less profoundly wounding for a man, for in addition to the propaganda for youth that puts both men and women on the defensive as they age, there is a double standard about aging that de-nounces women with special severity. Society is much more permissive about aging in men. . . . Men are 'allowed' to age, without penalty, in sev-eral ways that women are not. . . . Thus, for most women, aging means a humiliating process of gradual sexual disqualification. . . . Women are at a disadvantage because their sexual candidacy depends on meeting certain much stricter 'conditions' related to looks and age. (1975 : 32–5)

The early preoccupations of the feminists working in the tradition which began to develop during the 1960s were with the circumstances of younger women, domesticity, childbearing and childrearing. Now 25 years older, they and their successors are beginning to analyse issues relating to older women (Macdonald and Rich 1984).

What do we know of the circumstances and experiences of older women? Three pen portraits will serve to identify the themes of the discussion which follows. These women were interviewed during research by Evers (1984) on women's experiences of growing old. Some of the women were receiving support from lay carers and/or community health and social services. Each differs from the others and the three throw some light on why we need to study the sociology of the gender-related experience of old age. All live in the suburbs of a large Midlands city.

Older women: three pen portraits

Mrs Clark

Mrs Clark is in her early 80s and lives alone in a purpose-built bungalow for eld-erly people, which she rents from the council. Her husband, who had suffered with a heart complaint for many years, died very suddenly 3 years ago. Mrs Clark herself has troublesome arthritis in her knees and her eyesight has worsened with the years though she feels her health is generally very good 'for my age'. Mrs Clark has children and grandchildren, some close by and others further afield. She is in regular contact with all of them, exchanging frequent visits with a daughter who lives two bus rides away. Mrs Clark worked on and off during her married life as an enameller in the jewellery trade, but there was no occupational pension scheme for part-time and intermittent women workers and her income now consists of her old age and supplementary pensions.

Life nowadays is extremely busy: Mrs Clark is active in the local church and regularly visits 'some poorly old people' living nearby. She goes on frequent outings, stays with her children and, when at home, enjoys reading and cooking. Interviewing Mrs Clark was hard to arrange, as she was so often out. Her morale was high and she was cheerfully thinking ahead to a summer visit to her daughter in the south – and to various social events.

Mrs Dixon

Mrs Dixon is also in her early 80s. She is diminutive and rather frail in her appearance. She and her older husband occupy a first-floor, privately-rented flat. The flat is clean and neat, but with few signs of luxury: the couple have no savings to speak of and their sole source of income is the old age pension. Mrs Dixon had various part-time domestic jobs during the course of her younger married life. Although relatively well herself, she is effectively unable to go out because her husband is demented and cannot be left alone. The work of caring for him is considerable: he needs help with all the basic functions of daily living and his incontinence creates additional laundry.

Mrs Dixon's daughter, her husband and one of their daughters live in their own flat on the ground floor of the same house as Mr and Mrs Dixon. The daughter works full-time but helps her mother during the evenings and at weekends. She does the shopping, a certain amount of cooking and washing and helps to get Mr Dixon in to bed at night. Mrs Dixon is extremely devoted to her husband, and does not resent the work of caring for him. Her daughter is almost her sole lifeline with the outside world yet Mrs Dixon remains cheerful and physically and mentally resilient despite her relatively lonely life.

Mrs Erskine

Mrs Erskine lives alone in a council-rented house which she has occupied for about 60 years. She takes some pride in her appearance: she is always well dressed and has her hair done regularly. Now in her late 80s, Mrs Erskine has an extremely active mind and is a person who loves company, whether impromptu visitors or people she meets when she goes to the local church luncheon club. She devoted herself to nursing her severely disabled husband for 25 years: he died when she was herself turned 60. Then, having always been very short of money, she went out to work as a cleaner and later a shopworker until her own ill-health – hypertension and other cardiovascular problems – led her to stop work at the age of 64. Mrs Erskine needs to be very careful with money, being reliant on state benefits, but finds that she can just manage. She had no children, but is in regular touch with a nephew and his family who live some distance away. She has many friends – she received around 90 Christmas cards last year – whom she keeps in touch with by letter and telephone.

When interviewed, Mrs Erskine had not been out for over 12 months, for her worsening heart condition and a slight stroke had shaken her confidence. None the less, she is very resourceful in solving her own problems. The local shopkeepers all provide a delivery service and she has found a man to look after the garden for her. A home help calls twice a week, a female neighbour looks in daily for a chat and a young woman living nearby, whom Mrs Erskine has known since she was a child, visits regularly and helps in various ways.

These three examples lead us on to various questions about women in old age and the extent to which their social position and experiences of late life parallel, or differ from, those of old men. First, all three of the women live frugal lives. Having had only intermittent part-time jobs bringing them no occupational pension when they finally ceased paid work, they all had low incomes. The husbands of Mrs Clark and Mrs Dixon had no occupational pensions either and during their working lives had had low-paid jobs which did not allow much scope for saving. In any case, Mr Clark had retired early due to ill-health and Mr Erskine had been an invalid for 25 years and therefore not earning. Are these women's work histories typical of older women more generally? Do they differ systematically from those of men? Do women have, in general, lower incomes than men in old age?

A second set of questions relate to demography and the family life of older women. Two of the three have outlived their husbands and are now alone. Mrs Erskine is childless, but Mrs Clark's children are a central part of her life. Mrs Dixon's daughter is the mainstay of her parents' household, where Mrs Dixon cares for a very dependent husband. How representative are these three cases, with respect to demographic trends relating to older women more generally? What systematic differences are there from men and how can we account for them?

The final set of questions we shall address here concerns women's health in old age. How typical is it for older women to suffer chronic health problems as these three do? Are there distinctive patterns in morbidity and mortality as compared with men? If so, what are the reasons and effects?

Women, work and retirement

We know far less about women's retirement from paid work than we do about men's. Szinovacz discusses the emphasis on male retirement in the research literature, remarking that: 'women's retirement was not studied because it was not considered to constitute a salient social or research issue' (1982 : 15). Yet, with increasing numbers of women participating in the labour force, how could this view prevail for so long?

On an experiential level, retirement clearly is a salient issue. Mrs Pullan, one of the women interviewed in the study of old age by Ford and Sinclair is quoted as saying:

> I don't think I mind being old, I try very hard to accept that I am old, but what makes it harder is that other people think that old age is a write-off, so it makes it very difficult. . . . When I was very young I never thought I would ever, ever grow old . . . I couldn't imagine it at all, but you just journey through life and suddenly you are there. The reason it's brought home to you with such a jolt is because you give up work. You have to give up work – suddenly. (1987 : 107)

She goes on to say:

> In the last year of teaching I was thinking about retirement, but up until then I was content, with a reasonable life that was ticking over. The thing about life at work is that it has to run along these rails, so you feel safe inside the rails. When you've given up work there's no timing, no guidelines, nothing. I was absolutely bewildered. As I came up to leaving work I was bitter, cynical and very cross that I couldn't stay at work. (1987 : 108)

Mrs Pullan found that reaching retirement age had a fundamental effect upon her whole life, not only transforming the conditions of her existence but also altering her own view of herself.

Szinovacz offers various reasons for the neglect of women in retirement studies. First, a common assumption is that fewer women than men are in regular paid work and that, therefore, retirement simply is not an issue for them. This view, however, is mistaken. Between 1931 and 1985, the percentage of all women who were economically active between the ages of 16 and 60 rose from 34 to 49%: for married women, these figures rose from 10 to 52% (CSO 1987). In 1986, over 70% of women aged between 45 and 54 were economically active; as were half of those aged 55–59 and nearly a fifth of those aged 60–64. Even after the age of 65, 3% of women were economically active (*Employment Gazette* 1987). It must be pointed out that official statistics on women's work and those seeking work tend to be underestimates: unemployed women often fail to register and the part-time work of many women is often not separately documented or even recorded (Dex and Phillipson 1986a). Thus numbers experiencing retirement from work are greater than official statistics show.

Another commonly-held assumption is that while work may often be a central life interest for men and a key source of their self-identity, it seldom is for women. But there is little evidence that women's commitment to, or interest in work is any less than men's despite discontinuities in employment. Where women do retire early, this may be forced upon them through unemployment among older female workers – increasingly common since the recession of the 1970s – ill-health, or giving up work to care for a sick or dependent relative, commonly a husband (Parker 1980).

Following on from the – mistaken – assumption of lesser salience of work to women, a third common belief is that the retirement transition is a less important life event for women. Not only is parting from work regarded as less of a fundamental change, but also women have the 'benefit' of continuity in their role as housewife or homemaker, which can now become full-time. Mrs Pullan, however, whom we quoted earlier, found her work a central life interest and a source of identity: she was clearly ambivalent about becoming a full-time housewife.

Finally, Szinovacz (1982) argues that major life transitions have been treated as fragmented, independent events. There are, for example, no studies which address both retirement and widowhood of women, despite the fact that these two major life events frequently occur close together in time, and that a proper understanding of retirement is not possible without due attention to the wider individual and social context in which it takes place.

The experience of retirement

What do the few available studies tell us about women's retirement? As with men, there is great diversity in the range of anticipated and actual experiences of retirement and these are related to different facets of women's life and work histories. Crawford's (1971) study of 99 couples before and after the husband's retirement showed that retirement of husbands is also at least as much of a significant life event for their wives. While many of both sexes were looking forward to retirement and the freedom and opportunities for companionship it would bring, more women than men could think of nothing pleasant about impending retirement. Reduced income was one area of concern – for more women than men – as also was some women's resentment of retirement for what they saw as the imposition of old age and 'old' behaviour on them and their husbands. Class as well as gender was important: for both sexes, the non-manual group of respondents was far less likely to anticipate retirement as the herald of a series of anticipated losses and negative experiences than was the manual group.

The longitudinal study by Atchley (1982) showed that there were gender differences in the pre-retirement period – women were more likely to have no plans to retire. However, Cribier (1981) confirms that both men and women generally have positive expectations of retirement so long as they have good health and enough money. Atchley found very complex gender differences in the post-retirement period, though in general the evidence was that both sexes tended to adjust successfully, albeit in different ways.

Palmore *et al.* (1985) used other longitudinal survey data to compare men's and women's retirement and argued that the indicators employed are largely irrelevant to understanding the reasons for and outcomes of women's retirement. They conclude that a different theoretical foundation is needed for understanding men's and women's retirement. Variables measured in large-scale retirement studies usually relate to the typical parameters of male, rather than female employment. Thus the conceptual and methodological tools for exploring women's retirement in relation to the pre-retirement phase remain at present largely lacking.

The contrasting experiences of men and women regarding retirement must be seen in relation to trends in the division of labour in the market-place as well as in the home. Women's work histories vary with respect to educational level, age, generation and demographic variables such as ethnicity, health, marital status and number of children (Shaw 1983). Their paid working lives often feature discontinuities, such as breaks in employment for child bearing and rearing, and to care for relatives who fall ill or become disabled. Since occupational pension schemes and the state earnings-related pension scheme are organized around the assumption that employment is or should be full-time and not subject to interruptions of any length during the working life (Joshi and Ermisch 1982), these discontinuities discriminate against women in their access to pension schemes in their own right.

Women are also far more likely than men to be employed in part-time jobs in clerical and service sectors of the economy, which are lower-paid and without the benefit of occupational pension schemes (Martin and Roberts 1984; Thompson Rogers 1985; Dex and Phillipson 1986a; Peace 1986). Hence their access in retirement to resources in their own right tends to compare unfavourably with men's. Also, despite equal pay legislation, women in full-time work often occupy lower-status positions and earn less than men. In 1971, men in full-time work earned 80% more than women working full-time in the same sectors of the market-place. In 1981, in the wake of legislation, the gap had narrowed to 50%, but by 1985 the disparity showed signs of widening again: men on average earned 52% more than women. As well as affecting retirement income, these differences also mean that women have less opportunity to save during their working lives.

O'Rand and Henretta (1982) compared expected retirement income of married and unmarried women approaching retirement. They found relatively little difference between the two groups. In both cases, discontinuity of work history, a late age of starting a first job and the industrial location of work (which in turn affects both socio-economic status of jobs and favourability of pension schemes), have large effects on anticipated income in retirement. Old women are among the poorest members of society: in 1982, among widows aged 75–79, 43% were reliant on a supplementary pension, compared to 28% of lone men and 17% of married couples (Walker 1986, 1987).

Although it might once have been possible to argue that the needs of women in later life could and should be provided for by their spouses (Beveridge Report 1942), it is now obvious that this has become an insupportable myth. Quite apart from the increasing numbers without spouses, women tend to outlive their husbands by several years and the most common type of household situation in which older women are to be found, particularly in late old age, is living alone.

Other sources of social differentiation are important here. Townsend (1979) showed that people's resources in later life bore a relationship to those they enjoyed at earlier stages of the life-cycle. But as Delphy (1981) had argued, applying conventional social class categorizations to women is problematic, as they are predicated on men's positions and statuses. Categorizing older women

by social class on the basis of jobs is even more difficult: usually they have not
worked recently and their husbands may have died many years before. Neither
does using class of origin, based on the father's occupation – perhaps 80 years
earlier – provide a sensible yardstick for ranking the current circumstances of
elderly women. Ethnicity, too, which we discuss in the next chapter, is another
important variable relating to social stratification. We know of no studies in the
United Kingdom which have explored the retirement phase of the lives of
women from the ethnic minorities, in relation to their work histories, whether
inside the home or in the market-place.

It might be argued that the disadvantages of women in retirement relate to
the patriarchal and capitalist base of social organization and that changes
towards a socialist mode might result in improvements for elderly people in
general and women in particular. It is of course very difficult to test this
proposition empirically. Sternheimer (1985) uses Russian data to review the
position of Soviet women. This proves a difficult venture, as demographic
statistics in the USSR are often secret. But it seems that there are many
demographic parallels with Western societies. Older women vastly outnumber
older men and are also relatively disadvantaged. Despite younger women's
growing participation in the workforce and poor childcare facilities, the
traditional *babushka* grandmother role seems to be dying out. The independent nuclear family is becoming more common and older women are increasingly found living alone: nor do they seem to find the role of *babushka*
attractive these days. Sternheimer concludes that demographic factors far
outweigh ideological considerations in their influence on retirement policies
generally, and the position of older women in particular.

Women and retirement: summary

On an individual level, women and men have contrasting experiences regarding retirement. Gender, along with social class, is a major variable in relation to
understanding global trends in retirement and variations in individual experiences. The differences between men and women in retirement relate to trends
in the division of labour and power relations both in the home and the
market-place, along with the public policies which have shaped and reinforced
these trends. Development of a feminist social-gerontological theory is needed
to locate women's personal experiences of retirement in the wider social order.
The economic recession of the 1970s and early 1980s finds many Western
societies facing fundamental changes in the market-place as well as mass unemployment on an unprecedented scale. Thus the need for theory development
is particularly pressing if social gerontology is to render the structured inequi-
ties of the social order more visible as they affect both sexes in old age. This
is especially the case for older women whose experiences are the least visible.

Old women, social and family life

As we have noted, there are differences between men and women in basic
demographic parameters and these affect social and family circumstances in

old age. Because they live longer and tend to marry men older than themselves, a majority of women outlive their husbands – as did Mrs Clark and Mrs Erskine. Past retirement age, women are to be found living alone far more often than men. By the age of 80 and over, 61% of women and 35% of men live alone: 47% of men live with their wives only but no more than 11% of women live with their husbands only (CSO 1987).

The single-woman household is the most commonly-occurring household type among old people, the second most common consisting of couples only. Men tend to live with women who are younger than they are: the women in these partnerships are quite likely to spend a period of time caring for a sick or dependent husband prior to his death. The women may not always enjoy the best of health: we remember that Sheldon (1948) observed that men were either very fit or very sick, whereas women were often relatively disabled yet carried on as best they could with the daily round of activities. Approximately one-third of today's old people have no surviving children and, given the trend towards segregation, discussed in Chapter 1, old people have to 'cope' or 'manage' on their own resources, alone or as a couple (Wenger 1984; di Gregorio 1987).

What, then, do we know of women's lives in old age? Ethnographic studies offer a useful starting point. Matthews' (1979) North American study of a group of old women was informed by the interactionist concepts of Goffman (1963). Her initial assumption was that old age tends to be seen as stigmatizing and indeed is constructed as such in social and economic policy. Elderly people as a social minority are rendered economically dependent and this is legitimated by reference to the idea that biological ageing is synonymous with physical and mental deterioration – an untenable position, as we have shown earlier. However, older women are subject to sexist as well as ageist treatment and for them as individuals Matthews construed a major issue as being how to maintain their sense of positive self-identity in the face of the potentially stigmatizing experiences of daily life. She showed how vital relationships with the younger generation are. Social relationships are commonly analysed in terms of exchange theory (Homans 1961; Blau 1964): successful relationships depend upon each participant having resources to deploy. From this perspective, older women lack power and resources to create their own niches: a common strategy for maintaining integration with the family has therefore to be compliance, fitting in with the demands and expectations of their children.

Matthews also discusses the impact of moving away from a known locale, for example on the death of a spouse. As long as a woman is 'known' in her local community 'oldness', with its potentially stigmatizing character, is only one of a rich variety of social identities available to her. For older women who arrive, unknown and unknowing, in a new environment, 'oldness' becomes a 'master status', the main determinant of ascribed identity among strangers.

Implicit in Matthews' study is the importance of continuity in women's lives: of relationships, activities and identification with a 'home' area. Such continuities are not uniquely important to women, of course, but they are perhaps especially important in women's lives, given the powerful negative stereotypes which apply particularly to them (and to which they themselves may subscribe) and given also the structured disadvantages of old women with respect to income and other resources. The effects of disadvantage may to some extent be offset by the benefits of life's continuities. None the less, Matthews was not totally pessimistic regarding the position of older women: she suggested that the women's movement would raise their profile increasingly by analysing the shared and distinctive features of oppression of women of all ages and, thereby, improve the lifestyle options available to older women.

Continuities in women's lives also emerged as important in the study by Evers (1985) of 50 women aged 75 and over who lived alone. The focus was on their experiences (if any) of dependency and support in old age. It seemed that one of the factors which women with high morale tended to have in common was that they actively continued to structure their lives in relation to their own domestic order, established over a lifetime. Many transitions occur over the years – in household composition, loss of spouses and perhaps other confidants and friends as well as alterations in health status – and these all bring changes in the day-to-day domestic routine. Despite these transitions, maintaining continuity in and active control over the basic parameters of home life seemed to be associated with high morale. Examples ranged from importance of accomplishing domestic tasks such as changing curtains or spring cleaning to maintaining particular social roles and activities: for Mrs Clark, visiting sick old people and continuing her active role in the church seemed central to her own sense of well-being. Although comparison with men was not possible in this study, we can suggest that continuity in domestic and social activities and priorities represents continuity of a lifetime's 'women's work' both within and outside the home.

However, continuity of 'women's work' alone, wrongly devalued as it often is in a gender-ordered society (Land 1978), was not always enough. The women who were most active and positive in their outlook on life, irrespective of their health status, tended to have worked outside the home, and/or to have a longstanding interest or hobby – such as going to the theatre – which they had managed to sustain through much of their lives.

Evers' observations may be class- and generation-specific. Social class differences could not be examined since a majority of the 50 women were of social classes four and five. As to generation, there may be shifts over time in the gender-related division of labour in the home and in the market-place. If so, these will throw up new considerations regarding the relationship between older women's morale and continuities in the domestic order and social activities for future cohorts of older women.

Jerrome (1981) discusses the friendships of middle-class women living alone. While we have already noted that living alone and being lonely are not at all the same thing (see Chapter 1), for some of Jerrome's group of women being alone offered positive opportunities for initiating or further developing rich and new dimensions of social life. These often centred on shared activities. Relatively few of the women in Evers' study had such active social lives outside the home and contrasts between the two groups with respect to income and resources are doubtless relevant. The women lived in different social worlds as a result of a lifetime in a class-structured and gender-ordered society. Middle- and upper-class women perhaps have more in common with middle- and upper-class men – including more resources to sustain freedom of choice even in old age – than they do with lower-class women.

Social and family life: some surveys

Various surveys tell us something of social and family life in old age: Townsend's *The Family Life of Old People* (1957), although written 30 years ago, showed the importance of reciprocity, of patterns of inter-generational attachment and particularly the role of women of different generations in maintaining family contacts. The fact that this was typical and not just a feature of a traditional working-class community, was confirmed by the cross-national survey of Shanas *et al*. (1968). However, in neither study was conscious attention paid to the gendered basis of the social relations and activities which were revealed.

More recently, Abrams (1978b, 1980) drew attention to the distinctive features to emerge about women in his sample of 844 people aged 75 or older. He noted some differences between men and women and between women living alone and those living with others. Compared to those in shared households, women living alone spent more time in pursuit of passive activities such as watching television, listening to the radio, reading or resting: outings were more likely to be taken alone and they had fewer visitors at the weekend. They were more likely to be disadvantaged economically and least likely to have access to material resources such as cars, domestic appliances, a telephone or a colour television. The most striking difference Abrams identified was regarding family and social life. Women living alone were more likely never to have had children and generally engaged in less sociable contact with non-resident relatives. They were more likely to express feelings of depression and isolation, although they were no less likely to say that they had friends than women living with others. However, Jerrome's (1981) study suggests that it may be stigmatizing for women to admit to having few friends.

Abrams' survey begins to map out and quantify some aspects of women's distinctive situations in later life. From quite a different standpoint, the work of Hagestad (1985) on demographic change and inter-generational relationships highlights the contrasting circumstances of men and women. In cross-sectional surveys of elderly people men seem to have more intra-generational – or 'horizontal' – ties with brothers, sisters and cousins to a greater extent than women. The widows they leave behind have only 'vertical' ties with succeeding generations. These demographic trends, together with a gendered division of labour in which women are socialized to take the main responsibility for main-taining integration of families, mean that for those older people who have famil-ies, women are far more likely than men to have close relationships, featuring dependency and intra-dependency, across two or more generations. Multi-generation families are now becoming more common as a result of the increase in expectation of life at birth for both sexes and a reduced generation span:

The main change experienced with increasing age is for old people to find themselves nearer one of two extremes – experiencing the seclusion of the spinster or widow who lacks children *and* surviving brothers and sisters, or pushed towards the pinnacle of a pyramidal family structure of four generations which may include as many as four or five children, their husbands or wives and twenty or thirty grandchildren and great-grandchildren. (Shanas *et al*. 1968 : 151)

In addition, commentators note increasing diversity in patterns of family and household formation and dissolution. It is not only that marriage has become more common, but also that higher proportions of the population experience divorce (and often, remarriage); more one-parent families are found and, particularly in cities, a greater diversity of family forms including many variations within ethnic minority groups, as discussed in the next chapter. The implications of these trends – both as they affect older people today and in the future – remain to be examined (Matthews and Sprey 1984).

Old women, health and health care

A major factor which influences women's experiences of late life – and in which there are important contrasts with men – is that of health. Old women's health care – whether lay or professional – warrants separate consideration. As we shall see, health care relates not only to health status, but also gender-based assumptions about 'needs' of women and men. Although virtually no attention was paid to women in old age and their carers until very recently, there is now a growing body of work on this topic (see, e.g., Finch and Groves 1982; Walker 1983; Evers 1985). We shall draw selectively on this literature in sketching the main issues for a sociology of old age and for health and health care.

Women's own perspectives on their health and illness have lacked documentation as Qureshi and Walker (1986) note. This may reflect a trend which, although on the wane, is still to be seen in some studies: that is, the tendency to relegate old people, and particularly old women, to the status of 'objects' having 'dependency' characteristics (see, e.g., Clarke *et al*. 1984) rather than 'subjects' of importance in their own right (see also Chapter 1). Newton's (1980) account of her time of dependency – partially enforced – in a series of nursing homes in Australia is an exception, as is the discussion by Elder (1977) of growing old. Ethnographic studies begin to shed some light on this area. For example, Cornwell (1984) describes Mary, a woman who regarded herself as 'lucky' to have such good health. Her medical history included:

Having had such bad eyesight as a child that she was expected to be blind by the age of twenty, lung disease including tuberculosis in her late teens, a miscarriage, a thyroid deficiency which requires permanent medication, and . . . a hysterectomy. Confronted with the contradiction between her initial claim that she had never been ill and the facts of her medical history, Mary explained that she did not like to see herself or to be seen by anyone else as someone with poor health . . . she was worried that she would be mistaken for a 'moaner'. . . . 'If you can't go through

life without bearing a little bit of pain, you might as well die.'
(1984 : 124–5)

For this woman, to admit to ill-health was stigmatizing. Similarly, Evers (1984, 1985) found that old women living alone were prone to say their health was good despite a portfolio of specific health problems in some cases. Why is this? First, older people of both sexes often subscribe to the stereotypical view of old age as a time of decrepitude. Thus 'my health is very good for my age' is a common remark. (That they have survived to see old age is, of course, testimony to their good health relative to those of their generation who have already died.) Secondly, many people past retirement age do not see themselves as 'old' – 'oldness', and concomitant ill-health, is someone else's problem. Mrs Clark visited 'sick old people', she herself being 'only' into her 80s. These considerations may be true of men as well as women but what may perhaps be special to women is Mary's feeling that acknowledging ill-health is morally reprehensible. Williams (1981a,b) describes women to whom being healthy is being able to do their housework and go out: sitting down, being inactive, is a state to be dreaded and abhorred. So it was for some women in Evers' study: Mrs Jones, for instance, who had had a series of acute illnesses as well as chronic circulatory problems, said of her recent incapacity: 'I felt so ashamed, I couldn't do my work. I couldn't even manage to dust round the living room.'

It was her sense of shame at failing to fulfil her domestic duties, and not so much the suffering occasioned by her illness, which was Mrs Jones' major preoccupation and there were many similar examples. We may conjecture that sex-role stereotyping is so strong that we would hardly expect to find a man reporting guilt or shame at being unable to do his housework, although he may express shame or regret at being unable to (or being prevented from) carry on working.

As ever, it is dangerous to generalize too widely. Herzlich (1973) described some of the Parisians in her in-depth study of perceptions of health and illness as experiencing 'illness-as-liberator'. Illness provided an opportunity to take time out from everyday pressures. Parsons' (1951) notion of the sick role, too, offers legitimation for someone who is 'really' ill to be excused normative role expectations. Some of the women in Evers' study appeared to fit this mould. After a lifetime of caring for others – for example, husbands – illness presented an occasion to put up their feet and opt for passivity, once the former recipients of their care had died.

If these ethnographic studies are limited in scope, what can be learnt from larger-scale surveys relating to health and illness? Epidemiological data on health and illness of women in later life is also somewhat limited in the United Kingdom. Two important sources of information are now rather dated – *Handicapped and Impaired in Great Britain* (Harris 1971) and *The Elderly at Home* (Hunt 1978). However, the General Household Survey (OPCS 1982) which includes some self-reported data on health, is more up-to-date. Other sources include the Royal College of General Practitioners' Morbidity study, Hospital Activity Analysis and mortality statistics, all of which are aggregates of officially-collected statistical data within professionally- and administratively-defined categories.

The early studies show that from the age of 65–74 the prevalence of chronic, limiting conditions is not much greater than that at ages 55–64. It is after the age of 75 that the probability of suffering some disabling condition seems to climb rather steeply for both sexes. Even so, the proportion of people over 65 who report mild or no disabling conditions by far exceeds the proportion with moderate or severe disability in all age bands. More recent sources, for instance Wenger (1984), suggest that it is not until 80 years of age and older that the prevalence of disability rises steeply.

Having reminded ourselves that growing old is far from necessarily accompanied by becoming sick – by definition, older people are the 'survivors' – we will review some data about differential morbidity and causes of mortality between old men and old women:

> Daily life for older women has many aches and pains that are bothersome but not life-threatening. Ultimately the 'killer' conditions of heart disease, cancer and stroke do manifest themselves and lead to death. By contrast, older men tend to be more bothered in daily life by precisely the problems [circulatory and respiratory] that lead to their death. (Verbrugge 1985 : 58)

Verbrugge provides a useful summary of data from the United States on causes of death and morbidity in older women, which seem to parallel the situation in the United Kingdom. Major causes of death are broadly similar for men and women: heart disease, stroke and cancer account for about three-quarters of all deaths among the population aged 65 and over, but deaths of women are more likely to be attributed to several conditions than are those of men.

On self-rated health status, Verbrugge notes that patterns for men and women are similar and quotes American studies which show that 9% of both sexes rate their health as 'poor' and just over a fifth as 'fair', More specifically, self-reported data shows that arthritis tops the list of chronic conditions – in no less than 53% of old women, although not all those reporting a diagnosis of arthritis suffer significant limitations on their activities. Old men's self-reports of chronic health problems differ in that 30% report arthritis: resultant limitations on activity seem to be less prevalent among male than among female sufferers from this condition. Although cardiovascular conditions are also very common among women, heart and chest diseases are more common among men and pose limitations on activities. Overall, women have more chronic health problems than do men: causes of death and morbidity, then, differ – arthritis proves particularly common and troublesome for women yet it is not in itself a cause of death.

Men and women differ in their rates of consultation with health professionals. These differences are what one would expect in relation to differing patterns of morbidity. In the United States, Verbrugge reports that consultation of physicians for ambulatory care centres on musculoskeletal, cardiovascular and eyesight problems and respiratory illness. Hospitalization, on the other hand, is more commonly in connection with acute life-threatening conditions and injuries. Heart disease, cancer, fractures and strokes head the list for women: among men, genito-urinary problems are more common and fractures less common causes of hospitalization.

In the United Kingdom, women in all the older age groups are more likely than men to report disabling conditions (Victor 1987: 253). General Household Survey data shows that women are more likely than men to report longstanding illness and are also – particularly those living alone – more likely to find their illness limits their activities. For example, 23% of women over 75 living alone reported problems with going out unassisted, as compared with 11% of men of the same age who lived alone (OPCS 1982). Hunt (1978) found that a higher proportion of women than men had mobility problems and women tended to have more visual impairment. Men, however, reported more hearing difficulties.

On capacity for self-care, the General Household Survey showed some sex differences. Capacity was generally reduced in relation to increasing age but, within that, men were more often able to accomplish some domestic activities, for instance shopping, than were women – possibly because of their rather better mobility. Sex role stereotypes are evident: the capacity of women to prepare a main meal and manage the washing exceeds that of the men, despite women's greater propensity to suffer long-term illness which limits their activities. Some chronic morbidity results from conditions which are suffered only by women, notably osteoporosis (Kerzner 1983). Older women's greater morbidity and their greater numbers in the population means that they are prime targets for the drugs industry, which is not always benevolent in its effects or its intent (Burns and Phillipson 1986).

Data on the mental health of older women is scanty. Work on the epidemiology of dementing illnesses is fraught with difficulty because of definitional and identification problems and thus estimates of its prevalence in the elderly population vary (Clarke *et al*. 1986). Commonly-cited figures are that 10% of all people over 65 and 20% of all people over 80 suffer dementia. Evidence as to the relative prevalence among men and women suggests that the latter are at greater risk (Clarke *et al*. 1984, 1986). Milne (1985) summarizes the major findings of a longitudinal study of the health of some 400 people aged 65 years and over. He notes that women are twice as likely as men to suffer from depressive illness and observes that women are more likely to suffer from dementia, particularly in the oldest age groups.

The general picture confirms Sheldon's (1948) earlier observation that women suffer more disabling conditions, particularly arthritis, over long periods of time than do men. Men's disabling conditions more commonly tend to be manifestations of diseases which will ultimately cause their deaths, i.e. heart and chest conditions. These patterns have implications for health care provision. Are state policies congruent with the above picture of needs? To what extent does data on actual health care provision match policy aspirations? Policies and provision embody unwarranted, usually implicit, assumptions about sex roles, to the particular disadvantage of many old women.

Ill-health in old age: provision of care for dependent women

Current emphasis in state policies on the desirability of community care for dependent old people means that in practice lay people, usually women, provide the bulk of the care that is needed (EOC 1980, 1982; Finch and Groves

1982; Charlesworth *et al*. 1984; G. Parker 1985; Qureshi and Walker 1986). State policies on community care therefore institutionalize and confirm the division of labour between men and women so far as care-work for old people in a gender-ordered society is concerned.

What is meant by caring? The concept has been variously interpreted and has several aspects. It involves, first of all, physical work: what Parker (1981) has evocatively called 'tending'. But more than that, it involves feelings too – of concern, love, obligation, even resentment. Graham (1983) reflected on how caring as feeling seems intimately related to women's roles and identity in the family. Waerness (1984) usefully sets out a simply typology to distinguish everyday helping and supporting between people, e.g. in the family context, from caring. Where the activities done for someone could not be done by that person for themselves and where there is imbalance in reciprocity of activities as between the two parties, then it is care-work which is being done.

As Isaacs *et al*. (1972) showed (see Chapter 1), families are only in exceptional circumstances unwilling or unable to provide care. Daughters are often the mainstay: despite increasing workforce participation, there is little evidence that married and working daughters provide any less care where it is needed (Brody and Schoonover 1986). Brody's earlier work (1981), which draws particular attention to the widespread preference of the older generation for independent living, shows that mothers who may receive care from younger family members are reluctant to become a burden and are positively disposed towards the idea of receiving help from paid carers.

What contribution do services make in practice? Community services supporting the old commonly have caseloads with a preponderance of old women living alone. From the population structure and data on household composition, this is entirely what we would expect to find. However, gender-based assumptions mediate service provision. For example, Hunt (1978) found that for an equivalent level of disability, men were more likely than women to receive home help. Similar findings emerge in Evers, Badger and Cameron's current research. Women, it seems, are implicitly expected to be able to manage at home for longer and under more adverse circumstances than are men, perhaps because of their lifetime's experience of household management. Notwithstanding the findings of Brody, women may also be more reluctant than men to relinquish part of their day-to-day household and care-work to services: Mrs Jones, described earlier, felt a sense of shame and guilt when illness rendered her unable to do her own housework.

Evers found that professional care workers sometimes tended to 'impose' their perceptions on dependent women whom they visited, hence denying, as it were, the validity of their clients' own views of their situations. This came about in part perhaps because the professionals' first contact with the women tended to be at a time of crisis of ill-health or dependency, when the women were least able to communicate the nature of their 'usual' selves (Evers 1984, 1985).

Regarding provision of institutional care, there is some evidence that men and women are admitted to residential care under differing circumstances (Willcocks 1982): for example, men are much more likely to be admitted shortly after the deaths of their spouse than are women. This perhaps reflects the assumption that a newly-bereaved widow is better able to cope at home than is a widower. There may be some truth in this assumption: women, generally, must expect to outlive their husbands and, when widowed themselves, are not only surrounded by other widows as role models but also, in many cases, will have known their mothers, grandmothers and aunts as widows. Hence, some 'anticipatory socialization' (Jacobson 1970) for this stage of life is more common in women than in men.

If for whatever reason they may find themselves living in an institution, it seems that men and women may have different experiences once they have been admitted. In Evers' (1981) study, although they did not necessarily have a 'worse' time in geriatric wards, women patients were far more likely to be depersonalized, in that the nurses knew far less about them as people than they tended to know about their men patients. The care strategies of nurses – who are usually female – differed systematically in relation to men and women patients. Evers suggested that doing basic care-work with women was particularly hard for them: their patients had been 'experts' in care-work themselves – in their own homes – and confronted the nurses in a particularly poignant way with an image of their future selves. Caring for men did not raise these particular difficulties for the nurses and for the men being looked after by a female nurse was less of a discontinuity than it was for the women.

Conclusion

Social gerontology is at last seeing a rapid growth in interest in issues concerning older women (Peace 1986). Our discussion of the literature in this chapter has not been exhaustive. We have not, for example, looked particularly at women's sexuality in later life (see, e.g., Greengross 1986), at widowhood (Lopata 1979) or more generally at issues of older women's subordination and control in our gender-ordered society (Hutter and Williams 1981). We have, however, mapped out other major questions which serve to show that analysis of women's experience of old age warrants particular attention.

Although we noted at the start of this chapter that feminists are beginning to turn their attentions to ageing (e.g. Cohen 1984; Macdonald and Rich 1984), younger women's issues continue to be a major preoccupation. Thus it seems more likely that social gerontology will take the lead in further analysis of the position and experiences of older women; and in developing strategies for challenging older women's oppression. However, there is no great cause for optimism regarding revolutionary changes to improve the position of older women – or older men, for that matter. Old people's lives tend to be lived primarily in the 'private domain' of the home, rather than the 'public domain' of socio-political institutions (Stacey 1981). In the public domain, old people, and especially women, the predominant sex, are visible mainly – and mistakenly – in a negative light: as dependent consumers of scarce resources such as health care. An individualistic rather than collectivist gaze in our society makes it hard to establish as common currency the notion that dependency in old age, and particularly for old women, is socially created and sustained.

7

Race, ethnicity and old age

Introduction

This chapter will discuss some of the important contrasts between the ageing experiences of various ethnic minority groups, both with one another and with the majority group. The contrasts relate to differences in culture and religion, to patterns of migration and settlement and to continuities and discontinuities across the life-cycle. Responses of the dominant group are of course crucial, both at the level of individual attitudes and at the level of social and economic relationships in the society at large. Sociological analysis of old age must pay explicit attention to the ethnic dimension in societies which are already multicultural or increasingly are becoming so.

We will begin by setting out some limits to our considerations of this potentially vast topic: just as the socially-constructed category 'old age' must be considered critically and disaggregated, so too must the category 'ethnic minority' and we do this first. Three case studies then follow, drawn from research which will lead us to note *stereotypes* of old people from ethnic minority groups. We examine the demographic background of two minority groups and review recent studies, concentrating particularly on issues to do with health and social services. We conclude by arguing that sociological analysis of old age and ethnic minority status shows that socio-political systems are crucial influences on the extent to which disadvantage and dependency are created or, conversely and more rarely, confronted and averted.

Asians and Afro-Caribbeans as examples of ethnic minority elders

We shall take a relatively parochial view and discuss empirical data which relates to the above two major 'umbrella' groups in the United Kindom or, more specifically, parts of the United Kingdom. In this context, 'Asian' refers not only to people originating directly from the Indian subcontinent but also to those who came indirectly by way of East African countries. Taking just two groups is not meant to imply either that we are uninterested in the many other ethnic minority groups in the United Kingdom, or in cross-national theoretical and empirical comparison. However, focusing on the two major groups as case studies is sufficient to highlight the key issues of the ethnic minority dimension in the sociological analysis of old age. Indeed, given the rich diversity within different ethnic groups, to attempt a comprehensive review of all or even many of those represented in the United Kingdom would be unrealistic in a single chapter.

Our choice of parochialism, given the long tradition of minority studies elsewhere (particularly in North America) reflects our view that the United Kingdom context warrants attention in its own right and cannot be subsumed within theoretical and empirical frameworks deriving from other countries, although it can be informed by them. Since the mid-1970s sociological and policy interests in ethnic minority elders has awakened in the United Kingdom and grows apace. While there is much work yet to be done – and the level of analysis lags behind other areas of gerontology in this country by about 20 years – the field is developing rapidly (see, e.g., Mays 1983; Blakemore 1985; Fenton 1986; Holland and Lewando-Hundt 1987; McFarland *et al.* 1987).

Having said we will focus mainly on the United Kingdom, we must at the outset consider the referents of the term 'ethnic minority elders'. In the past, attempts have been made to define race in terms of distinctive biological inheritance. Today, it is widely agreed that ultimately racial groups are socially defined rather than solely biologically determined in any absolute or objective sense (Watson 1977; Manuel 1982; Donovan 1986a). Although *ethnicity* rather than *race* or racial descent appears to be more widely used as an analytical concept, both notions remain problematic and the subject of critical appraisal in sociology; not least their relationship with other concepts bearing upon issues of social stratification such as class and gender (for recent discussion of some key issues, see Cashmore and Troyna 1983; Cashmore 1984; Rex 1986).

For the purposes of this chapter we will assume that the term ethnicity encompasses that of race, or biological descent. Members of particular ethnic groups share and/or are influenced by cultural norms, biological inheritance and historical experiences which can be seen as relatively distinct from those of other ethnic groups. 'Minority groups' are not to be defined only or even primarily in numeric terms, but rather by reference to their shared cultural norms and heritage together with their aggregate social experience of relative powerlessness, discrimination and latent or explicit conflict in their relations with the dominant group.

The experience of discrimination and disadvantage is unlikely to be exclusively a consequence of ethnic minority status. Although their colour, their culture and – in the case of Asians – their religions and languages may seem to set them apart, ethnic minorities are often confronted with problems shared by other minority groups; for example, the relative poverty and deprivation of the inner cities, with their high concentration of unemployed people who find themselves relegated to the 'lowest' strata of society. British writers in the field tend to emphasize this point (see, e.g., Bhalla and Blakemore 1981; Barker 1984; Donovan 1986a). We will return later to the question of the ageing experience and interrelations among social class, ethnicity, inner-city domicile, and social indices of deprivation.

A brief note about figures is needed at this point. The lack of comprehensive statistics about numbers of people of ethnic minority groups reflects political sensitivities regarding any kind of 'ethnic monitoring'. In view of the idea that ethnicity is in any case a social construction, encapsulating relatively crude and arbitrary definitions in numerical form would not perhaps be any more illuminating than the convention adopted in the 1981 Census, which recorded country of birth (see Table 7.1). A certain amount of detective work is needed to gain a rough idea about numbers of ethnic minorities – crudely delimited – from such census data.

Table 7.1.   Numbers of middle-aged and pensionable people in the UK by country of birth.

	All persons		Males		Females	
	45–pens. age	Of pens. age	45–pens. age	Of pens. age	45–pens. age	Of pens. age
All countries of birth	10 527	9459	5862	3155	4644	6304
Irish Republic (including Ireland, part not stated)	223.0	132.0	122.1	43.8	100.9	88.3
Old Commonwealth	30.2	21.3	16.7	7.1	13.6	14.2
New Commonwealth						
East Africa	14.7	1.6	8.1	0.5	6.6	1.1
Rest of Africa	6.2	1.1	4.4	0.5	1.8	0.6
Caribbean	101.3	16.2	59.1	5.6	42.2	10.6
Bangladesh	9.4	3.8	8.0	0.4	1.3	0.2
India	104.0	44.1	61.4	15.6	42.6	28.5
Far East	12.5	3.9	7.0	1.1	5.5	2.7
Mediterranean	9.4	3.7	5.7	1.2	3.7	2.6
Pakistan	33.7	4.8	22.9	2.1	10.8	2.8
Other	287.5	155.3	257.9	103.2	139.9	99.7
Total born abroad	858.9	395.8	478.4	138.3	380.6	257.4

Source: OPCS (1983).

The figures include people of United Kingdom origin who were born overseas and exclude people of non-United Kingdom origin who were born in the United Kingdom. Thus they give only an approximate idea of the size of ethnic minority populations. The picture is more accurate for older than for younger age groups. Robinson (1986) estimates that the total population of wholly Asian ethnic origin was 1 054 000 in 1981. He quotes the 1979 estimate of the Immigration Statistics Unit that the population will be between 1.25 and 1.5 million by 1991. Anwar (1986) quotes 1981 census data which shows that of an ethnic minority population of 2.2 million (4.2% of the total population) about 1.2 million are of Asian origin and 0.55 million of Afro-Caribbean origin, the remainder originating from South-East Asia, the Mediterranean and other parts of the New Commonwealth. The distribution throughout the United Kingdom is highly uneven: for example, in parts of inner-city Birmingham the proportion of people of Asian origin in all age groups is around 50%. Numbers in and characteristics of ethnic groups other than Asians and Afro-Caribbeans are discussed, for example, by Watson (1977).

The population structure is undergoing many changes. In 1981 there were 16 000 Afro-Caribbeans of pensionable age or older, and 101 000 between 45 years and pensionable age. The ageing Asian population is larger: 45 000 people of pensionable age or older, and 110 000 aged between 45 years and pensionable age.

We will now turn to case material to highlight the issues we shall discuss in the remainder of the chapter. This is drawn from the current research of Evers, Badger, Cameron and Atkin, a survey of community health and social services' professionals' perceptions of their work with elderly and disabled clients, and the perceptions of a sample of Asian and non-Asian elders of their health and of health and social services in a large Midlands city.

Asians and Afro-Caribbeans: three pen portraits

Mr Sandhu

Mr Sandhu – who speaks no English – came to England from a village in the Punjab following the death of his wife about 6 years ago. Already suffering from tuberculosis and eyesight problems, he went to live with his son. Now in his mid-70s and barely able to care for himself, Mr Sandhu is looked after by his daughter-in-law and son. The couple have their own troubles: money is extremely short as the husband's business went bankrupt and he is now making a new start as a taxi driver. There are two teenaged children and a 2-year-old, and Mr Sandhu's daughter-in-law feels totally isolated: she is unable to leave Mr Sandhu by himself, even to do the shopping. The rest of her husband's family, some of whom are in the same city, are no help: the rift in relationships followed the business failure. Mr Sandhu is unable to go out and misses companionship of other men of his own generation and cultural background. His associates of a lifetime were left behind in his village of origin and he himself feels lost in a foreign land. Both he and his daughter-in-law would welcome the opportunity for Mr Sandhu to go to some kind of day centre to meet with other Asian men of his age, but they do not know of any such centre in their area.

Mr Morgan

Mr Morgan came from Jamaica with his mother more than 30 years ago. He is now 64 and his mother died several years ago. Mr Morgan has had two longstanding relationships with women but is now alone. His two relationships produced three children and he is in sporadic touch with a daughter who lives 'up north'. He worked and suffered accidents in heavy industry for over 20 years before being made redundant 2 years ago. Mr Morgan feels cheated and muses that although he has given this country so much, he's now thrown on the scrap heap. He lives in a flat in an inner-city tower block, admits to drinking a great deal and suffers with raised blood pressure.

Mrs Sharma

Mrs Sharma does not know her exact age, but she is probably in her late 50s. We first met her in the clothes shop of the family's small factory in an inner-city area, where she works every day until 6 p.m. The factory and shop serve the local Asian community. Mrs Sharma and her husband are at the centre of the extended family group and live in a large Victorian semi-detached house with one of their sons. The house is interconnected with its neighbour, where three married sons live, two of them with a baby apiece. Both houses are owned by the family and there are many other relatives in the same city. The family gives an impression of relative affluence, and have clearly done well in this country. Mrs Sharma's children were all born and educated in Britain and thus speak good English. She herself came to Britain 30 years ago following her husband from the Indian subcontinent and speaks very little English. When she needs to communicate across the boundaries of her own family and social group, she needs help from other family members both with English and with making sense of social institutions, such as the health service.

These pen portraits give us some points of reference in turning now to stereotypes of old people from ethnic minorities. There are various stereotypical views of ethnic minority elders in common currency and these are partially misleading.

Stereotypical views of ethnic minority elders

It is often assumed that black people live as part of extended families and that their needs for care and support in old age are almost always met within the family and cultural group. This is certainly more often true for Asian and Afro-Caribbean elders than it is for their white contemporaries in British society. (We have seen that Mrs Sharma is at the centre of her large multi-generation family. Mr Sandhu has partial support from his extended family and has no help from health and social services other than his GP, although arguably Mr Sandhu and his carers have unmet needs for social support.)

However, to be relatively isolated, like Mr Morgan for example, is far from uncommon. Ethnic elders, even if they live with other family members, may not receive the care and support which norms of their culture of origin might lead one to suppose and isolation may have a very different set of consequences for them. Black people may have difficulties with English, may often be unfamiliar with how British social institutions work and lack easy access to intermediaries who can help negotiate the British system. The ethnocentric organizational base of services on offer may be quite inappropriate and fail to address the problems of dependency among isolated old people from ethnic minorities. Pearson, for example, writes of the NHS:

> Its policies and practices have understandably evolved in response to the needs of the white British population, as perceived by professionals and planners. This has entailed the development of culture-bound and 'colour-blind' policies which do not consider that established practice might be inappropriate for ethnic minority users, and are insensitive to their beliefs and way of life. (1984 : 122)

Above all, isolation may be associated with the stigma and shamefulness of being without all the family support that is 'needed' in a cultural group where such support is so strong a normative expectation.

Stereotypical views also oversimplify with respect to the diversity of ethnic groups in terms of distinctive cultures and languages [Robinson (1986) reports 17 different dialects spoken in the Asian community of Blackburn] and also migration patterns and life histories, with their continuities and discontinuities. Mr Sandhu, who came to Britain when already old, clearly faces a wholly different set of contingencies from Mrs Sharma, who came as a young adult with her husband and has been here many years; and different again from Mr Morgan, living alone and approaching retirement age.

Another commonly-held stereotypical view is that ethnic minority groups such as the Asian or Afro-Caribbean communities are synonymous with 'social problems'. Elders of ethnic minorities have hitherto remained – perhaps surprisingly, in view of the projected increase in their numbers – relatively invisible in British social and health policies. The dominant group still tends to 'pathologize' members of ethnic minorities, particularly those who are to be readily distinguished by their colour. The strengths and contributions of older people and their family groups, like those of Mrs Sharma, are often overlooked.

Recognition of the rather more complex reality of the situation – that the problems which people of ethnic minorities face are in part created by the society in which we live – is growing but is not as yet common currency. It is not the older people of ethnic minorities who are themselves 'social problems' but, rather, their circumstances which cause or exacerbate disadvantages. Macintyre (1977), in a slightly different context, discusses how government policy on elderly people from 1834 oscillated between two basically incompatible sets of beliefs about old age: one is that old age is itself a social problem, in the sense that large numbers of old people pose a drain on the rest of society's resources, and that policy must therefore be directed towards minimizing the *burden on society* – the 'organizational' view of old age. The second is that old age can bring with it disadvantages, discomfiture and dependency for the individual, who deserves a humane and caring response from society at large in order that the *personal burden* of old age be eased – the 'humanitarian' view. To see ethnic minority groups as social problems corresponds to Macintyre's analysis of the 'organizational' perspective. Old people, whether of ethnic minorities or not, should not be seen as 'social problems'. Rather, the issue is that they are systematically disadvantaged by the socio-political organization of the dominant groups in society.

Older black people tend to suffer socio-economic disadvantage relative to other groups. Just like elderly people in the dominant culture, ethnic minority elders tend to be marginalized and devalued but they are doubly disadvantaged compared with older white people as a direct result of their ethnic minority – and frequently also for this generation, immigrant-status. They often live in deprived inner-city areas, like Mr Sandhu and Mr Morgan. Of our three cases, only Mrs Sharma has a home on the periphery of the inner city, having moved out a few years ago as a result of the growing prosperity of the family business and the strengthening of her British-based network of kin and friends.

Asians and Afro-Caribbeans: a demographic portrait

As we noted in Chapter 3, a proper understanding of the experience of old age is not possible without paying attention to people's life-histories. The life-histories of today's Asian and Afro-Caribbean elders resident in the United Kingdom (who are mostly immigrants) feature major discontinuities because of the upheaval they have experienced, so we shall look at trends in their migration.

Asian migration

The discussion of Sikh migration and settlement by Ballard and Ballard (1977) also gives some indication of migration trends from the Indian subcontinent more generally. The first phase was of individual pioneers, mostly seamen, who settled between the wars. Mass migration did not begin until after the Second World War – Robinson (1986) notes that in 1949 there were just 100 Indians in Birmingham.

The 1950s and 1960s saw immigration of lone men, mostly of rural origin, who served as a replacement unskilled labour force in areas of industrial decline and therefore outmigration, as well as in areas of industrial expansion where additional labour was needed (Robinson 1986). The early migrants acted as bridgeheads, helping newly-arriving migrants whether or not they were blood relatives. They often shared lodging houses and helped each other with the language, the bureaucracy and with finding jobs. As a result, migrants tended to be concentrated in particular locations and sectors of industry as, for example, textiles in Bradford. Robinson notes that often a whole night shift in a textile factory might be worked exclusively by Pakistanis all known to each other. An uneven distribution of settlement in Britain has resulted from the fact that migrants tended to follow one another through a network to indus-trialized areas where factory work was available. In Cornwall, for example, 1.3% of the population was born in the New Commonwealth and Pakistan, as compared with 6.2% of the population of the West Midlands Metropolitan County (OPCS 1983).

Many authors, including Khan (1977), Ballard and Ballard (1977), Anwar (1979) and Robinson (1986), discuss reasons for migration. One reason is that in Indian and Pakistani families, concern with status and honour is central and hence achievement is very important. The better opportunities for employment and economic advancement which were believed to exist in Britain as compared with India and Pakistan in the 1950s and 1960s offered a route to enhancing family status. The pioneers formed the link in the chain and the new migrants devoted themselves to earning as much as possible with a view to returning home in the longer term.

Another type of reason is displacement. A large number of Pakistanis from Mirpur came to Britain as a result of the construction of the Mangla dam in the early 1960s, a project which provided irrigation and electricity for large areas of the Punjab. About 100 000 people were moved from the area and the compensation paid to them enabled some to move elsewhere in Pakistan and others to come to Britain through arrangements at Government level (Rose 1969).

The experience of immigration was for most people a difficult one. Immigrants' views of Britain and British culture was based on experience of colonialism: this involved subordination, racial discrimination and exposure to a Western culture which was seen as morally base, for instance with respect to the role and behaviour of women. The reality of immigration did nothing to contradict negative images of Britain: only the lowest-paid, dirtiest jobs were available and the immigrants' status in the lowest stratum of society was reinforced. It is not surprising that there is little evidence of aspiration towards 'integration' or 'assimilation' among the majority of immigrants, notions made much of in British policy in the 1950s and early 1960s.

British attitudes to the new arrivals were also shaped by the long history of colonialism. Black people were seen as, at best, ignorant peasants or even savages and regarded with misunderstanding or suspicion even before they began to arrive in any numbers. Prejudice and discrimination were – and remain – widespread and can be seen as enshrined in legislative provision regarding restrictions on immigration, particularly from the 1962 Commonwealth Immigration Act onwards.

Immigrant settlements, comprising almost exclusively men, emerged. Networks of obligation and reciprocity developed between the new arrivals and those more established group members who helped them with lodgings and work. Stratification within the immigrant community meant that status and honour became a relevant dimension not just of the relationship between migrants and their kin overseas, but among migrants too. For example, immigrants began to buy property but were able to afford to do so only in decaying inner-city areas (Rex and Moore 1967; Ballard and Ballard 1977). Property owners could then provide lodgings for new immigrants and, therefore, acquire power and status.

Although the experience of British society did nothing to dispel its image as discriminatory and immoral – and therefore a dangerous place for women and children – families began to come to join the lone men. This was the beginning of the stage the Ballards call consolidation, when the men began to bring their families to join them, a phase which continued during the 1960s and 1970s. According to Robinson (1986) one important factor was that it became clear that the sojourn in Britain was to be longer than at first thought. If the men were to pursue the quest for status in Britain, rather than simply in relation to the community overseas, they needed to be able to offer the proper hospitality to others in suitable surroundings. This they were unable to do without womenfolk.

By this stage, the men could often afford the cost of establishing families here. Having invested in housing and, later, businesses, money was less readily available to be taken back to the immigrants' place of origin as had been the intention of most on arrival – another reason for consolidating the community in Britain. Because of the restrictions of purdah, the family reunifications of Muslims tended to take place much later than that of other subgroups. The timing of immigration during the consolidation phase was also influenced, of course, by Asians' strategies in responding to the restrictive legislation which was – and is – part of the British reaction to large numbers of black immigrants [see Anwar (1986) for a summary of the legislation and its impact].

Family consolidation means that in the 1980s members of a second generation of British-educated and often British-born Asians are beginning to create their own families here. Intergenerational cultural change is fast-moving and has implications for the now-ageing early migrants, as we shall see. It would be unwise to generalize from the experiences of today's older Asian migrants to the coming generations of elders, whose life experiences and expectations will be quite different.

The ageing experience of East African immigrants of Asian origin is likely to be shaped by differences in their life-histories from those of the majority of immigrants from the Indian subcontinent. Although some of the latter suffered the trauma of Partition and other major discontinuities, East African immigrants such as Ugandan Asians almost all came as exiles or as refugees. Most were from families which had been long-established in Africa as a result of recruitment in the last years of the nineteenth century to build the railways and they had come to control much of the economic life there. Some chose to leave – not all for Britain – when they saw the African threat to their futures; others left later as refugees to face a new beginning overseas. Thus, among migrants of Asian origin, it can be seen that there were a great variety of different reasons which precipitated a decision to emigrate to Britain.

Afro-Caribbean migration

Although there have been Afro-Caribbean people living in Britain for very many years (see Fryer 1984), mass immigration began after the Second World War. As a consequence of a post-war labour shortage, which also created pressures on older workers to postpone retirement (see Chapter 5), immigrants were even recruited in their countries of origin: British Rail and London Transport went to Barbados and Jamaica for this purpose. Between 1945 and the Commonwealth Immigration Act of 1962 there were no restrictions on entry and by 1960 the West Indian population had grown to 161 450 (Donovan 1986a). Poor economic circumstances at home and perceived job opportunities in Britain were both reasons for immigration. Single women as well as men came, particularly from some islands such as Montserrat (Philpott 1977). The first arrivals were usually semi-skilled workers; later, unskilled workers predominated. Chain migration developed: early immigrants helped kin and others to settle and to find housing and employment so there was a tendency for communities to arise in particular areas, as with Asian and Afro-Asian migrants.

A history of colonial domination influenced expectations of both immigrants and of the majority group, but in contrast to Asian migrants, the experience of relative deprivation on arrival for Afro-Caribbean settlers was heightened by a prior image of the United Kingdom as 'the mother country'. The operation of British social institutions and the attitudes and behaviour of individuals and groups among the majority population all embodied racial prejudice and discrimination to an extent which caused disillusionment.

Although most Afro-Caribbeans initially believed that they would return to the Caribbean, this was seen as a relatively long-term goal. In the meantime they established families here or brought dependants to join them in Britain. Many, perhaps, still subscribe to the 'myth of return' – described for Pakistanis by Anwar (1979) – but few actually do return. On visits they often find their memories and expectations at odds with reality; families are more often in Britain than the Caribbean; medical care and benefits in old age are often seen as less certain than in the United Kingdom. Further, the economic possibilities sought through immigration have sadly failed to fulfil their promise and only a minority can afford to return and establish a lifestyle befitting a 'successful' returned migrant (Barker 1984).

Elderly Asians and Afro-Caribbeans in Britain

What has been the experience of these groups of elderly people in Britain? There is great diversity in previous life-histories as we have shown: Asians include those who came many years ago either by choice or as exiles or refugees and have grown old here. They have different expectations and experiences from those who came in later life or old age to join families already established. Afro-Caribbean elders tend to have been living in Britain for many years as a result of the mass migration trends of the 1950s and early 1960s.

This rich diversity within the British Asian and Afro-Caribbean communities has fundamental implications for individuals' experiences of old age. The more recent migrants who are now old often face particular problems of poverty. Many have too few years' employment history in Britain to entitle them to a full pension; some, who understated their ages in order to facilitate gaining entry, are now not able to claim their pension rights until past pensionable age; those who came as elderly dependants are financially reliant on their sponsors and have no entitlement to state pensions at all. Given the rapid rate of cultural change among second and successive generations of Asian and Afro-Caribbean people, the extended family can no longer be taken for granted as the fount of all support.

There are still relatively few studies of elderly Asians and Afro-Caribbeans in the United Kingdom. The most interesting ones are those of Bhalla and Blakemore (1981), Berry *et al.* (1981) and Barker (1984), along with the overview of the literature on old people from ethnic minorities and service provision by Norman (1985). The survey of whites, Asians and Afro-Caribbeans in Bristol by Fenton (1986) is also relevant, although only a proportion of the respondents were elderly people. Another study is that carried out in Coventry (Holland and Lewando-Hundt 1987).

Bhalla and Blakemore's study was an interview survey of a random sample of 400 Europeans, Asians and Afro-Caribbeans over pensionable age living in inner-city areas of Birmingham. The Europeans tended to be relatively older and in the Asian sample women were under-represented, partly because they are only allowed restricted contact with outsiders.

Asians were far more likely to own their houses, whereas over two-thirds of Afro-Caribbeans and almost half of the Europeans rented their dwellings. More than half the whites wanted to move, usually because they had come to dislike the neighbourhood. A quarter of the Asians and a third of Afro-Caribbeans also wanted to move, often because their dwellings were too small; nearly half the sample felt improvements to their accommodation were needed. Thus all groups, despite differing patterns of housing tenure, showed evidence of housing problems.

Financially, the Europeans were better off. Only 46% of Asians received state pensions compared with 83% of Afro-Caribbeans and 94% of Europeans. This pattern no doubt relates to the fact that many Asians and Afro-Caribbeans will not have paid sufficient insurance contributions to acquire their full entitlement to an old age pension.

Over a third of both Europeans and Afro-Caribbeans lived alone but only 5% of Asians. Yet 26% of Asians had no family in Britain outside their immediate household, and thus they were probably at risk of particular isolation – in contrast to what their experiences might have been in the context of their communities of origin. Social activities differed. Even allowing for the Asian groups being relatively younger, they seemed to spend far more time going out and about than did the Europeans but sex differences were important here. It seemed that few Asian women went out daily, and hardly any more Afro-Caribbean women, whereas over half the European women, despite being older, went out daily. On the other hand, 83% of Asian men went out daily, doubtless a reflection of cultural influences in lifestyle. Given the high proportion of Asian respondents unable to speak English (88%), and the fact that older women in particular seldom speak English and also tend to stay at home, this group seems especially likely to be socially isolated where the traditional extended family is not in evidence.

People felt a lack of places to go when they went out – particularly Afro-Caribbeans. Religious institutions formed important meeting places for many Asians and Afro-Caribbeans, especially men. It follows that, since going out among the ethnic minority groups seems far more of a male activity, if community services like day centres – in which people expressed an interest – were provided, it would probably be predominantly men who would use these facilities. Only 6% of European elders, and even fewer Asians and Afro-Caribbeans were attending day centres but relatively few people were without some kind of social contact. Eighty eight per cent of Afro-Caribbeans, 78% of Asians and 77% of Europeans said they saw friends, relatives, neighbours or others on a daily basis.

The study of elderly West Indians – most of whom were Jamaican – in Nottingham by Berry *et al.* (1981) 'found' its 148 respondents by various means: initially contacting West Indian organizations to seek anyone they knew who might be over pensionable age and working outwards from them. The representativeness of the findings, therefore, as the authors are at pains to point out, must be regarded as very tentative. Also, there was no comparison group of non-Afro-Caribbeans. Even so, some interesting themes emerge, which partially echo Bhalla and Blakemore's observations. Socio-economically, this was a relatively deprived group. The majority had worked in low-paid occupations and over half those receiving old age pensions were in addition receiving supplementary pensions, as compared with a fifth of the retired population of the United Kingdom as a whole.

When Berry *et al.* asked about special problems faced in this country, the major points made were the problem of lower pensions and reliance on benefits, colour prejudice (a lifelong experience) and a belief that old age in the West Indies might have proved a better experience:

> The problem is they don't look on us as people, they look on us as black pensioners. They don't realise that we know we are black, and we are proud to be black. White people my age group is very selfish. They don't think we should even have a bus pass. I hear black people complain about some of the white pensioners who think black people should not have the things that are provided for pensioners. (1981:43)

> I didn't know about 'pensioners' until I came here . . . we don't call people old. We don't throw people on the scrap heap. (1981:42)

Although many of the study group were in close touch with children, approximately a third either had no children or had children living abroad. This obviously has implications for availability of family support. Contact with the church figured as a very important part of social life for many people, almost a quarter being visited regularly at home by a pastor of the church. More than half of those questioned – both men and women – felt they lacked places to go and meet with other retired people. Many would have liked access to some kind of day centre for elderly West Indians. Bhalla and Blakemore also found this: a third of Asian and two-thirds of Afro-Caribbean respondents in their study were interested in the idea of day centres.

Barker's (1984) study was a survey of 619 Asians, West Indians and Africans aged 55 or over living in parts of London and Manchester. (It is not clear how

the sample was chosen.) Barker, like other writers, emphasizes the hetero-
geneity of the categories 'Asian' and 'West Indian'. His findings illustrate
similar trends to those already noted in the Birmingham and Nottingham
studies discussed above. Only 5% of Asians lived alone, but 36% of Afro-
Caribbeans were by themselves. However, a sense of loneliness and social
isolation pervaded the comments of many respondents. The cold, damp
British weather and fear of racial harrassment mitigate against the 'casual'
meetings with friends and relatives out of doors which would be the norm in
their countries of origin.

A recent study covering about three-quarters of the ethnic minority population in Coventry, mostly Asians (Holland and Lewando-Hundt 1987),
produces parallel findings to other studies. It is particularly interesting that
60% spoke more than one language although only 17% of Asians spoke
English. Most of the sample were not in paid employment but had formerly
worked in low-paid manual occupations.

Elderly members of ethnic minority groups run the risk of what Norman
(1985) calls 'triple jeopardy'. The first is that they experience discrimination
because they are old. Secondly, many of them live in disadvantaged physical
and socio-economic circumstances of our inner cities (both these factors being
partly common to indigenous elderly people) and, thirdly, they experience
discrimination because their culture, language, skin colour or religious affili-
ation in effect preclude access to services or agencies which might address their
needs.

Our review of these demographic and social features shows that, sociologically, the circumstances of our chosen case study groups are often characterized by disadvantages which are in part distinct and in part overlap with those
experienced by indigenous elderly people. Many of these special disadvantages
derive from the experience of migration and settlement in a country where
social institutions, processes and stratification are affected by the legacy of
colonialism. We now turn to issues concerning the health, illness and use of
health and social services by ethnic minorities in old age.

Health, illness and service provision

Given some of the particular disadvantages experienced by many old people
from ethnic minorities and what is known of the association between ill-health
and poverty (Townsend and Davidson 1982; Whitehead 1987), we might
expect to find that they also suffer disadvantages with respect to illness. It is
worth noting that some groups of particular racial descent suffer from diseases
which are not found within the majority population, for example sickle cell
anaemia among Afro-Caribbeans. There also appear to be epidemiological
differences with respect to various conditions: osteomalacia is found in excess
among older Asian women. Hypertension and stroke is more prevalent among
Afro-Caribbeans and ischaemic heart disease among Asians. Prevalence of
diabetes is higher among both Asians and Afro-Caribbeans than among the

majority population. [Whitehead (1987) summarizes what is known of the causes of immigrant mortality.]

The causes of these differences are not as yet fully understood, due to the complexities of interrelationships among the physiological, environmental, lifestyle and social factors involved: see, for example, the discussion by Silman *et al.* (1987) of heart disease and the apparent lack of relationships to raised blood pressure in Bengalis. Further, the experience and understanding of illness, and its social consequences, may differ in some respects for members of different ethnic groups. Donovan draws attention to the tendency to 'pathologize' people from ethnic minorities by focusing on particular conditions from which they suffer:

> Mostly researchers have looked at conditions which they believe affect specific ethnic groups, such as sickle cell anaemia in people of Afro-Caribbean descent, and rickets in people of Asian descent; or on topics of special interest to themselves, such as schizophrenia, tuberculosis and venereal disease. On the whole, the approach employed has been to isolate black individuals and groups, to discuss them as 'problems', and then go on to suggest solutions that are couched entirely in terms of individuals themselves having to change their ways of life so that they will conform to the desired norm of the white majority. (1986b : 117)

Differences in culture and languages, together with implicit or explicit discrimination in social organization of health care delivery, may make for difficulties both in seeking for and providing health care but ethnic minority status of itself cannot be regarded as a cause of distinctive patterns of ill-health among old people. Rather, the disadvantages of years of employment in hazardous occupations or surroundings, low income, poor housing and restricted access to the good things of life – disadvantages shared by many old whites living in inner cities – compound the disadvantages experienced in access to appropriate health and social care.

Glendenning (1979), Donovan (1986c), Pearson (1986) and others also discuss the tendency to regard the sufferers, rather than the conditions suffered, as the problem. For example, osteomalacia and rickets may indeed be due to lack of sunlight and vitamin D deficiency in diet. But to identify the solution as persuading Asian women to spend more time out of doors and to modify their diets – for instance by taking Western foods rich in vitamin D – is to ignore the importance of social causation of ill-health. Rickets was not uncommonly associated with poverty in Britain before the Second World War, until rationing, the fortification of basic foods with vitamin D and the National Milk Scheme brought about radical changes in working-class diets (Burnett 1966). Why, then, cannot chappati flour be fortified with vitamin D, rather than the Asian community be expected to eat a Western diet? Regarding access to sunlight, poor inner-city environments and fear of racist attacks may serve to reinforce culturally-based proscription in confining some Asian women to their homes.

Community services

As Norman (1985) points out, there is relatively little information either about trends in health and illness more generally among Asian and Afro-Caribbean old people, or about their own perceptions and experiences of illness and treatment, whether by health services or traditional healers.

Donaldson (1986) reports a survey of 726 Asians, three-quarters of whom had lived in African countries before coming to Britain. They were aged 65 and over, and sampled from general practitioner lists in Leicester and Lough-borough. Demographic characteristics of the sample were not unlike those found by Bhalla and Blakemore in Birmingham: only 5% lived alone and a further 13% lived in households of only one generation. Most, therefore, lived with a child or children and often with grandchildren or great-grandchildren also. There were slightly more men in the sample, of whom 37% said they could speak English, but only 2% of the women could.

Examining the ability to carry out various activities of daily living, Donaldson finds that the older age groups in the sample reported more incapacity, as has been repeatedly shown for other population-based samples of older people in the community (Shanas *et al*. 1968; Hunt 1978). Very small numbers were receiving domiciliary services, although 12% were attending day centres. Respondents commonly lacked information about services, although when these were described, as many as 94% said they would like to go to a day centre. That so many people are interested in day centres may reflect various factors: social isolation in the home, or lack of places to go outside the home, particularly perhaps for older Asian men whose custom it is to leave the house during the day. Other studies show similar findings, as discussed above.

Cooper (1979), Berry *et al*. (1981), Bhalla and Blakemore (1981) and Barker (1984) all document low 'take-up' of domiciliary health and social services (e.g. home help), particularly among Asians. In the Coventry study (Holland and Lewando-Hundt 1987), Caribbeans were much better informed about services available than were the Asians: 80% had heard about many services, apart from sheltered housing, but 80% of the Asians had never heard of most services apart from day centres. Even allowing for the relatively young age of this sample of older people, service take-up was low: just two people had meals on wheels, only 2% used the home help service and 1% lived in sheltered housing. Five per cent used day centres (4% of the Asians, 32% of the 71 Caribbeans). Sustantial proportions of both ethnic groups expressed an interest in using all of these services in the future, assuming they could be provided in an acceptable way, most obviously in respect of meals and home help services.

Lack of information about what is available is no doubt partly responsible for low levels of service take-up. As Cooper (1979) points out, if policy and service provision is geared to whites, and if ethnic minorities have distinct needs, then they are in fact suffering discrimination unless these needs are given explicit consideration in their own right. The implication is that services in practice embody racist assumptions and stereotyped views. For example, the view that people from ethnic minorities are not in need of help because of their family and community support networks; that they are ignorant about what is on offer and require 'educating'; or that they are in a way to blame for their own needs as a result of deviant and 'unsatisfactory' lifestyles. The ongoing research by Evers *et al.* (forthcoming) into community services' work with elderly people provides some illustrations of professionals' viewpoints which seem to be in common currency:

> In reply to the researcher's comment that there are few old people of ethnic minority groups on the district nurses' caseload, given the high numbers known to be living in the area, a district nurse replies:
>
> > 'It's because Asian families tend to look after their own. They tend to live as extended families in a single household, and they respect their elderly people far more than we do. They don't usually need us.'
>
> A different district nurse, in response to the same comment from the researcher, offers the following view:
>
> > 'They have a different view of health and illness from us. What we have to offer them is often not what they want. I was visiting a man with a stroke, and his family were not helping at all with his rehabilitation – instead of encouraging him to do things for himself, they said "he's sick, we must look after him – it's against our custom to make him take care of himself."'
>
> A social worker observes:
>
> > 'We know that there are old people out there who may need support from services, or information on welfare rights, but we haven't begun to tackle the problems of making contact. They don't know what we can offer, and we don't know enough about what we should be offering.' (Evers *et al.* forthcoming)

It seems that among service providers, concern to learn more about needs of ethnic minority groups is growing but services still continue to fail in communicating what they have on offer, to find out what people's expressed wants really are and to identify culturally-appropriate ways of responding. Changes are needed in policy and practice aimed to redress the situation. Ethnic groups themselves could provide a higher profile for their own concerns and services must listen and learn if they are able to work together with ethnic groups in developing more appropriate services. Examples of particular challenges include housing, which needs to be of an appropriate size and in the right location. Special thought should be given to the provision of sheltered housing and residential accommodation. Home support services must be ethnically-sensitive. Day care provision is wanted by Asians and Afro-Caribbeans, having due regard to considerations of mixing religious, linguistic or gender groups and offering acceptable food and opportunities for activities which participants will enjoy. Seeking and providing further information is vital. Policy makers and service providers need more and better information about what ethnic minority groups require and a clearer understanding of the cultural and socio-economic contexts within which needs arise. In this way services may make practical progress towards providing for the different needs identified in these groups. Members of ethnic minority groups require access to comprehensible information, in their own language if necessary, and ready access to service organizations.

There is some room for optimism. Norman notes various new developments in service provision. For example, there are initiatives in the provision of housing, residential and day care and home care services, e.g. meals on wheels for Asians and Afro-Caribbeans incorporating appropriate choices of menu and culturally-sensitive modes of food preparation (Brent Social Services Department 1983). Some of these initiatives come from the state sector of service provision, but many derive from the voluntary sector or self-help groups. Blakemore (1985) considers that state and voluntary sectors must continue to work in parallel.

Medical services

In contrast with use of community and domiciliary services, use of general practitioner and in some cases hospital services tends to be high (Johnson *et al.* 1983). Donaldson (1986) found that 67% of the Asians in his study had seen their doctor in the last month. As M. R. D. Johnson's (1986) population survey shows, most people are registered with a GP: 99% in his study. Blakemore (1983) observed that elderly Asians and Afro-Caribbeans use GP services more than elderly white people.

Given what Pearson calls the ethnocentrism of the NHS, how is this usage of GPs to be explained? There may well be excess morbidity: according to an American study (Lawton 1980), older black people tend to suffer poorer health than do their white counterparts living in similar environments, probably due mainly to particularly disadvantaged circumstances of poverty, poor housing and inner-city environment. However, cultural factors play a part. Immigrants are familiar with the role of Western medicine before migration, but access to medical care was more restricted for most old people in their countries of origin. Also, elderly Asians and Afro-Caribbeans may face particular stresses in old age as compared with whites. For example, many older black people had anticipated returning to their countries of origin in old age, but had been unable to do so. Social and family networks in old age in the United Kingdom are usually unlike those which could otherwise have been expected, thus there may be particular disappointments in old age. These may contribute to morbidity, and directly to the decision to consult the GP.

Is treatment received from the GP generally efficacious, at least in the sense that patients are satisfied? We do not really know the answer to this question. However, Bhalla and Blakemore found that the proportion of Asians and Afro-Caribbeans who were not receiving treatment for problems they reported with eyes, feet, ears and teeth was higher than the proportion of Europeans not receiving treatment when they reported such problems, despite the higher proportions of the ethnic minority groups who had contacted their GPs during the month before interview. Sixty eight per cent of Afro-Caribbeans, 70% of Asians, but only 53% of Europeans – who were older, on average and therefore might have been expected to experience more health problems – had been to their GP in the month before interview.

Ethnographic studies of doctor–patient relationships (see, e.g., Webb and Stimson 1976) show that there are many barriers to communication and understanding between lay and professional people, where the patient is subordinated to the power and mystique of the professional. This would apply just as much to Asian patients registered with Asian GPs – M. R. D. Johnson (1986) reports that 66% of Asians are so registered – and even more so to Asians registered with non-Asian GPs. Cultural and language differences as well as lay and professional differences in perceptions, understanding and communication of symptoms and illness add to the complexities of the doctor–patient relationship. 'Hot' and 'cold' are very important concepts in relation to the health of Asians. A balance must be kept, by eating appropriate foods – some of which are associated with 'hot', others with 'cold'. Although Asians came to rely on GPs and Western medicine, medicines were seen as 'hot', and therefore not to be taken in excess. Thus patients often did not take all, or even any, of their prescribed medication (Aslam *et al.* 1979; Bhopal 1986; Donovan 1986a).

Afro-Caribbeans seem to have less confidence in the NHS, despite their higher use of GP and hospital services as compared with Europeans. They often seek second opinions privately and actively pursue their own strategies of treatment through traditional means. Weightman (1977) notes their strong preference for liquid medicines as compared with pills. Several studies suggest that traditional measures are used alongside Western medicine. For example, Donovan's (1986a) study found that the Afro-Caribbeans, particularly the older people, knew most about traditional remedies. Most respondents, including the younger ones, made use of such remedies, for instance herbal preparations.

The Asians could sometimes remember childhood use of traditional remedies, or contacts with hakims although none in Donovan's study had made use of these in this country, preferring to rely on Western medicine. In the study by Donaldson (1986), 6% of the sample reported using traditional healers. Bhopal (1986) found that three-quarters of the 65 Asian patients he interviewed in Glasgow had tried traditional remedies for such complaints as stomach ache, toothache and ear-ache and it was the older people in the sample who were more likely to know of and to have used these remedies. Only two people had consulted an Asian healer, though 13 out of 57 had done so on return visits to the Indian subcontinent, mainly in relation to chronic conditions. Very few people preferred traditional to modern medicine. Bhopal also documented the ignorance of GPs concerning traditional remedies, though of those he questioned, half thought they were to be encouraged provided they did no harm. A majority of GPs felt they needed to learn more about these measures to enable them to respond more sensitively and effectively to their Asian patients' needs.

Regarding use of hospital services, Blakemore (1982) found that Afro-Caribbeans made greater use of these services – particularly the women – than did either Asians or Europeans. This suggests a higher incidence of health problems in this group. Norman (1985) observes that there may be special difficulties which Asians have in using the present hospital services, including language problems, inappropriate food and culturally-unacceptable 'hands-on' delivery of care and treatment. Ebrahim *et al.* (1987) looked at hospital discharge rates of Asians, Afro-Caribbean and British born elderly people in Nottingham for a variety of diagnoses. They found no evidence of under-utilization of hospital services by black elderly people – lending support to Blakemore's (1983) surmise that lifelong familiarity with Western medicine means that medical services are those most likely to be well-used by Asians and Afro-Caribbeans. Ebrahim *et al.* found excess discharges among Asians and Afro-Caribbeans for tuberculosis, diabetes, asthma, gastrointestinal bleeding and cataract surgery. They argue that this probably reflects real differences in morbidity between Asians, Afro-Caribbeans and the majority white population.

Illness behaviour

There has been very little research into Asians' and Afro-Caribbeans' perceptions of health and illness, nor much in the way of in-depth analysis of health and illness behaviour. Donovan's (1986a) study is an exception. She carried out lengthy, informal interviews in respondent's homes (often there were several interviews with the one respondent) and her analysis sought particular themes which had been identified by the respondents themselves. Although the 30 Asians and Afro-Caribbeans in the sample were mostly below retirement age, aspects of the analysis are relevant to our concerns.

Donovan's respondents took a particularly gloomy view of life in Britain, some feeling they could never be healthy here. Most were immigrants and felt they had left behind – perhaps in an idealized view – factors associated with healthiness: warmth, friendliness, fresh food and good company. They tended to see Britain as associated with illness, depression, worries, coldness, damp-ness, stale food, racism and loneliness. Loneliness was a special problem to Asian women, who often spoke no English, and spent much of the time at home. New social relationships to replace those severed by migration were hard to make, for reasons previously discussed. Afro-Caribbean women found loneliness a less significant problem. They mostly went out to work, thus making sociable contacts and often went out to religious gatherings which Muslim women did not.

In describing attitudes to ill-health, Donovan suggests Afro-Caribbeans tend to carry on and put up with ill-health attempting to shrug it off – perhaps because of a necessity to keep on working. The Asians in her sample, who were all women, did not go out to work. They spent a lot of time thinking about ill-health, which was, for them, related to tiredness, pain in the body and depression. Donovan's conclusions here seem to mirror the findings of Brown and Harris (1978) for a predominantly European sample in Camberwell that depression in women is particularly associated with being 'trapped' in the home, often with several young children and having no confiding relationships. These other social factors may be as important as ethnicity here and may help to explain why, to Donovan, Afro-Caribbeans seemed to have the strength to bear ill-health, whereas the homebound Asians appeared to become preoccupied with illness – their own or other family members' – and seemed likely to consult the doctor.

Donovan's findings about the use by Afro-Caribbeans of health services are interesting in relation to Blakemore's finding, in a different research mode (a survey), that older Afro-Caribbeans, particularly women, tend to make greater use of GPs and hospital services than do elderly Europeans. There is clearly room for further analysis of health, illness and behaviour in different ethnic groups, in order that apparently contradictory findings may be better understood. In the area of mental health and illness, there is a growing body of literature concerning ethnic minorities (see, e.g., Rack 1982), but analysis of mental illness and old people remains largely lacking at present.

In thinking about health and illness of older Asians and Afro-Caribbeans, it is clear that 'exotic' illnesses of ethnic minorities are a very small part of the issue. More important are the trends in illness resulting from social disadvantage: poverty, poor housing and environment, compounded by racist assumptions and ethnocentric service organizations which fail both to inform themselves about culture and health needs of ethnic minorities, and to respond appropriately. Attention to the basics of communication is needed – written information in Asian languages and the availability of interpreters – and to the greater subtleties of religious and cultural norms.

Conclusion: the need for further analysis

We have described something of the particular circumstances of two 'umbrella' ethnic minority groups in the United Kingdom, Asians and Afro-Caribbeans. We have shown that stereotypical views regarding family life and social support networks for ethnic elders are not altogether without foundation but are misleading. That such stereotypes are incorporated into the organization and *modus operandi* of the state's services and benefits network results in widespread failure to consider and address the specific economic, health and social needs of these groups. It is not black elders themselves who are social problems, of course. The disadvantages they experience are sometimes socially created and certainly socially reinforced.

Along with social class and gender, ethnic minority status is an important variable in social stratification. Ours is an ageist society, where elderly people's access to socio-economic resources is systematically restricted, whether implicitly or explicitly. Racism tends to compound the socially-created disadvantages faced by older people who are also members of black ethnic minorities. Thus, in any rounded consideration of the ageing experience in a multicultural society, ethnicity must figure as a key variable.

While studies presently available – some of which we have discussed above – do much to illuminate the issues, further research is needed, perhaps more urgently than in any other area to do with the sociology of ageing. The relationships among age, ethnicity, social class and gender as factors in shaping the experiences of the aged in ethnic minority groups requires continuing analysis. Studies to date have often been initiated by white researchers. They need to be complemented by studies where the ethnocentrism of 'white' methodology and assumptions in sociological studies can be challenged. Currer (1986), for example, draws attention to the difficulty of carrying out individual interviews with Pathan women about health and illness. One-to-one discussions with outsiders, as in the standard survey interview, are not necessarily common currency in all cultures. The notion of speaking about oneself independently of the family group may be quite alien, even when the interviewer is of the 'right' ethnicity and sex and can speak the same language. Despite the formidable conceptual and methodological problems involved, a dearth of ethnographic research on the experience of old age among Asians and Afro-Caribbeans must be remedied if we are to further our understanding of old age and ethnicity.

In addition, besides generational changes to be expected in any group, intergenerational change in ethnic minorities is and will continue to be dramatic. The life experiences and aspirations of second and successive generations are moving away in crucial respects from cultural norms in the countries of origin of today's elderly people. This is not to say that 'assimilation' is taking place: the process of change is more complex than that by far. Not only will the experiences, lifestyles and needs of the next and succeeding generations of old people be different, so also will their social and care networks. Thus continuing study will be needed if we are to keep pace with unravelling some of the complexities.

Inter-ethnic comparison may prove particularly valuable in reconsidering some of the theoretical, methodological and conceptual issues discussed in Chapters 3 and 4. Comparative and preferably longitudinal studies – qualitative, to map out the key issues, quantitative, to test hypotheses regarding inter-ethnic differences – are needed. Analysing over time the experiences of older people of ethnic minorities in their own right and in relation to the experiences of the dominant group will clarify the relationships among ethnicity, class and gender as factors influencing disadvantage in old age.

PART III

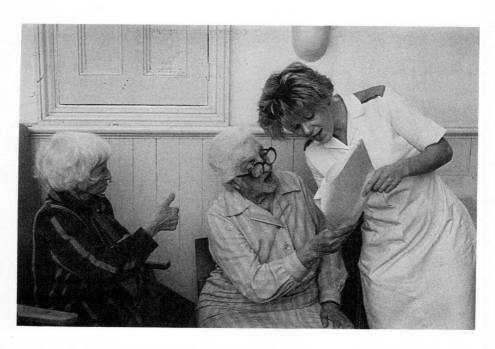

8

Old age in special settings

Outside are the Sunshine minibuses and the ambulances. Inside is oblivion. Thirty very aged people, almost all women, are sitting side by side, immobile around the walls of a large room. . . . They were lifted into the chairs where they now sit. They haven't moved since. (Owen 1977)

Introduction

As far as possible this book has concentrated on general issues in the sociology of old age, reversing the usual emphasis, which is to focus on the welfare and problem-related aspects of special provision for elderly people with its tendency to legitimate what Macintyre (1977) calls the 'organizational' perspective or Johnson (1976) the 'pathology' approach.

In Chapter 2 we noted that the proportion of elderly people living in institutions has seldom exceeded 5% in recorded history, but the sheer weight of research and the number of publications on institutional care are proportionately far greater and necessitate at least some discussion. Abrams examined the balance of projects reported in the *Register* of the National Corporation for the Care of Old People contrasting the work then being undertaken with the 'priority areas' identified by the DHSS:

Of the 27 priority topics listed by the Department only one is concerned with residential homes; in contrast, of all the 160 research projects in hand and listed in the NCCOP register over one-sixth are concerned with various aspects of the residential care of the elderly. (Abrams 1978a : 16)

Taylor's analysis of the 1978–9 register recorded 'a reduction in the number of projects which are concerned with residential care . . . from 13 per cent to 8 per cent' and noted that 'interest in sheltered housing remains strong' (1979 : vii), though the next year saw 'a reduction in the number of studies concerned with housing of the elderly, together with a renewed focus on residential care' (1980 : vii). Later, a bibliography of sheltered housing for elderly people recorded 450 publications on the subject in the previous decade (Way and

Fennell 1987). Clearly 'special settings' attract disproportionate attention, but few of these research projects and publications are sociologically informed (Fennell 1985). In this chapter, while grappling with a predominantly un-sociological literature, we examine what we regard as sociologically interesting questions.

What is a special setting?

By a special setting in old age we mean a physical place, predominantly or exclusively intended for the use of elderly people, where the users spend a substantial proportion of their time. To qualify to spend such a substantial proportion of time in the place one must, minimally, be an elderly person (or a member of staff) or have what Goffman (1963) terms a 'spoiled identity' – such as being labelled as disabled, mentally handicapped or prematurely senile – which legitimizes being 'lumped together' with another social minority category (Townsend 1973). By attending, or living in the special setting, one is brought into association with other elderly people and contact with other age groups is, in varying degrees, inhibited.

The special settings we have in mind include day centres for elderly people, geriatric day hospitals, sheltered housing schemes, residential homes and long-stay hospitals or wards of hospitals. We exclude voluntary associations of elderly people coming together once a week or so, as in a pensioners' club or bingo session; and also concentrations of elderly people arising unintentionally (by choice, or the operation of market or demographic factors) as we might see in a retirement resort or an ageing estate. Integral to the concept of a special setting is that someone (or some group), somewhere, at some time, has designated the place as especially suitable for people in old age; and also taken the decision that other age groups should be excluded.

Some of these special settings have their roots far back in the past and it might be said that no one, today, is actively responsible for the fact they exist. Many examples could be given: the new Health Authorities, for instance, created in 1974, found themselves administering all manner of institutions they inherited from previous bodies; the Social Services Departments (coming into being in 1971) took over specialized facilities from earlier Welfare or Health and Welfare Departments. In the 1980s, voluntary housing associations have been invited to take on the management of the retirement housing created in coastal and rural areas by the now-disbanded Greater London Council, which itself inherited the scheme from the previous London County Council. There are very specialized settings, for instance residential institutions for elderly European Jews, survivors of the Holocaust; and army camps housing ageing members of the Polish Free Army.

Sociologists have a shorthand term for this phenomenon: they refer to such institutions as being 'reproduced' or 'socially reproduced' by succeeding generations of voters, politicians, planners and administrators. Maybe we did not create the workhouses or the almshouses, but such institutions are successively reproduced by continuing to vote them funds or administer them for as long as their ethic is not explicitly challenged or dynamic attempts made to create alternatives. One perplexing theoretical problem is the inertia of institutions, their slowness to change even when denounced as out of date and unsuited to the needs of today's elderly people: a suspicion (even a hypothesis) develops that the survival of some forms of special settings is attributable to the fact that they serve wider social functions (such as custodial care) to which the needs of the elderly users become secondary.

The literature of dissent

This was why he did not agree with old people's housing, Dr Isaacs said. He hoped that would not be interpreted as a criticism of the wonderful work being done by housing managers to create special housing for the elderly. But one had to think of the society they wanted to create and Dr Isaacs did not think one wanted to create a society in which old people would be segregated in more and more special houses for the elderly. (Isaacs 1969 : 19)

This quotation encapsulates the dilemma of any commentator on special settings: they are someone's creation, someone's 'wonderful work'. They have been planned for elderly people – or at least designated for their use – to meet perceived needs and often they do meet them. The staff are confident of the value of their enterprise, elderly users are often grateful and express pleasure in what is provided, so what right do outsiders have to express reservations about 'the sort of society we want to create'?

Many people have a vested interest in special settings and it is hard even to find a dispassionate and value-free vocabulary with which to discuss them. To find a middle-ground in the literature is difficult: what appears to be another diatribe about 'abuse', 'segregation' and 'total institutions' demoralizes staff and undervalues the work they do; yet bland and uncritical accounts of special settings tend also to ring false, as if the observers have missed some obvious flaw. Perhaps we are all unconsciously influenced in this by 'news values'. Stories on the theme, '98% of users happy with day centres' are intuitively less newsworthy – even less plausible – than stories of the type, 'Old people's home of shame – report sent to Director of Public Prosecutions'.

This dilemma is clear in what Jones (1975) called 'the literature of dissent'. There was a period, particularly during the 1960s and early 1970s, when every fresh book appeared to be written from a critical perspective. Examples include Goffman's *Asylums* (1961), Townsend's *The Last Refuge* (1962), Robb's *Sans Everything* (1967), Morris's *Put Away* (1969), Meacher's *Taken for a Ride* (1972) and Miller and Gwynne's *A Life Apart* (1972).

This literature, in Jones's view was:

Concerned with what is wrong with institutions rather than with how they can be well run. . . . This is a generation which is unusually intolerant of authority in any form, and it may be that those who manage and work in institutions have become popular targets in the same sense that the Government (any government), God, the Royal Family and the Governors of the London School of Economics have become popular targets. (1975 : 290–91)

Jones is ambivalent about this 'anti-authoritarian' tradition, which is 'sometimes blind and seldom analytical' but, for all that 'may serve a purpose, and a very useful one'. This ambivalence is shown in her put-down of Goffman:

> Who attempted (from a fairly limited experience – one year as an assistant remedial gymnast in a federal mental hospital in Washington) an eclectic analysis of what he calls 'total institutions'. (Jones 1975 : 291)

This jibe misses the point. Participant observers have to assume a suitable role in carrying out their studies and a low echelon one is ideal for getting close to patients and seeing the institution as it is, rather than taking the word of senior staff who spend little time in the wards. Also, what matters more than the role adopted and the length of time spent in observation is the quality of the analysis and the extent to which it is theoretically informed and integrated with a wide range of reading. In these respects, Goffman's work is unsurpassed.

Goffman's model as exemplar

Goffman's mode of analysis exemplifies the use of a particular sociological technique, the *ideal-type* or model. As we have not previously discussed this technique, we need to observe that the 'ideal-type' total institution is not to be regarded as an 'ideal' or 'model' institution in the flattering sense, but as a scientific or abstract model like the ball and wire structures molecular biologists construct to help them understand the complexities of DNA, a way of understanding something in its 'pure' form and getting at the interrelationship of parts. Goffman's work is clear and accessible and is rehearsed in other sources (Jones and Fowles 1984), so we need only sketch the general propositions in order to draw out the utility of the approach, showing that this is not merely negative but can be put to constructive use.

One proposition is that a whole range of different institutions, set up with different objectives, have common features or can easily regress towards a common type where the differences in *aim* of, say, a long-stay prison, a monastery, psychiatric hospital or old people's home, become less significant than the fact that these are 'people-processing organizations' which – sometimes as an accidental by-product of their organization, and sometimes deliberately – make an assault on individuality in order to create compliance to the institutional regime.

Other propositions flow from this: the more total the institution, the more determined the assault on individual privacy, dignity and self-respect. Townsend reported instances which may seem safely remote to the contemporary reader:

> The staff took the attitude that the old people had surrendered any claims to privacy. The residents were washed and dressed and conveniently arranged in chairs and beds – almost as if they were made ready for a daily

inspection. An attendant was always present in the bathroom, irrespective of old people's capacity to bath themselves. The lavatories could not be locked and there were large spaces at the top and bottom of the doors. The matron swung open one door and unfortunately revealed a blind old woman installed on the wc. She made no apology. In a dormitory she turned back the sheets covering one woman to show a deformed leg – again without apology or explanation. (1962 : 5)

This ward is reached up twenty steep stone steps, the staircase walls being pitted and peeling. On the windswept landing are 12 wcs in two rows of six, with no doors, no wooden seats and divided from each other by only iron bands three feet high. (1962: 67)

In extreme cases, people lose their self-identities and means of keeping them in repair: their names are taken away, their personal clothing removed, 'self-repair' kits and props, such as pocket mirrors, nail scissors, razors, spectacles, dentures and hearing aids removed (for 'safe keeping') and the person's adult integrity attacked verbally – by abuse, sarcasm, hostile jokes – and sometimes physically:

'They have to be broken in when they come into a communal home. . . . There's a team of three men in the bathrooms – one dries, the other undresses them and the third baths them.' He meant that the bath was a kind of initiation . . . for it was accompanied by other actions. Hair was often cropped short and toenails cut. Clothing was taken away and replaced by institutional underwear and suits or dresses. A shapeless herring-boned suit or a print dress was doled out. Quite often each article of clothing bore the name of the institution, the name or number of the ward or block stitched in red or inked in black. (Townsend 1962 : 90)

However, although we may hope that these practices have been abandoned, problems in institutional care do not disappear simply through the passage of time and the publication of books, as Martin's analysis in the early 1980s reminds us:

It is an unhappy fact that despite all the efforts of the health authorities . . . there seems to be a steady stream of cases where members of staffs of hospitals or homes appear before the criminal courts on charges of maltreating those in their care. . . . An example was that of a nurse in a Yorkshire Hospital who was sentenced to six months imprisonment for ill-treating an 81-year-old patient by repeatedly punching him in the ribs and stomach while he was sitting in a chair. . . . The Judge said, '. . . I have no doubt that you took advantage of a situation, with that man in a chair, to bring him to a state of submission.' (1984 : 62)

Sequestration of personal effects, segregation from the wider community and seclusion from view help increase the totality of an institution and Goffman's analysis also points to the divide between 'the staff' and 'the inmates', both groups developing or inheriting a world view which explains why things are as they are and why they have to be so. This shows that protest is futile and punishment is deserved. He refers also to 'batch living' whereby the residents are got up when the lights go on, to suit the convenience of the institution, or bathed, because it is bath time, or put to bed, regardless of daylight or personal preference.

'You get funny things today, too. The other month one lot of old women went off on a coach trip and they weren't back until after 10 o'clock. Now just you remember that most of the old women go off to bed just after tea at 5 o'clock. When the other lot arrived and put the lights on the first lot thought it was time to get up. So there we were – with one lot of women putting their clothes on and the others taking them off.' (Townsend 1962 : 86)

These examples remind us that there is a constant risk that what Martin (1984) calls 'the corruption of care' can occur in institutional settings where vulnerable people are looked after. However, Goffman's work not only reminds us of the risks to avoid but also gives pointers about how to avoid them. If the totality of an institution is assisted by the 'membrane' which surrounds it (the visible barriers, such as high walls, locked doors, forbidding notices), then it makes sense to tear this down and 'open-up' the institution to view – as indeed, at many former workhouses the boundary walls were pulled down, the gates removed and flower beds planted.

If depersonalization arises from lack of privacy and batch living, this helps us to understand the necessity to break the monolithic institution down into smaller units, perhaps adopting the flatlet model advocated by Willcocks *et al.* (1987) and the need to train and support staff in encouraging and permitting individual activities and timetables. If personal identity is sustained by physical props and needs to be repaired in a private 'backstage' area – as Goffman calls it in another powerful analysis of *The Presentation of Self in Everyday Life* (1959) – then we more readily see the need for people to have their own clothes, their dentures, spectacles, hearing aids and means of keeping them in repair and replacing them. Hence the value of hairdressers coming in to visit, or of residents being helped to go out shopping or for beauty care in the widest sense.

If the general invisibility of what goes on in the institution is the problem, the more important it is to 'normalize' the setting by encouraging constant flows of people in and out – visitors, relatives, school children doing community work, doctors, support staff, central management – as well as making sure residents go on trips, have holidays, visit friends and relatives or go out to the shops. This message is probably well-understood in the higher echelons of the public sector, but may need to be reaffirmed constantly at lower levels there and to the proprietors of private residential establishments. 'Protection' of residents can easily lead to the recreation of the impermeable membrane which Goffman sees as encasing the institution, and behind this barrier can arise 'an enthusiasm for an extremely high degree of security . . . almost obsessional in intensity', 'an atmosphere of fear and frustration' and an 'ominous form of group loyalty [among staff]' (Martin 1984 : 21, 41, 50).

Beyond Goffman

Martin thinks that in one particular at least, Goffman was wrong. Goffman sees the inmates as living in the institutions, whereas he sees the staff as living 'in the community': the staff come and go, the inmates stay. In analysing more than 20 inquiry reports into abuses (particularly in long-stay hospitals) Martin concludes that this exaggerates the integration of the staff. Because their work is arduous, underpaid and devalued, staff can in some cases become as cut-off from the wider society as the patients, with the negative corollary that:

> In the hospitals which suffered major scandals, the fundamental failure had been of that self-regulating, self-evaluating function which lies at the heart of all effective social institutions. While it is alive reform is possible, but when it fails the sense of community is diverted into the cause of short-term self protection with all the dishonesty and victimisation that may entail. (1984 : 109)

Another point where we might go beyond Goffman, is to consider how far the 'totalitizing' effects of institutions may inhere to some extent in the characteristics of the residents as in the physical structure of the plant and aspects of the regime and, if so, what follows from this. Of course, in saying this we have to be wary of the pitfall known as 'blaming the victim', but the thrust of Jones' attack on the 'literature of dissent' is probably based on a sense that people do not come to be in institutions without having some 'deviant' characteristics (in the broadest sociological sense) which help to 'explain' the development of features that other observers deplore.

Many residents have special demographic characteristics which 'explain' why they are in the institution and reinforce their isolation – for instance, that they are older than average, having outlived their relatives; are more commonly drawn from the unmarried, the childless and the divorced; or that they have no known relatives (as Townsend shows).

Some people, as Miller and Gwynne (1972) argue, can feel so seriously deformed and handicapped as to prefer to hide themselves from the censorious or hurriedly averted gaze of 'normals'; others suffer from extremes of physical and mental frailty which render the notion of passing backwards and forwards across the barrier which separates the institution from the world outside problematic, to say nothing of those whose antisocial behaviour or other stigmatizing characteristics have led other 'carers' to reject them.

This is one extract from the many heart-breaking accounts in Sidell's study of confusion and formal and informal care:

> There was no element of self-pity in Mrs Pountney's story. Nor was there any guilty self-recrimination about having had Mr Pountney 'put away'. She could not and would not cope. But she was not unfeeling towards her husband; she hated to think of him 'shut up in there'. . . . She said, 'I dread going and seeing him like that – I shall burst out crying.' (1986 : 159)

However, by the time Mr Pountney was taken into hospital, Mrs Pountney was down to six stone in weight. Then 84, she had been caring for her heavy, confused and not infrequently violent husband for 2 years. She was knocked off her feet twice, on one occasion striking her head against an iron door-stop; she found he had hidden 'a great big chopper' in the sideboard; he smashed his false teeth with a hammer to deal with a 'rough bit on them'.

One night she tried to stop her husband drinking neat Dettol and he drove her out of the house. With only one slipper on and unable to walk without her stick, Mrs Pountney struggled painfully over gravel to two neighbouring houses, but no one was in:

> Then I went to the one on this side – Mrs Talmon – and they were at home. They're up on a hill. They've got a lot of steps to go up, and I couldn't get up the steps, so I went up the grass bank, and hung on to some rose bushes and whatnot, and I was shaking and crying and trembling – wondering if he'd drunk it you see – and I daren't come in to see, and Mrs Talmon came down. . . . It was still in the glass – he threw it outside – anyway, I said, 'I'm not going back; not yet, I'm not', and so I stopped up there. . . . They don't know what they're doing, you see.
> (Sidell 1986 : 158)

It is clear that there are people of extreme frailty and physical dependency, or whose behaviour and mental state apparently deprive them of the capacity for rewarding, reciprocal social relationships and that some such people will live in residential or nursing homes. How can staff, who are in the main probably kindly people with families they care for, become 'sucked in' to the negative aspects of the 'total institution'? What can be done, beyond securing openness of organizational boundaries and strengthening registration and inspection procedures to prevent the perpetration of suffering and abuse?

Stereotypical views of old people as sick and dependent, in part personified by a minority of old people in institutional care, reinforce other trends which accord low status to care-work with older people. Care workers are predominantly female and low paid (Finch and Groves 1980). They are in the main carrying out basic 'women's work' in caring for their charges, who are themselves mainly women. Clarke (1978), in an aptly titled chapter on 'getting through the work', describes how the 75 nurses she interviewed saw their job as comparable with factory work: a series of tasks to be 'got through'. This commonly-held view was reinforced by staff shortages.

Depersonalizing the people being cared for, disaggregating them into a series of tasks is a way whereby staff can protect themselves from confronting the pain of people-processing organizations where both carers and cared-for alike are devalued by and unsupported in their social context. It is one of several 'neutralization techniques' familiar to us from the sociology of deviance (Sykes and Matza 1957) such as the 'denial of injury' and 'denial of the victim' discussed by Martin (1984).

Maintaining open organizational boundaries as a strategy for improving the situation, including enabling staff to move in and out of institutional settings, could be complemented by actions to 're-value' not only residents but also staff. Proper resourcing could allow more widespread adoption of good practices pioneered in a few settings (as discussed, for example, by Wainwright and Burnip 1983). To secure institutional settings against possible future mal-practice, it would be fundamental to accord the prime carers – whether nurses or social care staff – proper status, accountability and responsibility for their work. This would mean paying them adequately, acknowledging their expertise and the social value of care work in its own right, independently of the curative aims often more highly prized in medical interventions.

Special training is needed, but this is preferably not located under the medical umbrella which so often tends to dominate and convey the hidden message that only 'cure-work' – but not 'care-work' – is valid and valuable. Protecting the frail resident or patients can be achieved only if staff needs are also carefully considered and given a proper response. However, as cost-cutting is at present a political requirement in the public sector and an organizational imperative in the private care market, we are pessimistic about prospects for this at least in the short-term.

Day centres and day hospitals

Fair evaluation of special settings of this type is problematic in the United Kingdom where, not only is under-resourcing of each unit commonplace, but also, total system under-resourcing is endemic, so that there is constant pressure to use/misuse/distort whatever local resources are available to solve critical problems for what Goffman calls the 'circuit of agents' who make decisions for, about or on behalf of elderly people. Self-initiated referrals to day centres or local authority residential care are rare: commonly the referral can be traced to another agent, or set of agents resolving a problem they have by making the referral.

Why have day centres for elderly people? The rationale is located in activity theory. If people are lonely, isolated, depressed, have problems keeping warm, run the risk of under-nourishment and lack stimulation, better to take them out for the day – it is argued – for company and a cooked meal in a warm, sociable and secure setting, rather than make feeble efforts to input services to the home, leaving the elderly person 'a prisoner of his or her own four walls'. Company stimulates us and (although sexual tastes are as variable in old age as in other age groups), many would acknowledge social and biological 'program-ming' to respond to heterosexual stimulus. So, if people are going out for the day in mixed company, they want 'to look their best', the outing creates an incentive to think about self-presentation, to care about appearance, take an interest in dress and so on. This is a counter-active to the risk of slipping into a spiral of self-neglect through depression and lack of stimulus, becoming unkempt, deviant and unloveable, and hence experiencing more social rejection and becoming more negative about oneself.

Also, it is argued, eating a meal is a social activity and one reason elderly women – quite capable of shopping, cooking and eating a meal – cease to bother and 'pick at bits' is that they do not have anybody to cook for or eat with. Better, then, to bring people together, and they will eat with pleasure and appetite, because the meal is a social event. Adequate nutrition, in turn, helps other bodily mechanisms maintain homeostasis, that dynamic, self-regulating system whereby the body adjusts to fluctuations in the internal and external environment.

We have noted in Chapter 7 that there is unmet demand for day centres among members of ethnic minorities who feel they lack meeting places and opportunities for company. Studies as different in their methodological approach as that by Carter (1981) and Fennell *et al.* (1981) are in agreement that the majority of day centre users enjoy their day at the centre and appreciate the opportunity to escape from the confines of their home. These are comments from day centre users who were well known to the researchers from months of acquaintance and interviewed in the privacy of their homes:

> Yes, it's beautiful, beautiful, I really look forward to going there. Mondays and Fridays don't seem to come quick enough for me.

> You meet people and they give you a good dinner.

> It gives you something to look forward to, and you see all the people and their problems and you think yours are not so bad.

> I do enjoy going and I enjoy doing the handicrafts and seeing other people doing things you've never seen before. It does you good. (Fennell *et al.* 1981 : 98–100)

If this social stimulus is the basic rationale for the day centre, more adventurous ideas can be added on. Perhaps interesting activities can be pursued while at the centre; perhaps the centre can be used as a jumping off point for other necessary or pleasurable excursions – to the dentist, to the opticians, to the shops, as well as the common summer outings. Perhaps the centre can be used as an educational forum, helping to offset the lack of time and educational opportunities which elderly people have experienced when they were younger. Perhaps the centre can act as a health education and welfare rights advice point, even the basis of 'out-reach' to those who do not attend regularly.

Well-resourced and imaginative centres certainly do these things, but, as always, standards vary from centre to centre and there is often scope for improvement (Bowl *et al.* 1979; Fennell and Sidell 1982). We quoted in Chapter 4 the findings by Godlove *et al.* that more than a fifth of the day centre users they observed spent 'more than half their time in isolated inactivity' and that the 'average inactive time' in day centres was 32% (1982 : 30). As one user commented in the study by Fennell *et al.*:

> If they gave me some eggs to sit on, I think they'd hatch.

Another commented:

> We just sit like mummies, we don't do anything. They throw some old magazines on the table and that's all.

And another:

You sit there watching the clock, waiting for five o'clock. (1981 : 100)

Debates about day centres

The day centre cannot be seen as the panacea for all ills. If an elderly person requires home help assistance, going to a day centre does not lessen the requirement. If there is a problem of loneliness and isolation, one day a week at a day centre will make only a marginal impact; as equally will a cooked mid-day meal one day in seven. If relative deprivation – lacking company when other people have it, such as weekends, Christmas and other public holidays – is a source of dismay, a day centre is hardly a palliative since it will typically be closed (Fennell 1979).

The conclusion to draw from this is that the day centre is a useful adjunct in the armoury of community resources for elderly people, but there is limited substitutability between services: going to a day centre will seldom reduce a need for meals on wheels or home help.

Then there are debates about the stimulus level in day centres and implicit debates between the protagonists of activity and disengagement theory. Quite often, it will be said that day centre users 'only want to sit and chat'; or (because of poor vision or arthritic fingers), 'there's nothing they can do, really'; or, 'they spoil too much material'. These attitudes, carried to extremes, lead to the occasional centre where the staff are hard at work on craft activities, making items for sale to raise money for the centre, but the attenders are not allowed to touch the machinery or materials for fear of accident or waste; or the diversion of goals, where users doze away the day under placards bearing the legends, 'art therapy', 'music therapy', 'reminiscence therapy' and so on; or where 'make-work' is created, and coarse materials are constantly knitted up into dishclothes, only to be unravelled by the staff for the next day's shift. Generalization is perhaps hazardous, but after visits to many centres one team of observers concluded that education and care inputs were hard to combine in one staff, and the most stimulating centres had education and craft inputs coming in from outside educationalists and craft instructors, rather than being supplied 'in-house' (Fennell *et al.* 1981).

Is the day long enough? Here, too, the question of under-resourcing muddies the waters. The welfare of the users can become secondary to the authorities' need to make use of transport which doubles up for the transporting of children to and from special schools, or comply with union stipulations that all care staff must be out and the doors locked by 5 p.m. Under these conditions, 'day care' often means a late start and an early finish, and this may be particularly important when we consider another function of the day centre, not so far discussed, namely to give respite to an 'informal carer' at home.

Here the primary welfare of the day centre user is admittedly secondary to that of the carer, or is regarded as being secured by giving temporary primacy to the needs of the carer. Many examples of this could be quoted. Often, the person cared for has as one of their diagnostic labels 'dementia' or 'confusion'.

Relief afforded to carers may be tempered by uncertainties interposed on finely-balanced routines, regarding, for instance, when transport will arrive to collect the old person and equally when he or she will be brought home. Carers may also have to cope with disorientation seemingly exacerbated by a once- or twice-weekly change of venue for their charges, not to mention guilt feelings about consigning the care of their relative (usually it is a relative, neighbours seldom 'count' as carers for whom relief is needed) and to others who may not know and love them.

While day care may provide welcome relief for many carers, it is not without its unintended – and problematic – consequences. Also, some carers who might welcome relief may be excluded from the day centre. Jones and Vetter (1985) found that carers of old people who were incontinent and/or aggressive were far less likely to be offered day care primarily for relief purposes, than were carers of less dependent old people. These potential users were presumably deemed 'too bad' to be coped with in day centres or day hospitals, although by default, not 'too bad' to be looked after 24 hours a day by a lay carer.

Like other special settings, allocation of day care as a resource is influenced by many factors besides dependency – whether it is too great, or not great enough – accidental and otherwise. Demographic factors are important – those living alone, more commonly women, are a major category of client. Gender, too, seems important in other ways. The work of Evers *et al.* (forthcoming) shows that in the case of elderly couples living in a two-person household where one partner is disabled or demented, men as carers tend to be offered different 'packages' of care from women. For example, where it is the wife who is caring, it appears more likely that the dependent husband will be receiving day care. But the husband supporting a demented or disabled wife is instead more likely to receive domiciliary support such as a home help, or perhaps a nursing auxiliary to help with bathing. The woman as carer seems implicitly deemed capable of managing the domestic duties without support as long as the 'object' of her care is removed from time to time, whereas the man as carer is not expected to cope in the house without help – though neither is he deemed to need 'relief' from his wife.

The ways that day care centre places and access to these and other special settings are controlled by those who run them, particularly the exclusion of very dependent or 'deviant' old people, in effect 'institutionalize' the old people (and particularly their carers) in the privacy and invisibility of their own homes. We must for a moment, then, consider the private household as becoming in some cases a kind of 'special setting'.

Parenthesis: the home as a special setting

Pulling (1987), writing of the 'caring trap', addresses the plight of demented old people and particularly of their daughters whose lives are devoted to the task of caring. As a journalist who has herself been in that role, she illustrates through case material the ambivalence of those who, while wishing to care for their elderly relatives, suffer emotionally, physically and financially through doing so. Spackman writes about Linda, a woman caring for her 81-year-old mother:

> On a good day Linda gets six hours' sleep. On a bad day, she is down to bursts of two hours. . . . 'I have never actually hit my mother. But I've come close to it', she admits. 'What really cracks me up is when she's ill and I'm up every two hours. It makes me resentful – not about my mother but towards outsiders. Why aren't there more resources?' (1987:10)

Research, too, has amply documented the situation of carers and cared-for in their private homes (see, e.g., Wright 1986; Nissel and Bonnerjea 1982; Levin *et al*. 1983).

It seems likely that the more competent the lay carer, the less likely he or she is to be offered help. This may particularly be the case for dementia sufferers. Badger (1987) shows that among demented people living at home and in touch with community care services, it is apparently differences in how 'deviant' and socially unacceptable they are, rather than how dependent, which influences their typical pathways through the network of services. There is little difference between those who get to see a specialist community psychiatric nurse or the psychogeriatrician and those who do not, other than that the former engage in more antisocial behaviour, are on average younger and have fewer physical health problems. Being younger and fitter, they are likely to pose social control problems for a period of longer time.

Where old people are known to community services and are living mainly at home, the professionals may in effect create a special setting through their interventions. This has positive and negative aspects. Very disabled people may be helped to continue living at home as they themselves wish, by provision of technical aids to daily living – 'Possums', for example – as a means of controlling their own environment, as well as intensive support and care, sometimes by volunteers who live on the premises for periods of up to 6 months at a time. Such intensive support as this, supplemented, perhaps, by regular calls from the district nurse and social worker, is of course expensive and rare. Recipients tend to be younger rather than older and such schemes are not without their problems: the clients may remain predominantly 'in charge' of their own lives, but are inevitably dependent on their facilitators to retain a semblance of personal autonomy.

Negative aspects of professional intervention in the home include the professionals who 'reorganize' the home to render it 'safer' for someone at risk and create unintended consequences: a blind woman in Evers' (1984) study found that she was more incapacitated in her own home as a result of intervention than before: the health visitor recommended moving furniture and rugs with the intention of reducing the woman's risks of falling and the home help who moved things around, created unseen hazards, from one visit to the next. The woman's solution was to give up receiving home help. Frequently, Badger *et al*. (1988) were told that a nursing auxiliary's visit to help with washing or bathing disrupted half a day or more, due to uncertainty regarding time of arrival, or the stress resulting from a hurried visit by the hard-pressed auxiliary.

On a more fundamental level, Evers (1984) found that, while professionally-engineered house moves – to bungalows or sheltered housing – could prove extremely liberating, sometimes a lack of attention to detail on the part of the professional could result in an old person agreeing to a move which proved disastrous. For people with mobility problems, a move even a short distance away removes them from the familiar – the shops, bus routes and neighbours – and is in danger of creating or reinforcing dependency and social isolation. Yet the power of the professional here, as in the provision of health care, is hard to resist.

Sheltered housing

By sheltered housing we mean specially built or adapted self-contained accommodation for elderly people which is characteristically grouped together – as in a block of flats or a cluster of bungalows – and where there is a resident warden with whom the inhabitants can communicate by means of an alarm system and (usually) a two-way speech intercom. Sheltered housing schemes often have additional facilities, such as a communal laundry room, one or more guest rooms and a communal lounge as well as, sometimes, a special bathroom for assisted bathing.

Sheltered housing is meant to be different from hospital or residential care and some would argue that it should simply be regarded as 'housing' provision and not be treated as a 'care environment' at all (Butler *et al.* 1983; Age Concern 1984). However, to go too far down this line lays sheltered housing open to a different form of polemical attack, namely, if it is simply a housing provision and the occupants no different from other elderly people with housing needs, why have a warden and communal amenities at all: why 'so much for so few'? (Middleton 1982).

Our view is that sheltered housing constitutes a special setting which distinguishes it from ordinary housing; it has some features of a care environment, but is very different from residential care. Its distinctive place in the spectrum of special settings can be shown by comparing and contrasting it with a residential home. One similarity, following Goffman, is that there is a staff attached to the premises (different, in other words, from the home help service, which is allocated to people, not to places); but the staff is minimal and, in theory at least, less obtrusive. The warden is there in case of need, and there will be some system of warden relief, some part-time cleaning input for the communal areas and someone who maintains the garden.

The difference is that elderly people living in sheltered housing are house-holders in their own right, secure behind their own front doors, so a much higher degree of independence is possible and encouraged. Goffman's dictum about a body of people who live, eat, sleep and spend their leisure time together cannot be applied to sheltered housing. People cater for themselves, separately, in their flats. There are no meals provided and no communal catering staff. People control their own lives: they can go to bed when they want, get up when they want; there is no set timetable, no set breakfast times, bath-times or bed-times; participation in informal gatherings or organized events (if any) in the common rooms is voluntary, not inescapable. People can come and go as they choose. Individuals retain their own doctor and (if tenants) their own rent book and do not experience confiscation of assets.

Certainly a typical sheltered housing scheme is far removed from a 'total' institution and also much different from contemporary residential care. If additional support is required, it is allocated on an individual basis via the social services and health authorities in the form of home help, bathing or district nurse help and so on; and some individuals may go out to a luncheon club or day centre, which is rarely the case for those living in residential homes for elderly people.

The justification for having any staff at all, and the distinctive rationale for sheltered housing, is the fact that (at least in the public and voluntary sectors) it caters for an 'at risk' population which distinguishes it from the wider population of elderly people. Tenants are older than the wider population of retired people and much more likely to be women and people living alone. For instance, in a study of tenants of the Anchor Housing Association, 80% were women, 63% of tenants were widowed (only 19% being still married) and their median age was 76 years (Fennell 1986a). Hence, although the tenants are an independent group, they are statistically more likely than the elderly population at large to experience illness, disability and falls, and to have no one living with them who can help with such contingencies.

This explains the importance of the warden service to the tenants. It is not that the tenants require constant care and attention (although, statistically, there are bound to be times when the warden is stretched and under stress) but that there is someone on call who can supply immediate help and mobilize other support in the event, for instance, of a fall or other health emergency. In Fennell's Anchor study, more than a quarter of the tenants had had to summon help in an emergency within the previous 12 months – a fall being the most common reason (1986a : 60–63). Again, what differentiates sheltered housing from residential care is that the warden's role in these emergencies is to provide stop-gap cover and mobilize *outside* sources of help (statutory or relatives) rather than cope with the situation with 'in-house' staff.

Debates about sheltered housing

Sheltered housing has suffered from two English maladies: a tendency for exaggerated claims to be made on its behalf, claims which are bound to be disappointed or disputed, and a tendency for debates to be polarized into very simple terms, like, is sheltered housing 'the most humane and successful formula for long-term assisted independent living in use today in Western society' (Heumann and Boldy 1982 : 203) or a 'disaster' (Bessell 1986): are we for it or against it?

With the passage of time and the accretion of experience and research, it becomes more possible to create a picture with more light and shade. Clearly, sheltered housing is not going to replace residential care, although it may postpone for some time, even postpone altogether, a move into residential care for some elderly people who might otherwise have been admitted. Funds for the continued expansion of the public and voluntary sectors have been cut back in the 1980s, and barely a 'lucky five percent' of the elderly population live in sheltered housing (Bytheway 1984). Given the projected increases in the higher age groups, overall demand for residential care will be only marginally affected.

Equally, even if private sheltered housing expands rapidly, the great majority of elderly people at any one moment are going to go on living in ordinary housing rather than in sheltered schemes and the special setting is unlikely to appeal – in the foreseeable future – to the majority of the population who do not identify themselves as having 'special' needs.

Even for those at risk, doubts will be expressed about sheltered housing as the complete panacea. Although warm and comfortable, it does not prevent hypothermia developing while standing outside, waiting for a bus to the shops (Keatinge 1986). Although offering care and support, disturbed behaviour arising from dementia and incontinence stretch the resources of the solo warden to breaking point (Fennell and Way 1986), so the need for more protective and/or nursing environments cannot be avoided. At a more general level, the warden may contribute to dependency in old age: treating residents like children or limiting their contribution to the running of schemes (Phillipson and Strang 1985). Although offering social opportunities and chances to re-engage, sheltered housing cannot in itself prevent or offset the impact of major life events such as bereavement or physical disablement with their 'desolating' or depressing effects.

Residential care

As an introductory disclaimer it must be stated that there are many sources of differentiation in residential homes: they vary in age, from those inherited from the Poor Law to the modern purpose-built home. They vary in size, from the very small private home with fewer than 20 residents to some in the public sector accommodating more than 250. They are provided by non-profit-making voluntary agencies, as well as by local authorities and businesses. Within the private sector, there are differences between the big business chains of establishments and the small owner/manager homes. Irrespective of these sources of variation, homes can vary in their 'regime', a short-hand term for the style of management and general feel of the place, as well as in the social composition of the resident population. To do justice to all these differences is impossible in a short compass. The early study by Townsend (1962) and a later one by Davis and Knapp (1981) review the spectrum of care from different perspectives.

Within sociology, it is a functionalist approach which immediately suggests itself in attempting to explain some of the paradoxes of residential care.

Observers have been puzzled by apathy and inactivity they observe and by the fact that the ethos of care in some homes appears to be more punitive and custodial than 'caring': they comment that the residents are not as physically incapable as they had supposed and wonder what they are doing there. They are sometimes so unimpressed by what they see that they call for the abolition of residential care.

Functional theorists such as Merton (1957) have a terminology which helps to explain these observations, contrasting the 'manifest' – or publicly acknowledged and socially acceptable – functions of institutions with their 'latent' or less obvious functions. The manifest function of residential care has always been to provide full board and lodging to those who, because of physical frailty and sometimes poverty, would otherwise be exposed to the hazards of what Isaacs *et al.* (1972) call 'insufficient basic care', lacking any combination of food, warmth, cleanliness and safety.

However, as Townsend has argued in 'The Purpose of the Institution' (1952), in any population where the social arrangements are such that poverty and homelessness for some are endemic, a latent motif has to weave some form of rationing or deterrence into the provision. This is to reinforce what is sometimes termed 'labour discipline' and 'family discipline' (Kincaid 1973). Following this line of reasoning (based on certain assumptions about human nature) it would be argued that to make residential provision too generous and attractive would undermine the motivation of adults during their working lives to provide for their old age (to avoid entering residential care at all costs) and the motivation of family carers to undertake unpaid care-work (to keep their elderly relatives out of residential care at all costs). The sanctions of rewards and punishments in old age for a working life well- or ill-spent and the possible psychological impact on working adults of tampering with these social controls are latent factors which underlie both pensions and residential care provision.

While there may be a social logic to this, since positive rewards for 'good' behaviour and 'punishment' in varying degrees for deviance are part of the fabric of social life and undoubtedly are part of the calculus which affect how individuals behave, its outcomes can conflict with our sense of natural justice when viewed from a different perspective. For instance, if entering residential care is a punishment, what are the residents being punished for (or is it like an execution 'to encourage the others'?) and is the punishment just? Regardless of the answer to this question, we understand that those who find themselves in the situation are bound to find ways of apparent compliance and token resistance.

Mrs Hatter, interviewed in the study by Ford and Sinclair, describes how she spends the day:

> Well, I get up by half past six, between six and half past, and of course it takes a bit longer getting dressed now . . . than it used to. Then we have a cup of tea about seven and they come and give you a tablet. It's a water tablet. . . . I don't need it but you have to take it from them so then I put mine down the sink. Breakfast is at half past eight. . . . We get a cup of tea around quarter past ten but I've already told them I won't bother this

morning because I don't want them coming in. After breakfast you just have to sit and shut your eyes. . . . I do an awful lot of just sitting. They bring more tea and you can have a biscuit but then at half past five it's supper. That's what they call it but it's really tea. Later they bring you a milk drink, you can have what you want. But I tell you what: least said, best said about lots of things here. (1987 : 34)

To try to understand how so many people came to be in residential care although apparently capable of leading an independent or semi-independent life at home, Townsend (1962) differentiated between 'predisposing' and 'precipitating' factors in admission, an analysis just as relevant today. We have said that at most 5% of the elderly population are in long-term care at any one time. Even if this does not tell us what proportion of each cohort experience it at some time in their lives, clearly most people avoid it. Townsend's predisposing factors identify the social categories most 'at risk' of admission. This is not to say that those with the predisposing or underlying factors are inevitably admitted, or that people not in such categories are invariably 'safe', because the precipitating factors, or immediate causes of admission are also important. However, these precipitating factors apply to those who are already at risk. As a later study by Booth (1985) confirms, many of the residents are too capable and alert for their admission to be attributed simply to 'physical dependency'.

Precipitating factors are most easily understood: these examples from Townsend's study show how some form of crisis makes a previous situation unviable and brings the circuit of agents into operation:

Mr Farmer . . . served for 21 years in the army before becoming a clerk. His wife had died 10 years ago and after that he was looked after by a neighbour, was in hospital for a year and went blind. 'My relatives couldn't or wouldn't put me up. I went into one of these institutions but I got my son to take me away. They put me in a nursing home and then I got another billet (outside, but) . . . I couldn't see my way about and they whisked me into another home; then here.' (1962 : 306)

Mrs Llandaff, widowed earlier in life, explained how she had helped her son in various business enterprises but:

He died five years ago without a will and my daughter-in-law got his money. I stayed with her for two years and then my niece offered me a room. I was with her for over a year and then she had a nervous breakdown. That's why I went to these Homes. I was three weeks in one in Gloucestershire, but I was unhappy and then I was advised to go back to the one in Wales. I do exactly what they tell me. I was there two years and then I went to hospital for nine months. The almoner said I should come here. (1962 : 296)

Precipitating events, then, include accidents and illnesses often leading to spells in hospital during which previous accommodation is lost, as well as the physical or social break-up of a previous home. As for predisposing factors, Townsend writes:

The chief theme which has emerged . . . has been the striking unrepresentativeness, as a group, of the old people entering institutions and Homes. . . . To sum up, homelessness, financial insecurity, social isolation and the absence of subsidiary or secondary sources of help on the part of those living with or near a relative – these appear to be the underlying social reasons for the admission of old people to residential institutions. They are the fundamental causes of social insecurity in old age. (1962 : 327)

Debates about residential care

Some questions about residential care, such as whether or not it is necessary and how boredom, apathy and abuse can be minimized are relatively timeless and have already arisen in our discussion. More time-specific issues have emerged in Britain in the last decade as a result of the dramatic reduction in the construction of new local authority residential homes and an unprecedented expansion of the private market following changes in DHSS regulations about support for residents (Bird 1984; Johnson 1984; Kane 1985).

We are conditioned to think in terms of 'onwards and upwards', automatically assuming that – whatever the problems and deficiencies revealed by Townsend in 1962 – the situation today must be better: buildings more modern, attitudes more enlightened. A reading of Booth's (1985) study is chastening, if we do subscribe to this comforting idea of linear progress. We quote just isolated sentences from Booth's carefully argued conclusions:

The findings of this study make rather depressing reading. . . . These findings may be added to the already substantial body of evidence about institutional failure. . . . Sociologically, the differences between regimes must . . . be seen as a veneer that decorates the massive uniformity of institutional life and catches the eye for precisely that reason. Underneath lies the same crushing panoply of controls over the lives and doings of residents. Changing the wrapper does not alter the contents . . .

[It] fails to address the real needs of a substantial proportion of residents, especially the large numbers of really quite independent people who still have the capacity for getting something out of life and giving something in return. For them, attempts to soften institutional regimes in line with current notions of good practice are not enough to relieve the torpor of their days. Residential care is not so easily saved from its critics. This study obliges us to face up to the fact that the only sure way of limiting its harmful effects is to stop admitting people who, given the chance, could manage with other kinds of support. (1985 : 205–10)

However, what this means in practice is not simply the expansion of housing alternatives such as sheltered and other specialist dwellings and 'staying put' adaptations to enable people to continue living in their existing accommodation but also upgrading the response to crises in old age. It is not only a matter of their being alternatives to residential care, but that these alternatives are known to the 'circuit of agents' involved in the decision-making and that they are prepared, enabled or required to explore these alternatives. Otherwise, 'I do exactly what they say' is bound to be the response of the relatively powerless elderly person, whether Ellen Newton (1980) bowing to the dictates of her sister and doctor or Mrs Llandaff deferring to the hospital almoner as reported by Townsend in 1962.

The expansion of private residential care opens, for those with a critical perspective, another large area of anxiety. Lenski (1966) draws attention to pervasive differences in values and approach between 'radicals' and 'conservatives' across continents and centuries. Titmuss (1974) referred persistently to the differences between those who favoured a 'universalistic' as opposed to a 'selectivist' or 'residual' approach to social welfare, leaving the private market to deal with most contingencies. George and Wilding (1976) identify four schools of thought about the welfare state, of which the most significant today are probably what they call the 'anti-collectivists' and the 'Fabian socialists'. Other ways of splitting up the political spectrum are advanced (Mishra 1984), but a basic cleavage is between those who believe that market competition is a force which must lead to high standards of service and those who feel that – even if the proposition was true in conditions of perfect competition – where consumers are weak in physical and financial resources, the need to extract profit from care must act to depress rather than raise standards.

Geriatric hospitals

Trends in geriatric hospital care have their roots in the historical development of institutional care for elderly people, and the emergence of geriatric medicine as a speciality (Carboni 1982; Means and Smith 1985; Burns and Phillipson 1986; Evers 1986). In contrast to its legacy of custodial, long-stay care for inert, immobile old people, the geriatric department of the 1980s is usually characterized by a major emphasis on medical care for acutely ill old people – often now defined as more than 75 years old – and multidisciplinary rehabilitation. Many geriatric departments see themselves as a resource concerned with maintaining and improving the health of the elderly population within their geographical catchment area. None the less, geriatric departments may also provide long-term or – more euphemistically – continuing care for those who cannot be 'cured' or rehabilitated to a level where they can be discharged. Thus geriatric hospitals serve a vastly varied group of old people, who have in common only that they are more than (roughly) 75 years old.

Policy documents (DHSS 1978; DHSS 1981) have stressed the imperative for equality of access to the best of acute care services for older people, and geriatric departments have achieved some success in that regard, if average length of stay is anything to go by. This has decreased from 79.7 days in 1978 (DHSS/OPCS 1981) to 49.6 days in 1985 (DHSS/OPCS 1987). Long-stay care, though, remains a reality, however much geriatricians might wish it to be otherwise.

What do we know of patients' experiences? Where these have been documented, there are many themes in common with experiences in other special settings discussed earlier. For example, in Evers's (1981, 1984) study, it appeared that the quality of patients' experiences was related to the extent to which they 'fitted in' with the implicit goals aspired to by (most importantly) nursing staff. For short-stay patients (those seen for acute care/cure/discharge/ rehabilitation) the suffering and inhumane treatment observed – caused, usually unintentionally, by the actions or inactions of staff – tended to be much less when patients 'complied' with the expectations which staff had of them for their futures.

For long-stay patients, the perceived legitimacy of the caring task in its own right, within the curative ethos of the hospital, was related to the type of care patients received. Unintended suffering and inhumane treatment was markedly less in wards where the consultants subscribed to the importance of care-work, carried this belief through into their own work with long-stay patients, as well as acknowledging and actively supporting the primacy of the nursing role in care-work. The nurses – most importantly, the ward sisters – working with these consultants carried out their work in a distinctive style. They were more likely to make concerted efforts to care for patients as individuals than as work objects and sets of tasks to be accomplished. Despite similar staffing levels, in wards where 'batch processing' and a view of care-work as low status and second-rate prevailed, patients' sufferings as a consequence were observed to be more common.

Debates in geriatric hospital care

Dealing with the 'problem' of long-stay care remains a key topic. Writing initially in 1949, Thomson remarks:

> My most vivid impression of the chronic wards . . . is of an atmosphere of profound apathy. The patients seldom spoke to each other; they rarely moved, and . . . it was exceptional to see one reading. Contact with the patients was not difficult; histories of their social background and infirmities were . . . readily given, but what made them remarkable was the conspicuous absence of emotional overtones as they recounted them. . . . One old lady told us a strange story of many years of colourful life. . . . Her face was immobile as she spoke; the glory and the zest had departed; she was interested mainly in her tea, which was a little late. Food, indeed, was their major interest: the wards came momentarily to life at mealtimes. (Thomson *et al.* 1951 : 15)

In 1983, we still find Denham writing:

> In spite of upgrading, these wards can still look depressing, lack privacy for the patient, are often noisy and may smell of urine. The patients may be dressed in clothing which is not their own, and sit in rows along the

wall, staring vacantly into space and doing nothing. . . . In such an establishment, where staff may consider there is nothing further to be done, institutionalisation can rapidly develop. (1983 : 12)

A response to the 'problem' of long-stay care which has become widespread, is that of rotating and relief admissions. (This is true also in residential care.) Patients who might well in the past have been candidates for permanent institutional care are admitted for a period (a week, a fortnight) on a regular basis. Often the aims are two-fold: to maintain or improve the elderly person's health status, and to provide relief to a lay carer in the expectation that their part in community care will be prolonged by means of this intermittent support. Holiday relief – an occasional admission for 1 or 2 weeks – is more overtly geared to relieving carers, but essentially serves the same purpose.

Related to the 'problem' of long-stay care is the debate about whether geriatric hospital care should be segregated or integrated – with general medicine as the most usually-proposed partner, or psychogeriatrics or psychiatry. By bringing geriatric medicine back into the mainstream, it is argued, better staff and more resources will accrue and elderly patients receive a better service. This may be so, but what may be overlooked in this argument is the possibility that general medical or psychiatric patients – at least a proportion of whom will be younger and more amenable to curative intervention – may 'steal the show' and the older patient, particularly the long-stay patient, may in the end lose out. Both forms of organization have their merits, and local contingencies – the array of care services more generally, the location of hospital beds in relation to the major catchment area, whether or not these are on the site of the District General Hospital or in a specialist geriatric hospital – will in the end quite rightly determine local choice. It is to be hoped that the existence of a variety of organizational permutations will stimulate further comparative evaluation of outcomes for patient care, qualitative as well as quantitative (see, e.g., Horrocks 1982; Grimley Evans 1983).

Conclusion

Our discussion has not exhausted the range of phenomena which might be covered by the term 'special settings': space does not permit coverage, for instance, of retirement settlements like Sun City in the United States, where nearly 50 000 elderly people live (Jacobs 1974, 1975), the 'old people's village' as in Scandinavia (Donahue 1961; Donahue *et al.* 1977), or the semi-permanent 'trailer parks' in America where the majority of the residents are elderly people (Hoyt 1954; Johnson 1971).

A feature common to the settings we have discussed is that complex social selection processes determine who ends up in them: they are seldom 'chosen' by the user and the user seldom initiates the application or referral. This lack of positive choice is coupled with what often seems to observers to be an unattractive and unstimulating result: 'inside is oblivion'.

Different features can be distinguished analytically which moderate or accentuate this tendency. The length of time spent in the setting is one variable: if the regime in a day centre is boring, at least the users are not there continuously; depersonalization and regimentation in hospital environments may be more tolerable if the patient will soon be going home. The degree of privacy and autonomy allowed to the individual (both by the architecture and the regime) influences the ability of individuals to make friendships and pursue activities. (Hence, sheltered housing has to be exempted from most of this discussion, since it is designed to give individuals as much privacy and independence in their own dwellings as they desire.) The extent of staff surveillance and control is another variable affecting the quality of life. These variables are often correlated with others such as the age, scale and isolation of the setting, which influence staff culture and morale. We have also touched on the social control aspects of special settings for people who either lack supportive networks or whose 'carers' break down, perhaps because *they* lack support.

While the settings we have examined are ranged in terms of intensity, we do not endorse the 'conveyor belt' notion, that each type of setting is particularly appropriate to an identifiable stage in the ageing process and that individuals should therefore 'progress' from one to another. On the contrary, the research evidence is full of examples of people whose placing in special settings *cannot* be explained by their physical dependency levels and this is part of the critique of inadequate stimulus. It would be simplistic, however, to suggest that there is no need for special settings: the expansion of private residential care and private sheltered housing – and the existence of large retirement communities elsewhere – indicates that *some* elderly consumers positively endorse such choices. (Not all do, by any means. Some are forced into private care, against their preference, through government imposed cuts in public provision, as well as through a lack of more desirable alternatives.) Also, it was noted in Chapter 7 that there is unmet demand for day centres among, for instance, elderly Asians. These preferences clearly relate to the other options, or lack of them, which older people have available.

Special settings attract and repel investigators: they receive disproportionate attention for reasons discussed in Chapter 4 and the critiques may demoralize staff without necessarily improving life for older people. The nub of the anxiety about special settings turns on their 'specialness'; long-stay residential institutions, in particular, have an immense inertia which makes them difficult to change. The sociological instinct is to normalize the special setting as far as possible. This means encouraging continuous movement over the boundaries which separate them from the environing society, trying to modify the historical pattern of long periods of invisibility punctuated by the sudden searchlight of inquiries into abuse.

9

Death and dying

Introduction

This chapter considers the nature of death and dying, exploring its impact on the social world of older people. Some of the policy responses to the range of problems and stresses faced by older people and their carers in the final phase of life are also reviewed.

Traditionally, the topic of death and dying has been given limited attention in sociology textbooks (see, e.g., Worsley 1987). By contrast, psychologists and psychiatrists (from Freud onwards) have devoted considerable attention to the topic and have almost certainly exercised greater influence on public awareness and understanding [the work of Kubler-Ross (1973) is an outstanding example].

The task of this chapter is to explore some of the issues raised in the sociological and psychological literature on death and dying: what does it tell us about the position of older people in society; what are current attitudes towards death and dying; how do we respond to those who are bereaved; what problems and concerns do they face? Finally, what are the policies currently being devised to support those facing a terminal illness and those who have lost a partner?

The experiences of death and dying

The literature on death invariably describes the act of dying as a lonelier event now in comparison with the past; just as funerals and mourning itself are seen to be more discreet and muted in their outward forms. Before the present century, according to writers such as Ariès (1983) and Elias (1985), dying was experienced in the company of other people, especially friends and relations, but also on occasion other members of the community. Now, according to Ariès, we have 'removed death from society, eliminated its character of public ceremony, and made it a private act' (1983 : 575). Elias (1985) describes the way we have removed the dying from social life and have achieved technical perfection in moving the corpse from the death-bed to the grave.

As we shall see, there is much to suggest that the act of dying, particularly for those in hospital, is a lonely event. But it is unclear whether this is exclusive to the twentieth century. The study by McManners of attitudes towards death in eighteenth-century France, found evidence for a shift towards more private expressions of dying and mourning. He related this change to the emergence of the nuclear family and the experience of greater longevity. He writes:

> The rise of the small nuclear family as the emotional centre of existence coincides with the beginning of the conquest of death. Husband, wife, and children were to have a longer time together and a new assurance that this will be so, the inherent desire for emotional enrichment antedating, or at least coinciding with, the means of obtaining it. With a longer time together, the affections could more often deepen and diversify. At the same time, the old community and neighbourhood life was beginning to disintegrate; guilds, the village youth organisations, kinship groups, the nexus of conformity around the parish church would exercise less power over young people's minds. (1985 : 462)

McManners concludes from this that:

> With this new focusing of the emotions, attitudes to death changed. Death was seen, not as a public event with the whole community taking part, not as a religious crisis in which all the faithful share, but as an intense, introverted family affair. The last will and testament became a family document, rather than a public and religious manifesto: the details of funeral ceremonies and, even, of masses can be left to the affection of the heirs – the important question is, has generosity and fairness been shown within the family circle? (1985 : 463)

A major strand in the argument presented by Ariès and other writers is that our culture is one which now tries to deny the very existence of death. Ariès writes dramatically about 'death being driven into secrecy', as we construct a trail of elaborate deceits around and with the dying (1983). Kubler-Ross, author of a major study on the impact of terminal illness, argues that death has become a 'dreaded and unspeakable issue in our society' (1973). In a similar vein, Sontag writes: 'All this lying to and by cancer patients is a measure of how much harder it has become in advanced societies to come to terms with death' (1983 : 12).

Arguments such as the above, if true, carry enormous implications for older people. In an ageing society, deaths cluster towards the end of the normal life-cycle and elderly people are the most directly affected by social attitudes towards death. They regularly experience the loss of relations and close friends; they are increasingly aware of their own mortality; and they experience themselves, of course, the process of dying. Under these circumstances, to live in a world which denies death is to face a very heavy burden in the final period of one's life. Indeed, this must also be a problem for those who are bereaved and who seek support and comfort from friends and family. Thus, the other side of denying death is to restrict expressions of grief among those who lose their partners. Weeping, according to Ariès, becomes synonymous with hysteria and mourning itself is now viewed as morbid. The consequence of this, it is suggested, is to marginalize the bereaved from the rest of society:

> Society avoids them, whether they are young or old, but especially if they are old, for in that case they are doubly distasteful. They have no one to talk to about the only subject that matters to them, the person they have lost. There is nothing left for them to do but die themselves, and that is often what they do, without necessarily committing suicide. (1983 : 583)

Awareness of death

How accurate is it to say that we deny the reality of death? Is this true of young and old? How far are older people accepting death? Let us examine different types of evidence on this issue. First, there is considerable survey evidence suggesting that thoughts about death are relatively commonplace. American research using the technique of consciousness sampling (where the interviewer asks the individual: 'what were you thinking about in the last five minutes?') found no less than 17% of males and 23% of females mentioning the topic of death (cited in Baum and Baum 1980). Another study by Scheidman (1973) which asked people whether they ever thought about death, found only 6% of Americans denying that they did so. Even allowing for significant cultural variations, such figures indicate that denial of death is commonplace only among a minority in Western culture and may be more of a taboo topic in the public domain than in private thoughts.

Secondly, some of the theories we reviewed in Chapter 3 (for example, disengagement theory and biographical perspectives on ageing) suggest that people experience a turning inwards in late middle-age as they review their lives and their own future death. This development may be triggered by particular events in the life-cycle. According to Marshall:

> Recognition of our mortality grows from the middle years and becomes quite strong around the 70s for most people. It grows in relation to deaths of people connected to us, especially our parents. . . . Something quite psychologically important happens to people when their first parent dies, and something in addition when the second parent dies. Experiencing these deaths brings people to a fuller sense of their own maturity, and it points to the fundamental truth that people come into the world and pass out of it, that one generation succeeds another. (1986 : 137–8)

It may be argued, therefore, that far from denying death, people may think about it when young and with increasing frequency as they grow older (Kalish 1976). Moreover, some contexts (for instance, retirement communities and older people's homes) may increase people's awareness of death; indeed it may be a regular topic of conversation in such environments. Hochschild (1973) writes that among her 'community of grandmothers' the subject of a 'good death' was an engrossing topic of conversation when the widows were with one another. However, in deference to what they perceived to be the sensibilities of younger people, they switched from discussing death to topics more suitable for younger ears, such as the remarriage of Jackie Kennedy. Marshall (1975) shows that in grouped living arrangements people may socialize one another into a more accepting attitude towards death. Elderly couples in independent households may also discuss and prepare themselves for impending death.

Yet at the same time, it might still be the case that with the onset of a terminal condition people experience the kind of deceit and half-truths described by Ariès and others. The sociological evidence would give some support to this view. Indeed, Glaser and Strauss described a number of what they term 'awareness contexts'. These they define as follows:

> There is the situation where the patient does not recognise his impending death even though everyone else does. There is the situation where the patient suspects what the others know and therefore attempts to confirm or invalidate his suspicion. There is the situation where each party defines the patient as dying, but each pretends that the other has not done so. And, of course, there is also the situation where personnel and patient both are aware that he is dying, and where they act on this awareness relatively openly. We shall refer to these situations as, respectively, the following types of awareness context: closed awareness, suspected awareness, mutual pretence awareness, and open awareness. (1965:11)

At one level, these examples might be taken as good illustrations of the way we avoid telling the truth to those who are dying. Equally, they suggest that denial of death is only one strategy among many and the extent to which it occurs will depend on factors such as the type of illness a person has (see, e.g., Bowling and Cartwright 1982), the stage of the illness, the setting in which dying takes place and the type of relationship between the people involved.

However, if denial only occurs on some occasions and in some contexts, both the dying and the bereaved may still feel unprepared for death when it comes. The uncertainty is one problem and it must be acknowledged that accurate advance prediction of death is highly problematic, even for professionals regularly involved in terminal care. The study by Cartwright *et al.* (1973), found that although the majority of respondents were aware that their relation was going to die only one-fifth expected them to die when they did (for one-quarter the death occurred earlier than expected) and uncertainty may be increased by inadequate information from professional workers. Bowling and Cartwright, in a study of the problems faced by the elderly widowed, found one-third of their sample saying they had been unable to find out all they wanted to know about their spouse's illness. On the other hand, only 10% said they would have liked to have talked or talked more about the illness and what was likely to happen. Bowling and Cartwright's comment on this is revealing.

> The apparent contradictory attitudes among those who said they had not been able to find out all they wanted to know, but did not want to talk

about it more, reflect people's uncertainties and fears over communication about terminal illnesses – many may have a desire for knowledge but are still afraid to possess it. One widow commented: 'I often felt like it [asking] but I dare not.' (1982 : 49)

A further reason for our being unprepared for death relates to the setting in which it now occurs. Over 70% of deaths in urban areas now take place in hospital (Taylor 1983). Of those who die in hospital, roughly half will do so with no relatives or friends present. As Bowling and Cartwright point out in their study, being with the person at the time of death to say 'goodbye' may affect the immediate adjustment to, and acceptance of, the death, as well as feelings of guilt or anxiety which the bereaved person may have. They report the following comments from their respondents:

> I always look back and say 'I wish I could have said so and so, or done this or that.' The last time I saw him he had a mask over his face.

> Yes, I'd like to have been with him – seen the last of the poor old soul – especially as they said he was sensible at the end.

> I'd like to know what happened – a chance to say 'bye-bye' and 'thanks for what you've done'. I'd like to know if he called out or suffered before he went.

> I think I would have liked to have said a few things to him, to thank him for all the good years we had and to reassure him that I'd be able to manage without him. I would really have liked to go at the same time because when you're as close as we were you feel like that. (1982 : 44)

Emotional support for the dying patient may be lacking compared with the physical care and attention. Life may be prolonged to the detriment of patient dignity and comfort (Parkes 1972). Sociological research suggests that organizations designed to care may often be insensitive to the needs of the terminally-ill and those closest to them. In such settings, the routine of the organization may frustrate the individual's need to control the final stages of dying or, in life-review terms, to make a good ending to life (Marshall 1975).

Finally, it might also be argued, that our lack of preparation for death is part of a wider problem – that death is rarely perceived, as de Beauvoir (1966) points out, as a 'natural event'. Instead, it is invariably experienced 'as an unjustifiable violation' whether coming at the end of a long life or much earlier. Moreover, while questioning whether death is especially lonely and isolating in our society, there are many features which make it a difficult and stressful experience. It is to one of these that we now turn, restricting our discussion to the individual's contemplation of his or her own death or that of a long-term sexual partner.

Roles and rituals

Coming to terms either with a partner's death or one's own terminal illness may be frustrated by a number of barriers. First, death may be difficult to accept because it undermines the basis of one's identity and perception of self. For the sociologist, the individual's identity is formed and maintained through social interaction and through playing a variety of social roles. From this vantage point, death is indeed a terrifying prospect as it represents the loss of all the most significant roles and relationships that the individual has ever experienced (Baum and Baum 1980).

Equally, for the bereaved, the death of a partner may represent the loss of a unique source of support and sense of who one is. This can be seen in the following extracts from interviews with widowed men interviewed for a study of retirement:

> Losing my wife altered circumstances completely. There was nothing much left to look forward to then. Even now I wonder sometimes what the point is, coming home with nothing there.

> Well, when the wife was here, yes . . . we thought a lot about retirement . . . you know like . . . we were looking forward to retirement when she was here . . . we had a lot done on the house just for when we retired and, of course, it was only about 12 months before she passed away . . . I still had 12 months to go . . . course you know how you feel then . . . you don't care two ruddy hoots.

> Terrible . . . terrible . . . for the first 9 months as I say. Well, I don't know . . . er . . . I should have gone out and looked around but I just didn't want to meet people at the time. I suppose when you're young it's not too bad but when you retire and you do need someone . . . you haven't got that someone . . . and that's all it amounts to really.

> No . . . the only time we used to think about retirement was when the wife was alive . . . we'd always had visions of selling this and getting a little bungalow in the country see . . . of course . . . that finished it completely when she died. (Phillipson 1978 : 263–5)

We might also agree with Ariès that death creates a problem, in part, because of the difficulty of finding emotional substitutes either within the family or elsewhere. For couples who have lived together for 40 or 50 years and who may have outlived many of their close friends and relations, the loss of a partner may represent – depending on the nature of the relationship – a major crisis. Lopata (1971) suggests that for women there may be special difficulties in adjustment because of gender inequalities. Because they have lived in a male-dominated society and have been socialized into restricted roles, women may face considerable difficulties in developing social activities following widowhood though, as we noted in Chapter 6, Matthews' study suggests that this may be critically affected by the local environment, and whether the woman moves away or not. Men face problems which differ because of gender roles – such as a learned inability to cook or cope with housework – though this may be an example of cohort effects: later generations of men may show a different pattern of aptitudes and inabilities.

Adjustment to widowhood will also depend on age, with younger widows and widowers more likely to find loneliness a problem and have greater difficulties in adjustment (Marris 1958; Bowling and Cartwright 1982). Cumming and Henry (1961) refer to the 'society of widows' open to elderly women, a society not available for the young widow who is less likely to have contemporaries who have been widowed. Older age groups may also adjust better because they may more readily accept death if they feel they have fulfilled their lives. This point was made in a study by Tunstall in the 1960s. His study of older people found:

> There is one striking difference in attitudes in widowhood in old age – the virtual unanimity with which old people seem to accept death and do not feel guilty about it. The median age at which their spouses had died was over 70 and many had said spontaneously that their spouse had had a good long life. There is little evidence of the disbelief and astonishment reported by Marris for his younger widows, or any tendency to blame the doctor or some other person for the death. (1966 : 155)

Despite accepting the inevitability of death, it still needs to be placed within a framework which gives it meaning and significance. Here again, the individual may encounter difficulties within contemporary culture. This may arise partly because of the decline in religious beliefs but also because, as Marshall observes, the bulk of religious meanings have dealt with the legitimation of death in the young. Moreover, at a practical level, the ambivalence towards religion has created a problem in terms of the rituals surrounding death and dying. The ability of religious ceremonies to give help and support has diminished and secular equivalents have not emerged to replace them. Social and religious responses are, in some senses, running behind the demographic changes described in this book. This must be attributed, in some degree, to the novelty of the ageing experience. Men and women are just beginning to realize the implications of the inevitability of growing old (in Britain, it is only since 1950 that a majority of people living at age 25 would survive to the age of 70).

Social institutions have provided little help in the way of providing positive attitudes towards old age. On the contrary, the view that old age is a burden and problem for society has been a strong impulse over the past 20 years (Phillipson 1982). This perception has inevitably affected the way death itself is seen, perhaps contributing to the idea of death in old age as less traumatic and emotionally fraught than in other periods of the life-cycle. In this restricted sense, the idea of the loneliness of dying has a degree of accuracy. The loneliness may be in terms of people (invariably with a chronic illness) perceiving they are a burden on their family and society and that death is both a solution to a problem while at the same time representing an abandonment by those closest to them.

Conclusion: supporting the dying and their carers

This chapter has concentrated on the problems of couples and the surviving partner and focussed on what has hitherto been the dominant monogamous pattern in Britain. But it is important to remember that death affects the kinship network as a whole and, in particular, informal carers such as daughters and other familiars. Further, rising rates of divorce and remarriage, as well as a developing variety of alternative household structures, mean that the dominant pattern will require more qualification in years to come. There will, in addition, be important class and ethnic variations in response to death, particularly in the rituals associated with the period of mourning.

None the less, some general themes emerge from our analysis. For example, we have indicated some doubts over how far our culture is one which denies the reality of death. We have also questioned whether dying is especially lonely now in comparison to the past. Yet it does, as we have suggested, have problems and difficulties which make it very different when compared with previous centuries. These differences include the fact that only a minority of people will die in their own homes, that major adjustments may be acquired for a partner trying to cope alone after spending 40 or 50 years in close proximity to just one other person and that the survivor may have no obvious emotional substitutes to whom to turn (due to geographical mobility of the rest of the family or to the fact that the person has outlived many friends and relations).

Responding to the needs of dying people (as well as their carers) has become an important component in policies for older people. The growth of the hospice movement has been a significant development, with approximately 70 hospices currently operating in the United Kingdom. According to Hockley:

> Within a hospice, basic nursing care is the same as that in hospital but the working environment and philosophy differ greatly. All members of a hospice ward team are motivated to the individualised care of each patient, who in turn receives continual assessment of his or her physical and psychosocial needs as well as sensitive spiritual care. Honesty and openness allow patients to feel secure in the answers to their questions and time is given to talk things through. Families are considered an important part of the patient's emotional well-being and every effort made to meet all the different needs from the youngest grandchild facing his or her first loss, to the wife, mother, sister or husband of the person dying. (1986:286)

Techniques developed inside hospices are increasingly being used to help support dying people in their own homes for as long as possible. This is achieved by providing specialist domiciliary nursing services which are increasingly attached, not to in-patient units, but to the existing primary care teams. Taylor observes that these specialist nurses working alongside other primary care colleagues are beginning to enable larger numbers of dying persons to remain in the comfort and familiarity of their own homes. However, he also notes that existing evidence is unclear about the extent to which this is achieved at the expense of the caring relatives or whether the additional support provided appreciably eases their burden. Taylor concludes, however, that:

Both in the hospice and in the community, the existence of an alternative model of care for the dying, which does not regard the death ultimately of a patient as a 'failure' but as a natural process requiring specialist sensitive medical, nursing and support services, is beginning to challenge the neglect and poor quality of service available in many traditional hospital settings. (1985 : 137)

While some improvement is beginning in the treatment and support for the dying, we are some way from establishing proper support either for the bereaved or their carers. Bowling and Cartwright (1982) found a lack of support given to widowed people from professional carers. Many general practitioners, for example, appeared unwilling to take the initiative and either contact their elderly widowed patient or arrange for an appropriate member of their team to do so. Indeed, Bowling and Cartwright found a tendency 'to prescribe pills rather than give supportive care to the bereaved' (1982 : 223). The problems of the bereaved may be compounded through poverty, which we have discussed in earlier chapters, restricting the woman's ability to reconstruct her social network after her partner's death, as well as by feelings of physical insecurity which, as Parkes (1972) observes, are not wholly imaginary: the elderly widow living alone is more vulnerable than she was before.

For carers, too, many difficulties have to be faced. Research has confirmed that the family (particularly daughters) remains a crucial source of support to elderly widowed people (Bowling 1984). At the same time pressures on a single carer can often be considerable and will require a range of supportive services to provide the necessary relief. Among these we might include: day centres for frail older people; voluntary visiting; and support from self-help groups for elderly widowed people.

In addition, there must be help, where appropriate, for the older person to grieve and to share their loss with others. It may be that our culture, while not one which necessarily denies death, may be one which finds it difficult to allow older people to express the loss they may feel. Inability to express grief may lead to clinical depression and morbidity at a later stage of life. Just as the dying should be helped to a good death, so we should also help the bereaved to envisage the possibility of a new life despite the loss of a partner. That so few older people gain the skilled help that is required or the economic resources to achieve a new life in late old age, reflects the low priority accorded to older people in general and to widowed elderly people in particular.

10
Conclusion

We have not entered into technical or philosophical debates about either what ageing is or when it begins, for our concern in this book has been with the period of old age. Yet it is abundantly clear that, however we define 'old' age and whenever we think it begins, ageing itself is a process which occurs throughout life. Hence we have not called this book *The Sociology of Ageing* – because we do not want to stand accused of saying nothing about transitions from infancy and through childhood to adolescence, maturity, middle age and beyond – but *The Sociology of Old Age*, in order to flag the fact that it is the older age groups in our society who form our predominant concern.

In referring to those of pensionable age and above as 'old', we are perfectly aware that *they* would generally *not* define themselves so, reserving the term for a later age group. Also, we recognize that there are discernible differences between the younger old (sometimes called 'green' or 'silver' aged) and the older old or very old (not precisely designated by the euphemistic term 'frail' or 'infirm'). But we talk about the sociology of old age for semantic convenience. We also do not particularly favour euphemistic usages, such as 'Senior Citizens', 'good' or 'ripe' old age, although we do try to avoid perjorative ones.

Regardless of these niceties, the fact remains that there has not previously been a book published in the United Kingdom with a title explicitly linking sociology and old age and we regard this as symptomatic of the under-development and neglect of the subject hitherto.

In our concluding chapter, as well as drawing together some of the themes of the earlier ones, we want to speculate about the reasons for this underdevelopment and make the case for a sociology of old age. We would expect this case to be acknowledged more readily overseas than in Britain; or if in Britain, not in the present 'historical conjuncture' when sociology is being subject to severe cuts – whether we look at the numbers of students being permitted to study the subject at undergraduate level in universities, the reductions in faculties (and in particular the decimation of the professoriate), the cuts in postgraduate student support or the attenuation of research funding.

Laslett (1987) has argued that, in Western society generally, we have simply not come to terms with the ageing of human populations which he regards as no less than a revolutionary change. Since, for a variety of reasons, Britain virtually leads the world in this demographic development, it is our contention that to cut back on free intellectual enquiry in one of the few subjects which might help in making adjustments to these massive changes in social structure is untimely and short-sighted.

The neglect of old age in sociological analysis

Trying to approach this in a slightly more timeless way, however, how do we explain the underdevelopment of the sociology of old age in Britain? There is a considerable literature about old age – most of it written in what we would think of as a social welfare tradition, concerned with the 'problems' of old age and the 'needs' of elderly people. In addition, and we have tried to draw on them where possible, there are *some* studies by sociologists and social anthropologists. But it is perhaps significant that, of the three seminal studies we reviewed in Chapter 1, only one of them (Townsend's) was the work of someone with a background in sociology and/or social anthropology, and Townsend is one of the very few members of that generation of sociologists who have had a demonstrable career-long commitment to this field of study.

Any sociologist working on old age (in England at least) knows self-evidently how marginal the subject has been to sociology as a whole and how under-represented has been the sociological perspective within the conglomeration of disciplines working under the umbrella of social gerontology. Indeed, this book has its origins in the concern we felt that gerontological debates were so ill-informed by the sociological imagination. Documenting the point to a sceptic is more difficult and requires a research project in itself. However, an analysis by one of us in 1982 is of some interest.

Examination of all the entries in three editions of the British Sociological Association's *Register of Postgraduate Theses* shows that in a registration period extending over a decade to 1981, only about 1% of Masters and Doctoral theses' titles in sociology were concerned with the topics we have discussed in this book and which we regard as of major human and social importance.

The British Sociological Association's *Registers* allows members to volunteer their research interests and publications (only about half of them do so). These registers can be used as another partial source of information about the salience of old age in the discipline. Of course, not all sociologists join the professional association. Those who do might feel that to express an interest in old age would invite marginalization; those with specifically gerontological interests might join a more specialized group. None the less, anticipating the predictable attempts to refute this type of evidence and acknowledging the indicative rather than conclusive nature of the date, Fennell notes:

> The Register still yields only 34 separate entries for sociologists who have had anything to do with elderly people in any shape or form at any time, of whom only two figure in all three distinguishable time periods (1960–1981). . . . Of these . . . 16 identify a (personal) publication in a period which in practice extends back to the early 1960s. (1982 : 23)

One reason for this underdevelopment is that sociology itself in Britain has experienced a very brief flowering season. At university level there were only limited opportunities to study the subject and to pursue it to high levels. There was a dramatic expansion in the years 1968–75 since when the subject has been on the retreat, and the highly selective attack on the social sciences now mounted within universities under stimulus from central government threatens to turn this retreat into a rout.

Since there were few practising sociologists in England in the period 1945–65, it is understandable that in the early drive for professional status and accreditation they went out of their way to define what the subject was about and what it was not. To establish its scientific credentials, this phase was definitely a 'hard-nosed' one. Certain types of methods (surveys, statistical analysis, modelling) were acceptable: life-histories, unstructured interviews, case studies, participant observation were not. Particular sorts of intellectual activities and issues were 'in' – for example, theory and the traditional preoccupations of the Founding Fathers of Sociology (Comte, Marx, Weber, Durkheim, Pareto), such as stratification, conflict and the nature of industrial society; other sorts were 'out'.

Those who carried the torch of the Founding Fathers emphatically disclaimed interests which, in the 1980s, came to be defined within the political spectrum as 'wet': they stressed that sociologists were *not* interested in people, that happiness was not a sociological concept, that welfare was the domain of social administrators and of no interest to them. Sociologists were interested in the real world of industrial conflict and whether or not the revolution was coming or going.

It was a male-dominated profession until the 1970s and the preoccupation with power, conflict and people en masse rather than as individuals, might, from one perspective, be regarded as reflecting typically patriarchal concerns. The marginalization of elderly people within the discipline, however, might not stem simply from the fact that the majority are women and the predominantly male investigators felt ill at ease or uninterested in their lives, but also from a cluster of other associations – with welfare, with 'deference' (or lack of overt conflict) and the dominance of psychological concepts such as 'morale'.

It is certainly the case that the battery of concepts developed for handling social conflict, industrial unrest and political struggles does not seem to apply very well to our field. Social class is an example. This has been a major intellectual problem within sociology, but straightforward class categorization and analysis often seems to collapse when applied after retirement age. By and large, class theorists have not seen fit to grapple with the theoretical and conceptual issues involved in integrating older women into models based on economically active males.

The one exception to this general rule about the inapplicability or irrelevance of the traditional armoury of sociological concepts to old age has been life-course transitions, where clearly 'retirement' and 'widowhood' are potentially as fruitful for study as 'social mobility' or 'divorce'. Other than that, traditional role theory seemed the most relevant approach. However, the central paradigm in sociology began to collapse in the 1960s and other flowers came to bloom amid the ruins: paradoxically, the subject expanded concurrently with the loss of theoretical and methodological consensus. From the late 1960s onwards, students flocked to study sociology when it became available to them. Many of these students were women, feminism was rediscovered and the composition of the British Sociological Association changed out of all recognition. A new permissiveness developed about what was regarded as legitimate to study. So, for those who had the curiosity, it became more acceptable to take an interest in issues related to happiness/depression, welfare/caring, health/ illness. Soft methodologies became more in vogue and women's studies became an important area of research.

None the less, it has taken a historian – Peter Laslett – more than any sociologist, to remind us that the ageing of society raises issues just as profound as others on which ink has been expended (for example, 'convergence theory', 'embourgeoisement', 'the managerial revolution' or 'post-industrial society' to quote some popular examples in general sociology over the last two decades). In this context we think it significant that, perhaps the most widely used/ multi-authored sociology textbook in Britain (Worsley 1987) devotes barely two pages to ageing or the ageing population.

An agenda for a sociology of old age

In our various chapters we have suggested that common issues crop up in the literature which does exist. Demography, for example, is a theme of central importance. Estes (1986) says that one task is to help the nation understand its own demography and we have noted Laslett's belief that this task has barely begun. This understanding is not advanced by the occasional moral panics about the 'growing burden' of dependency, the 'unaffordability' of pensions, the 'hard-core' of the iller than the ill, the older than the old and so on.

So, since endless demographic statistics and projections litter the pages of books on old age, wherein does this lack of understanding lie? It lies, we would argue, in the absence of the sociological imagination. Sheer numbers mean increasing diversity. People actively construct their lives with the resources at their disposal. A sociology of old age is essential if we are to further our understanding about the meaning and implications of an ageing population. We would cite three *general* reasons for this, along with a number of more *specific* benefits provided by a sociological perspective.

General

First, sociology can be used to provide a broader framework and perspective for interpreting old age. The sociologist starts from the view that old age is interesting because – although it is an enduring human phenomenon handled differently by different societies – it is changing and influencing social behaviour. He or she will want to explore the processes involved and how they are being interpreted by men and women. This approach contrasts with social administration and government interest in old age. In these cases, old age is regarded as a problem (for the economy or the health service, for instance), hence the need for some analysis and collection of data. This approach has its own validity and justification but it leads to a distorted view of older people, together with a limited selection of topics to be analysed and discussed. It leads, in addition, to a focus on the weaknesses of older people, rather than on their strengths, together with an emphasis on their similarities rather than their differences.

Secondly, as we discussed in Chapter 2, a historically-informed sociology can undermine some of the myths surrounding old age. Such a sociology tells us that it is wrong to believe that people 'care less' now than in the past about their aged kin; it shows, indeed, that there is as much continuity as discontinuity in patterns of care and support. Above all, it suggests that we cannot rely upon past customs or household structures to provide guidance for future models of care. We shall need, in fact, quite different approaches and perspectives, in line with altered circumstances, priorities and patterns of behaviour.

Thirdly, sociological perspectives are valuable because they can assist a clearer understanding of long-term social trends. The emergence of retirement is one example. This can be viewed as an economic problem – for the individual and for society – or as a psychological issue leading to problems of adjustment. However, retirement may also be seen as creating major changes in social relationships and activities. Earlier retirement (see Chapter 5), for example, is leading to a reevaluation of the balance between work and leisure, with a greater emphasis on constructing a lifestyle which either combines elements of paid work with longer periods of leisure or which focuses exclusively on recreational pursuits.

This raises many important questions: will this trend stimulate yet further the expansion in the service sector of the economy (Pahl 1984); who will gain and who will lose as the period of time spent in full-time work contracts; what are the implications for the family; will patterns of care change or remain the same as the work/leisure balance is changed; will the household division of labour be modified, with some older men taking on a broader range of domestic and caring responsibilities?

None of the above questions can be answered in the absence of a sociological perspective. Indeed, the fact that they await answers (and are the subject of much confusion in policy circles) reflects the current weaknesses in the sociology of old age.

Specifics

Having looked at these three general areas, we now examine some key points of departure for a sociology of old age, drawing on earlier chapters. There are the issues raised by secular trends. We discussed three of these – segregation, rising living standards and widening social cleavages – in Chapter 1. By a secular trend is meant a long-term and essentially continuous underlying movement in patterns of social life and conditions of existence. It is always a mistake to project such patterns far into the future because, even if they are unlikely to be reversed, they can stop or be succeeded by new ones. The segregation trend is an example. We would not expect to see ever larger residential concentrations of elderly people developing in the future, but rather a continuation of the trend towards what we might call increased micro-segregation, a continuing tendency for people to become more concentrated in small residential pockets (like sheltered housing schemes) adjacent to other semi-segregated residential developments for different age groups.

Another example is the issue of health in old age. The general trend in Western industrial nations seems clear: each successive cohort coming into old age *appears* to be somewhat healthier and with an improved expectation of life. Along with this goes an apparent widening of the differential expectation of life between men and women. However, we cannot be sure such trends will continue in a linear fashion: the immediate cohorts entering their 70s may prove to have been affected (in ways as yet unknown) by childhood in the years in and around the First World War and the depression which followed (with whatever consequences for infant nutrition that may have had). Women born in 1920 would have been 20 years old in 1940 and therefore part of a cohort at much greater risk of induction then into paid labour and of adopting the smoking habits of male workers. Aged 70 in 1990, such women may begin to show signs of aggravated ill-health and reduced expectation of life on that account. The intersection of general trends and particular cohort effects require continuing study.

Ethnicity is another important issue. As we discussed in Chapter 7, the population is becoming ethnically more diverse and we have shown that, within the ethnic minorities, major changes may be expected from one generation to another. With respect to the majority group, radical changes are occurring in respect of basic vital statistics like birth rates, age at first marriage, divorce and remarriage rates. The rates of household formation, dissolution and re-formation are increasing, with ever widening numbers of people acquiring partial connections with quite different kinship networks, while at the same time partially severing ties with previous ones (Vaughan 1987).

It has been commonplace in gerontology to associate divorce earlier in life with complications later in life, but we cannot be sure that a linear increase in divorce will necessarily lead to a linear increase in the number of elderly people cut off from their kin. People are not simply the passive victims of social change (although, as we note in the discussion of early retirement, they may not be able to resist the change itself on an individual basis) but they do actively construct and reconstruct their lives within the options available to them and which they themselves perceive and help to create.

We do not favour the imagery of old age which speaks only of the 'burden of dependency', or of the 'rising tide' of dementia or the 'crisis' of the ageing population, but there are *real difficulties* here which we do not mean to brush aside: the growing literature on 'caring for the carers' and 'elder abuse' – added to the existing critical literature about residential institutions which we looked at in Chapter 8 – indicates that there are problems here which must not be ignored. However, as sociologists we must always be wary of being stampeded with the latest 'moral panic', whether the now obviously dated Mods and Rockers analysed by Cohen (1972, 1980) or, contemporaneously, AIDS, hypothermia, dementia and child abuse. Part of the imagery of the moral panic is that of the floodgates opening and people being 'swamped' by whatever the latest supposed threat is. Juggling with figures is always part of this approach, whether the subject under inflammatory review is 'immigrants', 'muggers' or the 'burden of the ageing population'. This is one reason why we have tried, in this book, to distance ourselves as far as possible from the hysterical use of statistics. Sociology can offer an alternative to the moral panic by rigorous and dispassionate analysis of the circumstances and implications of data which highlight mass 'problems', whether of or for elderly people or those who care for them.

Also, although we eschew hypothetical arguments generally, it would be inappropriate to ignore the speculation in gerontological literature associated with the concepts of increasing rectangularity of population, the compression of morbidity hypothesis and the interest in 'terminal drop'. The rectangularity hypothesis is that, if we can continue to expect improvements in expectation of life at birth and continue to expect reductions in mortality at all ages between then and old age, the traditional age pyramid of population will be replaced by one more rectangular in shape. Associated with this is the 'compression of morbidity' hypothesis: people will stay healthy until extreme old age, when there will be a relatively short period of illness and rapidly declining functional competence (terminal drop), so that anxieties about the alleged burden of dependency will be shown to be unfounded.

Whether or not these changes are occurring or will occur is still a matter for debate. Whatever happens, the political economy perspective reminds us that it will not happen in a hurry or to all sections of the population equally. While some old people are buying second homes in the Costa del Sol and enjoying a longer and healthier old age, Frank White and Mr Morgan are mixing time with alcohol to help pass their solitary existence; many, many old people will continue to suffer chronic ill-health inherited from previous patterns of work, diet and environmental hazards. We recollect the analysis by Halsey which was quoted in Chapter 1: social inequality is an inescapable fact of life for the sociologist: while some elderly people are more comfortable than ever before, others stay at home for fear of racist attacks. Many suffer depression and arthritis and cannot get a hip transplant or their cataracts operated upon because of cuts in the National Health Service.

One task for the sociology of old age is to help make these inequalities visible and to remind us of the limitations to progress. Older people are not so much in the public domain: they are more hidden from view in the private domain of the home. If this is true for old people in general, it is particularly true for women, who make up the majority. It would be easy to regard them as particular 'problems' within the total elderly population: they live longer, have higher rates of morbidity than men and are, in aggregate, major consumers of services and state benefits. Older women figure little in common parlance, apart from in the negative stereotypes which abound.

A sociological perspective, informed by the feminist thought which has been developing in relation to younger women, guides us to look again: in Chapter 6 we mapped out some of the themes which emerge. We begin to see that the predominance of male-defined paradigms in sociology has blinkered our view of how distinctive women's experiences and concerns are and the extent of women's subordination in our patriarchal society.

A case in point is the fact that older women have not even figured on the agenda: women's retirement, for instance, has become a subject for serious study only recently. By leading us to examine the rich variety in women's perspectives on late life (as well as their differences from men in, for instance, social and family life, health and socio-economic status) a sociological approach can begin to clarify a number of conceptual and practical questions. For example, what are the implications for older women, as carers and as recipients of care, of changes in patterns of marriage, divorce and opportunities for paid work; what are the particular strengths on which older women can draw from the context of their life-histories; are these likely to change as patterns in the division of labour in the home and market place shift – or fail to – in the future? Much remains to be done to address these and other such questions: in our application of a sociological perspective we have sought to outline a fruitful approach.

Similarly, regarding old and ageing people from ethnic minority groups, a sociological approach leads us to consider quantitative and qualitative data from various disciplines, in order to understand something of the special positions of the different groups of black immigrants who are now old. By taking a historical view, we see that the life-histories of this generation of elderly people, together with the rapid and fundamental changes in cultural and family life in ethnic minority communities, mean that continuing and systematic study will be needed if the circumstances of future cohorts of old people are to be properly understood.

The importance of this in a multicultural society needs no justification. Methodological and conceptual development will be essential if proper account is to be taken of cultural imperatives. Sociology itself could in some respects be considered ethnocentric and there is no room for complacency on this front. In a multicultural society, sociological analysis of ethnicity and old age must also be multicultural.

In Chapter 8 we reviewed a variety of places where elderly people are found living or spending substantial periods of time together, relatively segregated from other age groups: we group these together under the heading of 'special settings'. Special settings for older people are of intrinsic sociological interest: they are tangible physical and social phenomena and they exert a perhaps disproportionate attraction to researchers. One reason for this is their 'special-ness', their sheer curiosity value. Another is that they provide an inexpensive but non-random sample for those simply seeking access to a group of older people for study purposes and an attractive option for those who wish to experiment with observation methods. A third reason (although only a minority of elderly people are found in special settings) is the fact that they are in the broadest sense of the term 'designed' for elderly people by others – they perhaps represent in distilled and visible form the particular attitudes and resources which go into the prevailing social construction of old age in any one time or place.

Two further reasons might be noted: on the one hand, the anxiety about abuse, neglect or lack of stimulus in special settings which concerned enquirers want to make known; on the other, the complex evaluative motives which mainly prompt the disproportionate volume of research on special settings. This may have a humanitarian ethos, concerned to discover the extent to which social planning is succeeding in meeting older people's needs, often mixed with a measure of organizational concern to discover if provision is over-generous, inappropriate, over-expensive and a useful target to attack.

The term special settings covers a wide range of types and, within each type there is great variability. Facile generalizations on the subject should therefore be avoided because these settings, while they may be the ideal answer to some people's problems and therefore enhance the options available, for others *represent* the problem that there is apparently no other option. As so often in sociology, we have to stress the diversity of the population and the relativity of subjective assessments. Any one example will suffice to make the point: for some people, conditions in geriatric wards are so unattractive and inferior to the standards of privacy and amenity which they are used to at home that the prospect of admission to care is almost a fate worse than death; for others, being fed regularly without effort, being warm and cared for and seeing other people represents a real temporary bonus, a genuine respite from the struggle of daily living. While trying, therefore, not to give disproportionate attention to special settings, we have indicated both their sociological interest and the contribution with sociological research and reflection can make in this area. We have touched on areas of concern and possibilities of improvement, without dwelling exclusively on issues of welfare.

This exemplifies our general stance in this book. The sociological approach we advocate would not start from the premise that old age is a problem, nor do we see our role as simply identifying new 'needs' and discovering fresh agendas for action. Our priority has been to demonstrate both the 'normality' and diversity of older people and to encourage more wide-ranging perspectives than the functionalist, welfarist or pathological models which have dominated the field. We hope we have succeeded in achieving the goals we stated in Chapter 1 of not only providing an introduction to this important topic but in conveying some of the particular interest and potential of applying sociological theories and approaches to the study of older people.

Bibliography

Abrams, M. (1978a). *The Elderly: An Overview of Current British Social Research.* London, National Corporation for the Care of Old People and Age Concern.

Abrams, M. (1978b). *Beyond Three Score and Ten: A First Report on a Survey of the Elderly.* Mitcham, Age Concern.

Abrams, M. (1980). *Beyond Three Score and Ten: A Second Report on a Survey of the Elderly.* Mitcham, Age Concern.

Abrams, P. (1978). 'Community care: some research problems and priorities', in Barnes, J. and Connelly, N. (eds), *Social Care Research.* London, Policy Studies Institute.

Achenbaum, W. A. (1978). *Old Age in the New Land.* London, John Hopkins Press.

Age Concern (1974). *The Attitudes of the Retired and Elderly.* London, Age Concern.

Age Concern (1984). *Sheltered Housing for Older People.* Report of a Working Party (Examining) the Role of Sheltered Housing Within the Spectrum of Care and Accommodation Needed by Elderly People. Mitcham, Age Concern.

Amoss, P. T. and Harrell, S. (eds) (1981). *Other Ways of Growing Old, Anthropological Perspectives.* Stanford, Stanford University Press.

Anderson, M. (1974). *Family Structure in Nineteenth Century Lancashire.* Cambridge, Cambridge University Press.

Anderson, M. (1985). 'The emergence of the modern life-cycle in Britain'. *Social History*, **10**, 69–88.

Anderson, W. F. and Cowan, N. (1956). 'Work and retirement: influences on the health of elderly men'. *Lancet*, **ii**, 1344–7.

Anwar, M. (1979). *The Myth of Return, Pakistanis in Britain.* London, Heinemann.

Anwar, M. (1986). *Race and Politics.* London, Tavistock.

Ariès, P. (1983). *The Hour of Our Death.* London, Peregrine.

Armstrong, D. (1983). *Political Anatomy of the Body: Medical Knowledge in Britain in the Twentieth Century.* Cambridge, Cambridge University Press.

Aslam, M., Davis, S. and Fletcher, R. (1979). 'Compliance in medication by Asian immigrants'. *Nursing Times*, 31 May, 931–2.

Atchley, R. (1972). *The Social Forces in Later Life: An Introduction to Social Gerontology.* Belmont, Wadsworth.

Atchley, R. (1982). 'The process of retirement: comparing women and men', in Szinovacz, M. (ed.), *Women's Retirement: Policy Implications of Recent Research.* London, Sage.

Badger, F. (1987). Personal communication.

Badger, F., Cameron, E. and Evers, H. (1988). *Who gets a Bath?* Birmingham, University of Birmingham, Department of Social Medicine.

Bailey, P. (1982). *At the Jerusalem*. Harmondsworth, Penguin.

Ballard, R. and Ballard, C. (1977). 'The Sikhs', in Watson, J. (ed.), *Between Two Cultures: Migrants and Minorities in Britain*. Oxford, Basil Blackwell.

Barker, J. (1984). *Black and Asian Old People in Britain*. Mitcham, Age Concern Research Unit.

Barley, N. (1983). *The Innocent Anthropologist: Notes from a Mud Hut*. London, British Museum Publications.

Bateson, N. (1984). *Data Construction in Social Surveys*. London, George Allen and Unwin.

Baum, M. and Baum, R. (1980). *Growing Old: A Societal Perspective*. New Jersey, Prentice-Hall.

Bechhofer, F. (1967). 'Too many surveys'. *New Society*, 8 June, 838–9.

Beeson, D. (1975). 'Women in studies of aging: a critique and suggestion'. *Social Problems*, **23**, 52–9.

Bell, B. (ed.) (1976). *Contemporary Social Gerontology*. Springfield, Charles Thomas.

Bell, C. and Newby, H. (1977). *Doing Sociological Research*. London, George Allen and Unwin.

Benjamin, B. (1968). *Demographic Analysis*. London, George Allen and Unwin.

Berger, P. L. (1966). *Invitation to Sociology, A Humanistic Perspective*. Harmondsworth, Penguin.

Berry, S., Lee, M. and Griffiths, S. (1981). *Report on a Survey of West Indian Pensioners in Nottingham*. Nottingham, Social Services Department, Research Section.

Bertaux, D. (ed.) (1981). *Biography and Society, the Life History Approach in the Social Sciences*. London, Sage.

Bertaux, D. and Bertaux-Wiame, I. (1981). 'Life stories in the bakers' trade', in Bertaux, D. (ed.), *Biography and Society, the Life History Approach in the Social Sciences*. London, Sage.

Bertaux-Wiame, I. (1981). 'The life history approach to the study of internal migration', in Bertaux, D. (ed.), *Biography and Society, the Life History Approach in the Social Sciences*. London, Sage.

Bessell, B. (1986). 'Very sheltered housing in the public and private sectors'. Address to British Association for Services to the Elderly Conference 'Housing Options for Older People', 5 December. London, King's Fund Centre.

Beveridge Report (1942). *Social Insurance and Allied Services*. Cmd. 6404. London, HMSO.

Bhalla, A. and Blakemore, K. (1981). *Elders of the Ethnic Minority Groups*. Birmingham, All Faiths For One Race.

Bhopal, R. (1986). 'Inter-relationship of folk, traditional and Western medicines within an Asian community in Britain'. *Social Science and Medicine*, **22**, 99–105.

Bird, N. (1984). *The Private Provision of Residential Care for the Elderly*. Social Work Monograph 23. Norwich, University of East Anglia.

Blaikie, A. and Macnicol, J. (1986). 'Towards an anatomy of ageism: society, social policy and the elderly between the wars', in Phillipson, C., Bernard, M. and Strang, P. (eds), *Dependency and Interdependency in Old Age – Theoretical Perspectives and Policy Alternatives*. London, Croom Helm.

Blakemore, K. (1982). 'Health and illness among the elderly of minority ethnic groups living in Birmingham: some new findings'. *Health Trends*, **14**, 69–72.

180   *The sociology of old age*

Blakemore, K. (1983). 'Ethnicity, self-reported illness and use of medical services by the elderly'. *Postgraduate Medical Journal*, **59**, 668–70.
Blakemore, K. (1985). 'The state, the voluntary sector and new developments in provision for the old of minority racial groups'. *Ageing and Society*, **5**, 175–90.
Blau, P. M. (1964). *Exchange and Power in Social Life*. New York, John Wiley.
Blau, Z. (1973). *Old Age in a Changing Society*. New York, New Viewpoints.
Booth, C. (1902–3). *Life and Labour of the People in London*, 3rd Edition. London, Macmillan.
Booth, T. (1985). *Home Truths: Old People's Homes and the Outcome of Care*. Aldershot, Gower.
Bornat, J., Phillipson, C. and Wand, S. (1985). *A Manifesto for Old Age*. London, Pluto.
Bosanquet, N. (1987). *A Generation in Limbo: Government, The Economy and the 55–65 Age Group in Britain*. London, Public Policy Centre.
Bowl, R. (1986). 'Social work with old people', in Phillipson, C. and Walker, A. (eds), *Ageing and Social Policy: A Critical Assessment*. Aldershot, Gower.
Bowl, R., Clegg, P., Emerson, A. R., Fennell, G., Sidell, M. and Thomas, N. (1979). 'Not just a day out'. *Community Care*, 14 June, 26–27.
Bowling, A. (1984). 'Caring for the elderly widowed – the burden on their supporters'. *British Journal of Social Work*, **14**, 435–55.
Bowling, A. and Cartwright, A. (1982). *Life After A Death: A Study of the Elderly Widowed*. London, Tavistock.
Brent Social Services Department (1983). *Services for the Ethnic Minority Elderly*. London Borough of Brent, Social Services Department Report No. 114/83.
Brody, E. (1981). '"Women in the middle" and family help to older people'. *The Gerontologist*, **21**, 471–9.
Brody, E. and Schoonover, C. (1986). 'Patterns of parent-care when adult daughters work and when they do not'. *The Gerontologist*, **26**, 372–81.
Brown, G. W. and Harris, T. (1978). *Social Origins of Depression, A Study of Psychiatric Disorders in Women*. London, Tavistock.
Brown, G. W., Ní Bhrolcháin, M. and Harris, T. O. (1975). 'Social class and psychiatric disturbance among women in an urban population'. *Sociology*, **9**, 225–54.
Brubaker, T. H. (1983). *Family Relationships in Later Life*. Beverly Hills, Sage.
Bruyn, S. T. (1966). *The Human Perspective in Sociology: The Methodology of Participant Observation*. Englewood Cliffs, Prentice-Hall.
Bucher, R., Fritz, C. E. and Quarantelli, E. L. (1956). 'Tape recorded interviews in social research'. *American Sociological Review*, **21**, 359–64.
Bulmer, M. (1986). *Neighbours: The Work of Philip Abrams*. Cambridge, Cambridge University Press.
Burgess, E. W. (ed.) (1960). *Aging in Western Societies*. Chicago, University of Chicago Press.
Burnett, J. (1966). *Plenty and Want*. London, Nelson.
Burnett, J., Vincent, D. and Mayall, D. (eds) (1986). *The Autobiography of The Working-Class; An Annotated Critical Biography*. Brighton, Harvester.
Burns, B. and Phillipson, C. (1986). *Drugs, Ageing and Society: Social and Pharmacological Perspectives*. London, Croom Helm.
Burns, T. (1966). 'The study of consumer behaviour, a sociological view'. *Archives Europeenes de Sociologie*, **7**, 313–29.
Butler, A. (1981). 'Dispersed alarm systems for the elderly'. *Social Work Service*, **25**, 17–22.

Butler, A., Oldman, C. and Greve, J. (1983). *Sheltered Housing for the Elderly: Policy, Practice and the Consumer*. London, George Allen and Unwin.

Butler, R. (1963). 'The life-review: an interpretation of reminiscence in the aged'. *Psychiatry: Journal of the Study of Inter-Personal Processes*, **26**, 65–76.

Butler, R. (1975). *Why Survive? Being Old in America*. New York, Harper and Row.

Bytheway, B. (1984). 'The lucky five per cent'. *Roof*, March–April, 30.

Bytheway, B. (1986). 'Making way: the disengagement of older workers', in Phillipson, P., Bernard, M. and Strang, P. (eds), *Dependency and Interdependency in Old Age – Theoretical Perspectives and Policy Alternatives*. London, Croom Helm.

Cain, M. (1971). 'On the beat: interactions and relations in rural and urban police forces', in Cohen, S. (ed.), *Images of Deviance*. Harmondsworth, Penguin.

Carboni, D. (1982). *Geriatric Medicine in the United States and Great Britain*. London, Greenwood.

Carter, J. (1981). *Day Services for Adults: Somewhere to Go*. London, George Allen and Unwin.

Cartwright, A., Hockley, L. and Anderson, J. (1973). *Life Before Death*. London, Routledge and Kegan Paul.

Cashmore, E. (1984). *Dictionary of Race and Ethnic Relations*. London, Routledge and Kegan Paul.

Cashmore, E. and Troyna, B. (1983). *An Introduction to Race Relations*. London, Routledge and Kegan Paul.

Cavan, R. S., Burgess, E. W., Havighurst, R. J. and Goldhamer, H. (1949). *Personal Adjustment in Old Age*. Chicago, Science Research Associates.

Central Statistical Office (CSO) (1987). *Social Trends*, **17**. London, HMSO.

Chapman, S. J. and Hallsworth, H. M. (1909). *Unemployment: The Results of an Investigation made in Lancashire and an Examination of the Reports of the Poor Law Commission*. Manchester, University of Manchester.

Charlesworth, A., Wilkin, D. and Durie, A. (1984). *Carers and Services: A Comparison of Men and Women Caring for Dependent Elderly People*. Manchester, Equal Opportunities Commission.

Clarke, M. (1978). 'Getting through the work', in Dingwall, R. and McIntosh, J. (eds), *Readings in the Sociology of Nursing*. Edinburgh, Churchill Livingstone.

Clarke, M., Clarke, S., Odell, A. and Jagger, C. (1984). 'The elderly at home: health and social status'. *Health Trends*, **16**, 3–7.

Clarke, M., Lowry, R. and Clarke, S. (1986). 'Cognitive impairment in the elderly – a community survey'. *Age and Ageing*, **15**, 278–84.

Cohen, L. (1984). *Small Expectations: Society's Betrayal of Older Women*. Toronto, McLelland and Stewart.

Cohen, S. (1972, 1980). *Folk Devils and Moral Panics: The Creation of Mods and Rockers*. Oxford, Martin Robertson.

Coleman, A. (1982). *Preparation for Retirement in England and Wales*. Leicester, NIAE.

Coleman, P. (1986). *The Ageing Process and the Role of Reminiscence*. London, John Wiley.

Cooper, J. (1979). 'West Indian elderly in Leicester: a case study', in Glendenning, F. (ed.), *The Elders in Ethnic Minorities: A Report of a Seminar, University of Keele*. Stoke-on-Trent, Beth Johnson Foundation Publications.

Cornwell, J. (1984). *Hard Earned Lives*. London, Tavistock.

Counter Information Services (1980). *NHS: Critical Condition*. London, CIS.

Cowgill, D. O. (1974). 'The aging of populations and societies'. *Annals of the American Academy of Political and Social Science*, **415**, 1–18.

Cowgill, D. O. and Holmes, D. (eds) (1972). *Aging and Modernization*. New York, Appleton-Century-Crofts.

Craib, I. (1984). *Modern Social Theory*. Brighton, Wheatsheaf Books.

Crawford, M. (1971). 'Retirement and disengagement'. *Human Relations*, **24**, 255–78.

Crawford, M. (1972). 'Retirement and role playing'. *Sociology*, **6**, 217–36.

Crawford, M. (1981). 'Not disengaged: grandparents in literature and reality'. *Sociological Review*, **29**, 499–519.

Cribier, F. (1979). 'Estimation de l'état de santé et pratiques medicales. Une enquete auprès des nouveaux retraites Parisiens'. *Gerontologie*, **29**, 12–30.

Cribier, F. (1981). 'Changing retirement patterns of the seventies: the example of a generation of Parisian salaried workers'. *Ageing and Society*, **1**, 51–72.

Cumming E. and Henry, W. E. (1961). *Growing Old, the Process of Disengagement*. New York, Basic Books.

Cunningham-Burley, S. (1986). 'Becoming a grandparent'. *Ageing and Society*, **6**, 453–70.

Currer, C. (1986). 'Concepts of mental well- and ill-being: the case of Pathan mothers in Britain', in Currer, C. and Stacey, M. (eds), *Concepts of Health, Illness and Disease: A Comparative Perspective*. Leamington Spa, Berg.

Davidoff, L. and Hall, C. (1987). *Family Fortunes: Men and Women of the English Middle Class*. London, Hutchinson.

Davis, B. and Knapp, M. (1981). *Old Peoples' Homes and the Production of Welfare*. London, Routledge and Kegan Paul.

Day, L. (1981). 'Health visiting the elderly in the 1980s – do we care enough?' *Health Visitor*, **54**, 538–9.

de Beauvoir, S. (1966). *A Very Easy Death*. London, Andre Deutsch and George Weidenfeld.

Delphy, C. (1981). 'Women in stratification studies', in Roberts, H. (ed.), *Doing Feminist Research*. London, Routledge and Kegan Paul.

Denham, M. (1983). 'The elderly in continuing care units', in Denham, M. (ed.), *Care of the Long-Stay Elderly Patient*. London, Croom Helm.

DHSS (1978). *A Happier Old Age: A Discussion Document*. London, HMSO.

DHSS (1981). *Growing Older*. Cmnd. 8173. London, HMSO.

DHSS (1985). *Reform of Social Security: Programme for Change*. Cmnd. 9518. London, HMSO.

DHSS (1986). *Tables on Families with Low Incomes – 1983*. London, HMSO.

DHSS/OPCS (1981). *Hospital In-Patient Enquiry 1978*. Main Tables (England and Wales), Series MB4, No. 12. London, HMSO.

DHSS/OPCS (1987). *Hospital In-Patient Enquiry 1985*. Main Tables (England), Series MB4, No. 27. London, HMSO.

Dex, S. (1985). *The Sexual Division of Work, Conceptual Revolutions in the Social Sciences*. Brighton, Wheatsheaf.

Dex, S. and Phillipson, C. (1986a). 'Social policy and the older worker', in Phillipson, C. and Walker, A. (eds), *Ageing and Social Policy: A Critical Assessment*. Aldershot, Gower.

Dex, S. and Phillipson, C. (1986b). 'Older women in the labour market: a review of current trends'. *Critical Social Policy*, **15**, 79–84.

di Gregorio, S. (1986a). 'Understanding the "management" of everyday living', in Phillipson, C., Bernard, M. and Strang, P. (eds), *Dependency and Interdependency in Later Life: Theoretical Perspectives and Policy Alternatives*. London, Croom Helm.

di Gregorio, S. (1986b). 'Growing old in twentieth century Leeds: an exploratory study based on the life histories of people aged 75 years and over, with specific reference to their past and present management of every-day living – at home and at work'. Ph.D. Thesis. London, London School of Economics.

di Gregorio, S. (1987). '"Managing" – a concept for contextualising how people live their later lives', in di Gregorio, S. (ed.), *Social Gerontology: New Directions*. London, Croom Helm.

Dobson, C. (1983). 'Sex-role and marital-role expectations', in Brubaker, T. H. (ed.), *Family Relationships in Later Life*. Beverly Hills, Sage.

Donahue, W. (1961). 'Housing the aged in Europe', in Burgess, E. W. (ed.), *Retirement Villages*. Ann Arbor, University of Michigan.

Donahue, W., Thompson, M. and Curren, D. J. (eds) (1977). *Congregate Housing for Older People: An Urgent Need, a Growing Demand*. Washington, US Department of Health.

Donaldson, L. (1986). 'Health and social status of elderly Asians: a community survey'. *British Medical Journal*, **293**, 1079–82.

Donovan, J. (1986a). *We Don't Buy Sickness, It Just Comes*. Aldershot, Gower.

Donovan, J. (1986b). 'Black people's health: a different approach', in Rathwell, T. and Phillips, D. (eds), *Health, Race and Ethnicity*. London, Croom Helm.

Donovan, J. (1986c). 'Ethnicity and health: a research review'. *Social Science and Medicine*, **19**, 663–70.

Douglas, J. D. (ed.) (1970). *The Relevance of Sociology*. New York, Appleton-Century-Crofts.

Douglas, M. (1963). 'Tribal policies for the old'. *New Society*, 25 April, 13–14.

Dowd, J. (1980). *Stratification Amongst the Aged*. Monterey, Brooks/Cole.

Doyal, L. (1979). *The Political Economy of Health*. London, Pluto.

Ebrahim, S., Smith, C. and Giggs, J. (1987). 'Elderly immigrants – a disadvantaged group?' *Age and Ageing*, **16**, 249–55.

Elder, G. (1977). *The Alienated: Growing Old Today*. London, Writers' and Readers' Publishing Co-operative.

Elias, N. (1985). *The Loneliness of the Dying*. Oxford, Basil Blackwell.

Equal Opportunities Commission (EOC) (1980). *The Experience of Caring for Elderly and Handicapped Dependants*. Manchester, EOC.

Equal Opportunities Commission (EOC) (1982). *Caring for the Elderly and Handicapped: Community Care Policies and Women's Lives*. Manchester, EOC.

Estes, C. (1979). *The Aging Enterprise*. San Francisco, Jossey-Bass.

Estes, C. (1986). 'The politics of ageing in America'. *Ageing and Society*, **6**, 121–34.

Evers, H. (1981). 'Care or custody? The experiences of women patients in long-stay geriatric wards', in Hutter, B. and Williams, G. (eds), *Controlling Women: The Normal and the Deviant*. London, Croom Helm.

Evers, H. (1984). *Experiences of the Elderly with Health and Social Care Support and Services* (unpublished report). Coventry, University of Warwick.

Evers, H. (1985). 'The frail elderly woman: emergent questions in ageing and women's health', in Lewin, E. and Olesen, V. (eds), *Women, Health and Healing: Towards a New Perspective*. London, Tavistock.

Evers, H. (1986). 'Organisation of care of the elderly in the UK', in Redfern, S. (ed.), *A Textbook of Geriatric Nursing*. Edinburgh, Churchill Livingstone.

Evers, H., Badger, F. and Cameron, E. (forthcoming). *Community Care Project Working Papers*. Birmingham, University of Birmingham, Department of Social Medicine.

Featherstone, M. (1987). 'Leisure, symbolic power and the life-course', in Horne, J., Jary, D. and Tomlinson, A. (eds), *Sport, Leisure and Social Relations*. Keele, Sociological Review Monograph No. 33.

Fennell, G. (1966). 'Two theories of ageing, a discussion and a test'. M.Soc.Sc. Thesis, University of Stockholm.

Fennell, G. (1979). *Day Centres for the Elderly: An Overview of Three Studies*. London, Department of Health and Social Security.

Fennell, G. (1982). 'Social interaction in grouped dwellings for the elderly in Newcastle-upon-Tyne. Ph.D. Thesis, University of Newcastle-upon-Tyne.

Fennell, G. (1985). 'Sheltered housing: some unanswered questions', in Butler, A. (ed.), *Ageing: Recent Advances and Creative Responses*. London, Croom Helm.

Fennell, G. (1986a). *Anchor's Older People: What do They Think?* Oxford, Anchor Housing Association.

Fennell, G. (1986b). 'Structured dependency revisited', in Phillipson, C., Bernard M. and Strang, P. (eds), *Dependency and Interdependency in Old Age: Theoretical Perspectives and Policy Alternatives*. London, Croom Helm.

Fennell, G. (1987). *A Place of My Own: A Consumer View of Sheltered Housing in Scotland*. Edinburgh, Bield Housing Association.

Fennell, G. and Sidell, M. (1982). *Day Centres for the Elderly: Good Practice Guide*. Norwich, University of East Anglia, Centre for East Anglian Studies.

Fennell, G. and Way, A. (1986). 'Sheltered housing: the limits to care'. *Voluntary Housing*, May, 16–17.

Fennell, G., Emerson, A. R., Sidell, M. and Hague, A. (1981). *Day Centres for the Elderly in East Anglia*. Norwich, University of East Anglia, Centre for East Anglian Studies.

Fennell, G., Phillipson, C. and Wenger, G. C. (1983). 'The process of ageing, social aspects', in DHSS, *Elderly People in the Community, Their Service Needs; Research Contributions to the Development of Policy and Practice*. London, HMSO.

Fenton, S. (1986). *Race, Health and Welfare: Afro-Caribbean and South Asian People in Central Bristol: Health and Social Services* (unpublished report). Bristol, University of Bristol, Department of Sociology.

Ferguson, S. and Fitzgerald, H. (1954). *History of the Second World War: Studies in the Social Services*. London, HMSO.

Finch, J. and Groves, D. (1980). 'Community care and the family: a case for equal opportunities?' *Journal of Social Policy*, **9**, 487–514.

Finch, J. and Groves, D. (1982). 'By women for women: caring for the frail elderly'. *Women's Studies International Forum*, **5**, 427–38.

Fischer, D. H. (1977). *Growing Old in America*. New York, Oxford University Press.

Fletcher, C. (1974). *Beneath the Surface: An Account of Three Styles of Sociological Research*. London, Routledge and Kegan Paul.

Ford, J. and Sinclair, R. (1987). *Sixty Years On: Women Talk About Old Age*. London, The Women's Press.

Forsyth, G. (1966). *Doctors and State Medicine, A Study of the British Health Service*. London, Pitman.

Friedmann, E. A. and Havighurst, R. J. (1954). *The Meaning of Work and Retirement*. Chicago, University of Chicago Press.

Fryer, P. (1984). *Staying Power: A History of Black People in Britain*. London, Pluto.

Gans, H. J. (1962). 'Urbanism and suburbanism as ways of life: a re-evaluation of definitions', in Rose, A. (ed.), *Human Behaviour and Social Processes*. London, Routledge and Kegan Paul.

George, V. and Wilding, P. (1976). *Ideology and Social Welfare*. London, Routledge and Kegan Paul.

Glaser, B. and Strauss, A. (1965). *Awareness of Dying*. London, Weidenfeld and Nicolson.

Glendenning, F. (ed.) (1979). *The Elders in Ethnic Minorities: a Report of a Seminar, University of Keele*. Stoke-on-Trent, Beth Johnson Foundation Publications.

Godlove, C., Richard, L. and Rodwell. G. (1982). *Time For Action: An Observation Study of Elderly People in Four Different Care Environments*. Sheffield, University of Sheffield, Joint Unit for Social Services Research.

Goffman, E. (1959). *The Presentation of Self in Everyday Life*. New York, Doubleday.

Goffman, E. (1961). *Asylums: Essays on the Social Situation of Mental Patients and Other Inmates*. New York, Doubleday.

Goffman, E. (1963). *Stigma: Notes on the Management of Spoiled Identity*. Englewood Cliffs, Prentice-Hall.

Goldthorpe, J. H., Lockwood, D., Bechhofer, F. and Platt, J. (1968–9). *The Affluent Worker*, 3 Volumes. Cambridge, Cambridge University Press.

Graebner, W. (1980). *A History of Retirement*. New Haven, Yale University Press.

Graham, H. (1983). 'Caring: a Labour of love', in Finch, J. and Groves, D. (eds), *A Labour of Love: Women, Work and Caring*. London, Routledge and Kegan Paul.

Greengross, S. (1986). 'Sexuality and older people', in Wyld, S. (ed.), *Sexuality in Later Life*, working papers on the health of older people, Health Education Authority in association with Department of Adult and Continuing Education, University of Keele.

Grimley Evans, J. (1983). 'The appraisal of hospital geriatric services'. *Community Medicine*, **5**, 242–50.

Guillemard, A.-M. (1982). 'Old age, retirement and the social class structure: toward an analysis of the structural dynamics of the later stage of life', in Hareven, T. K. and Adams, K. J. (eds), *Ageing and Life Course Transitions: An Interdisciplinary Perspective*. London, Tavistock.

Guillemard, A.-M. (1986). 'Social policy and ageing in France', in Phillipson, C. and Walker, A. (eds), *Ageing and Social Policy: A Critical Assessment*. Aldershot, Gower.

Haber, C. (1983). *Beyond Sixty-Five: The Dilemma of Old Age in America's Past*. Cambridge, Cambridge University Press.

Hagestad, G. (1985). 'Olde. women in intergenerational relations', in Haug, M., Ford, A. and Sheafor, M. (eds), *The Physical and Mental Health of Aged Women*. New York, Springer.

Halsey, A. H. (1987). 'Britain's class society'. *Guardian*, 13 July, 9.

Hanawalt, B. (1986). *The Ties That Bound*. Oxford, Oxford University Press.

Hannah, L. (1986). *Inventing Retirement*. Cambridge, Cambridge University Press.

Hareven, T. K. and Adams, K. J. (eds) (1982). *Aging and Life Course Transitions: An Interdisciplinary Perspective*. London, Tavistock.

Harris, A. (1968). *Social Welfare for the Elderly*. London, HMSO.

Harris, A. (1971). *Handicapped and Impaired in Great Britain*. London, HMSO.

Harris, D. (1985). *The Sociology of Aging, An Annotated Bibliography and Sourcebook*. New York, Garland.

Harris, O. and Cole, W. (1980). *The Sociology of Aging*. Boston, Houghton Mifflin.

Harrison, P. (1985). *Inside the Inner City*, Revised Edition. Harmondsworth, Penguin.

Hart, C. M. and Pilling, A. R. (1960). *The Tiwi of North Australia*. New York, Holt, Rinehart and Winston.

Havighurst, R. J. (1954). 'Flexibility and the social roles of the retired'. *American Journal of Sociology*, **59**, 309–11.

Havighurst, R. J. (1960). 'Life beyond family and work', in Burgess, R. (ed.), *Aging in Western Societies*. Chicago, University of Chicago Press.

Havighurst, R. J. and Albrecht, R. (1953). *Older People*. London, Longmans, Green.

Haynes, S. G., McMichael, A. J. and Tyroler, H. A. (1978). 'Survival after early and normal retirement'. *Journal of Gerontology*, **33**, 269–78.

Hazan, H. (1980). *The Limbo People: A Study of the Constitution of the Time Universe Among the Aged*. London, Routledge and Kegan Paul.

Held, J. (1987). 'Between bourgeois enlightenment and popular cultures: Goya's festivals, old women, monsters and blind men'. *History Workshop Journal*, **23**, 39–58.

Herzlich, C. (1973). *Health and Illness: A Social Psychological Analysis*. London, Academic Press.

Heumann, L. and Boldy, D. (1982). *Housing for the Elderly: Planning and Policy Formulation in Western Europe and North America*. London, Croom Helm.

Hochschild, A. R. (1973). *The Unexpected Community*. Englewood Cliffs, Prentice-Hall.

Hochschild, A. R. (1975). 'Disengagement theory: a critique and proposal'. *American Sociological Review*, **40**, 553–69.

Hockley, J. (1986). 'Death and dying', in Redfern, S. J. (ed.), *Nursing Elderly People*. Edinburgh, Churchill Livingstone.

Holland, B. and Lewando-Hundt, G. (1987). *Coventry Ethnic Minorities Elderly Survey: Method, Data and Applied Action*. City of Coventry, Ethnic Minorities Development Unit.

Homans, G. C. (1961). *Social Behaviour: Its Elementary Forms*. London, Routledge and Kegan Paul.

Horrocks, P. (1982). 'The case for geriatric medicine as an age-related speciality', in Isaacs, B. (ed.), *Recent Advances in Geriatric Medicine*. Edinburgh, Churchill Livingstone.

House of Commons (1908). *Hansard*, 190, Col. 575.

House of Commons (1924). *Hansard*, 184, Col. 79.

Hoyt, G. C. (1954). 'The life of the retired in a trailer park'. *American Journal of Sociology*, **59**, 361–70.

Huff, D. (1954). *How to Lie with Statistics*. London, Gollancz.

Hunt, A. (1970). *The Home Help Service in England and Wales*. London, HMSO.

Hunt, A. (1978). *The Elderly at Home, A Study of People Aged Sixty-five and Over Living in the Community in England in 1976*. London, HMSO.

Hutter, B. and Williams, G. (eds) (1981). *Controlling Women: The Normal and the Deviant*. London, Croom Helm.

Isaacs, B. (1969). 'Sheltered housing, the viewpoint of a geriatrician'. *Journal of the Institute of Housing Managers*, **5**, 18–22.

Isaacs, B. (1974). 'The silver age'. *New Society*, 14 November, 417–18.

Isaacs, B., Livingstone, M. and Neville, Y. (1972). *Survival of the Unfittest, A Study of Geriatric Patients in Glasgow*. London, Routledge and Kegan Paul.

Jacobs, J. (1974). *Fun City, An Ethnographic Study of a Retirement Community*. New York, Holt, Rinehart and Winston.

Jacobs, J. (1975). *Older Persons and Retirement Communities, Case Studies in Social Gerontology*. Springfield, Charles Thomas.

Jacobson, D. (1970). 'Attitudes towards work and retirement in three firms'. Ph.D. Thesis. London, London School of Economics.

Jerrome, D. (1981). 'The significance of friendship for women in later life'. *Ageing and Society*, **1**, 175–98.

Jerrome, D. (1986). 'Me Darby, You Joan!', in Phillipson, P., Bernard, M. and Strang, P. (eds.), *Dependency and Interdependency in Old Age – Theoretical Perspectives and Policy Alternatives*. London, Croom Helm.

John, R. (1984). 'Prerequisites of an adequate theory of aging: a critique and reconceptualization'. *Mid-American Review of Sociology*, **9**, 79–108.

Johnson, M. L. (1976). 'That was your life: a biographical approach to later life', in Munnichs, J. M. A. and Van Den Heuval, W. J. A. (eds), *Dependency or Interdependency in Old Age*. The Hague, Martinus Nijhoff.

Johnson, M. L. (1982). 'Editorial: observations on the enterprise of ageing'. *Ageing and Society*, **2**, 1–6.

Johnson, M. L. (1984). 'Privatising residential care: a review of changing policy and practice', in Laming, H. (ed.), *Residential Care for the Elderly*. London, Policy Studies Institute.

Johnson, M. L. (1986). 'The meaning of old age', in Redfern, S. J. (ed.), *Nursing Elderly People*. Edinburgh, Churchill Livingstone.

Johnson, M. L., di Gregorio, S. and Harrison, B. (1980). *Ageing, Needs and Nutrition*. Leeds, University of Leeds, Nuffield Centre for Health Services Studies.

Johnson, M. R. D. (1986). 'Inner city residents, ethnic minorities and primary health care in the West Midlands', in Rathwell, T. and Phillips, D. (eds), *Health, Race and Ethnicity*. London, Croom Helm.

Johnson, M. R. D., Cross, M. and Cardew, S. (1983). 'Inner-city residents, ethnic minorities and primary health care'. *Postgraduate Medical Journal*, **59**, 664–7.

Johnson, S. M. (1971). *Idle Haven, Community Building Among the Working Class Retired*. Berkeley, University of California Press.

Jones, D. and Vetter, N. (1985). 'Formal and informal support received by carers of elderly dependants'. *British Medical Journal*, **291**, 643–5.

Jones, K. (1975). 'The development of institutional care', in Butterworth, E. and Holman, R. (eds), *Social Welfare in Modern Britain*. London, Fontana.

Jones, K. and Fowles, A. J. (1984). *Ideas on Institutions: Analyzing the Literature on Long-term Care and Custody*. London, Routledge and Kegan Paul.

Joshi, H. and Ermisch, J. (1982). 'The trend to increased female labour force participation and women's pension rights in the transition to maturity', in Fogarty, M. (ed.), *Retirement Policy: The Next Fifty Years*. London, Heinemann.

Kalish, R. (1976). 'Death and dying in a social context', in Binstock, R. and Shanas, E. (eds), *Handbook of Aging and the Social Sciences*. New York, Nostrand Reinhold.

Kane, E. (1985). *Quality Control in Public and Private Homes for the Elderly*. Social Work Monograph 39. Norwich, University of East Anglia.

Karn, V. A. (1977). *Retiring to the Seaside*. London, Routledge and Kegan Paul.

Kart, G. (1987). 'Review essay: the end of conventional gerontology?' *Sociology of Health and Illness*, **9**, 76–88.

188   *The sociology of old age*

Keating, N. and Cole, P. (1980). 'What do I do with him 24 hours a day? Changes in the housewife role after retirement'. *Gerontologist*, **20**,84–9.
Keatinge, W. R. (1986). Radio interview.
Kent, R. A. (1981). *A History of British Empirical Sociology*. Aldershot, Gower.
Kerzner, L. (1983). 'Physical changes after the menopause', in Markson, E. (ed.), *Older Women: Issues and Prospects*. Lexington, Lexington Books.
Khan, V. (1977). 'The Pakistanis', in Watson, J. (ed.), *Between Two Cultures: Migrants and Minorities in Britain*. Oxford, Basil Blackwell.
Kincaid, J. C. (1973). *Poverty and Equality in Britain*. Harmondsworth, Penguin.
Kohli, M. (1986). 'The world we forgot: a historical review of the life course', in Marshall, V. (ed.), *Later Life*. London, Sage.
Kubler-Ross, E. (1973). *On Death and Dying*. London, Tavistock.
Kuhn, M. (1986). Prologue to Phillipson, C. Bernard, M. and Strang, P. (eds), *Dependency and Interdependency in Old Age: Theoretical Perspectives and Policy Alternatives*. London, Croom Helm.
Laczko, F. (1987). 'Older workers, unemployment and the discouraged worker effect', in di Gregorio, S. (ed.), *Social Gerontology: New Directions*. London, Croom Helm.
Laczko, F. and Walker, A. (1985). 'Excluding older workers from the labour force: early retirement policies in Britain, France and Sweden', in Brenton, M. and Jones, C, (eds), *Year Book of Social Policy in Britain*. London, Routledge and Kegan Paul.
Ladurie, E. le Roy (1980). *Montaillou*. Harmondsworth, Penguin.
Land, H. (1978). 'Who cares for the family?'. *Journal of Social Policy*, **7**, 357–84.
Laslett, P. (1965). *The World We Have Lost*. London, Methuen.
Laslett, P. (1977). *Family Life and Illicit Love in Earlier Generations*. Cambridge, Cambridge University Press.
Laslett, P. (1984). 'The significance of the past in the study of ageing: introduction to the special issue on history and ageing'. *Ageing and Society*, **4**, 379–89.
Laslett, P. (1987). 'The emergence of the third age'. *Ageing and Society,* **7**, 133–60.
Laslett, P. and Wall, R. (1972). *Household and Family in Past Times*. Cambridge, Cambridge University Press.
Lawton, M. P. (1980). *Environment and Aging*. Monterey, Brooks/Cole.
Lemmon, B., Bengston, V. and Peterson, J. (1976). 'An explanation of the activity theory of aging; activity types and life satisfaction among in-movers to a retirement community', in Bell, B. (ed.), *Contemporary Social Gerontology*. Springfield, Charles Thomas.
Lenski, G. (1966). *Power and Privilege, A Theory of Social Stratification*. New York, McGraw-Hill.
Levack, B. (1987). *The Witch Hunt in Early Modern Europe*. London, Longmans.
Levin, E., Sinclair, I. and Gorbach, P. (1983). 'The supporters of confused elderly people at home'. London, National Institute for Social Work, Research Unit.
Lipman, A. (1967). 'Chairs as territory'. *New Society*, 20 April, 564–6.
Loether, H. J. (1967). *Problems of Aging*. California, Dickenson.
Logan, W. P. D. (1953). 'Work and age: statistical considerations'. *British Medical Journal*, 28 November, 1190–93.
Long, J. (1987). 'Continuity as a basis for change: leisure and male retirement'. *Leisure Studies*, **6**, 55–70.
Lopata, H. (1971). 'Widows as a minority group'. *Gerontologist*, **11**, 67–77.
Lopata, H. Z. (1979). *Women as Widows, Support Systems*. New York, Elsevier-North Holland Inc.

Macdonald, B. and Rich, C. (1984). *Look Me in the Eye*. London, The Women's Press.
Macintyre, S. (1977). 'Old age as a social problem', in Dingwall, R., Heath, C., Reid, M. and Stacey, M. (eds), *Health Care and Health Knowledge*. London, Croom Helm.
Maddox, G. (1966). 'Retirement as a social event', in McKinney, J. C. and de Vyer, F. T. (eds), *Aging and Social Policy*. New York, Appleton-Century-Croft.
Maddox, G. (1970). 'Themes and issues in sociological theories of human ageing'. *Human Development*, **13**, 17–27.
Malinowski, B. (1922). *Argonauts of the Western Pacific* (reissued 1966). London, Routledge and Kegan Paul.
Malinowski, B. (1932). *The Sexual Life of Savages in North-West Melansia* (reissued 1957). London, Routledge and Kegan Paul.
Manuel, R. (1982). 'The minority aged: providing a conceptual perspective', in Manuel, R. (ed.), *Minority Aging: Sociological and Social Psychological Issues*. Connecticut, Greenwood Press.
Markson, E. (ed.) (1983) *Older Women: Issues and Prospects*. Lexington, Lexington Books.
Marris, P. (1958). *Widows and Their Families*. London, Routledge and Kegan Paul.
Marris, P. (1974). *Loss and Change*. London, Routledge and Kegan Paul.
Marshall, M. (1983). *Social Work with Old People*. London, Macmillan.
Marshall, T. H. (1965). *Social Policy*. London, Hutchinson.
Marshall, V. (1975). 'Age and the awareness of finitude in developmental gerontology'. *Omega*, **6**, 113–29.
Marshall, V. (1980). *Last Chapters, A Sociology of Aging and Dying*. Monterey, Brooks/Cole.
Marshall, V. (ed.) (1986). *Later Life*. London, Sage.
Martin, J. P. (1984). *Hospitals in Trouble*. Oxford, Basil Blackwell.
Martin, J. and Roberts, C. (1984). *Women and Employment: A Lifetime Perspective*. London, HMSO.
Matthews, F. (1977). *Quest for an American Sociology: Robert E. Park and the Chicago School*. Montreal, McGill-Queens University Press.
Matthews, S. H. (1979). *The Social World of Old Women*. London, Sage.
Matthews, S. H. (1986). *Friendships Through the Life Course, Oral Biographies in Old Age*. London, Sage.
Matthews, S. H. and Sprey, J. (1984). 'The impact of divorce on grandparenthood: an exploratory study'. *Gerontologist*, **24**, 41–7.
Mays, N. (1983). 'Elderly South Asians in Britain: a survey of relevant literature and themes for future research'. *Ageing and Society*, **3**, 71–98.
McFarland, E., Dalton, M. and Walsh, D. (1987). *Personal Welfare Services and Ethnic Minorities*. Research Paper No. 4, Glasgow College of Technology, Edinburgh College of Art and Heriot Watt University.
McFarlane, A. (1970). *Witchcraft in Tudor and Stuart England*. London, Routledge and Kegan Paul.
McGoldrick, A. and Cooper, C. (1980). 'Voluntary early retirement – taking the decision'. *Employment Gazette*, August.
McManners, J. (1985). *Death and the Enlightenment*. Oxford, Oxford University Press.
Meacher, M. (1972). *Taken for a Ride: Special Residential Homes for Confused Old People*. London, Longman.
Means, R. and Smith, R. (1985). *The Development of Welfare Services for Elderly People*. London, Croom Helm.

Merton, R. K. (1957). *Social Theory and Social Structure*. London, Collier-Macmillan.

Michelon, L. C. (1954). 'The new leisure class'. *American Journal of Sociology*, **59**, 371–8.

Middleton, L. (1982). *"So Much For So Few" – A View of Sheltered Housing*. Liverpool, University of Liverpool, Merseyside Improved Houses/Institute of Human Ageing.

Miller, E. J. and Gwynne, G. V. (1972). *A Life Apart*. London, Tavistock.

Miller, J. (1968). In Johnson, B. S. (ed.), *The Evacuees*. London, Gollancz.

Miller, S. J. (1965). 'The social dilemma of the aging leisure participant', in Rose, A. M. and Peterson, W. A. (eds), *Older People and Their Social World*. Philadelphia, F. A. Davis.

Mills, C. W. (1959). *The Sociological Imagination*. Harmondsworth, Penguin.

Milne, J. (1985). *Clinical Effects of Ageing: A Longitudinal Study*. London, Croom Helm.

Minkler, M. and Estes, C. (eds) (1984). *Readings in the Political Economy of Aging*. New York, Baywood.

Mishra, R. (1984). *The Welfare State in Crisis: Social Thought and Social Change*. Brighton, Wheatsheaf Books.

Morris, P. (1969). *Put Away*. London, Routledge and Kegan Paul.

Murphy, E. (1982). 'Social origins of depression in old age'. *British Journal of Psychiatry*, **141**, 135–42.

Myerhoff, B. (1978). *Number Our Days*. New York, Touchstone.

Newton, E. (1980). *This Bed My Centre*. London, Virago.

Nissel, M. and Bonnerjea, L. (1982). *Family Care of the Handicapped Elderly: Who Pays?* London, Policy Studies Institute.

Norman, A. (1985). *Triple Jeopardy: Growing Old in a Second Homeland*. London, Centre for Policy on Ageing.

O'Donnell, M. (1971). *The Impossible Virgin*. London, Souvenir Press.

Office of Population, Census and Surveys (OPCS) (1982). *General Household Survey for 1980*. London, HMSO.

Office of Population, Census and Surveys (OPCS) (1983). *Census 1981: Country of Birth; Great Britain*. London, HMSO.

Okely, J. (1986). Contribution to Economic and Social Research Council Seminar, 'The Ageing Initiative', September, University of Surrey.

O'Rand, A. and Henretta, J. (1982). 'Midlife work history and retirement income', in Szinovacz, M. (ed.), *Women's Retirement: Policy Implications of Recent Research*. London, Sage.

Owen, L. (1977). 'Over the hill and far away'. *Guardian*, 17 November, 13.

Pahl, R. E. (1984). *Divisions of Labour*. Oxford, Basil Blackwell.

Palmore, E. G., Cleveland, W., Nowlin, J., Ramus, D. and Seigler, I. (1979). 'Stress and adaptation in later life'. *Journal of Gerontology*, **34**, 841–51.

Palmore, E. G., Burchett, B., Fillenbaum, G., George, L. and Wallman, L. (1985). *Retirement: Causes and Consequences*. New York, Springer.

Parker, G. (1985). *With Due Care and Attention: A Review of Research on Informal Care*. London, Family Policy Studies Centre.

Parker, R. (1981). 'Tending and social policy', in Goldberg, E. and Hatch, S. (eds), *A New Look at the Personal Social Servies*. London, Policy Studies Institute.

Parker, S. (1980). *Older Workers and Retirement*. OPCS: Social Survey Division. London, HMSO.

Parker, T. (1985). *The People of Providence, Interviews from an Urban Housing Estate*. Harmondsworth, Penguin.

Parkes, C. M. (1972). *Bereavement: Studies of Grief in Adult Life*. London, Tavistock.

Parsons, T. (1942). 'Age and sex in the social structure of the United States'. *American Sociological Review*, **7**, 604–16.

Parsons, T. (1951). *The Social System*. London, Collier-Macmillan.

Peace, S. (1986). 'The forgotten female: social policy and older women', in Phillipson, C. and Walker, A. (eds), *Ageing and Social Policy: A Critical Assessment*. Aldershot, Gower.

Pearson, M. (1984). 'An insensitive service', in Harrison, A. and Gretton, J. (eds), *Health Care UK 1984: An Economic, Social and Policy Audit*. London, Chartered Institute of Public Finance and Accountancy.

Pearson, M. (1986). 'Racist notions of ethnicity and culture in health education', in Rodmell, S. and Watt, A. (eds), *The Politics of Health Education: Raising the Issues*. London, Routledge and Kegan Paul.

Phillips, D. L. (1971). *Knowledge From What? Theories and Methods in Social Research*. Chicago, Rand McNally.

Phillips, D. L. (1973). *Abandoning Method*. London, Jossey-Bass.

Phillipson, C. (1978). 'The experience of retirement'. Ph.D. Thesis. Durham, University of Durham.

Phillipson, C. (1981). 'Women in later life: patterns of control and subordination', in Hutter, B. and Williams, G. (eds), *Controlling Women: The Normal and the Deviant*. London, Croom Helm.

Phillipson, C. (1982). *Capitalism and the Construction of Old Age*. London, Macmillan.

Phillipson, C. (1987). 'The transition to retirement', in Cohen, G. (ed.), *Social Change in the Life Course*. London, Tavistock.

Phillipson, C. and Strang, P. (1983). *Pre-retirement Education: A Longitudinal Evaluation*. Stoke-on-Trent, University of Keele, Department of Adult Education.

Phillipson, C. and Strang, P. (1985). 'Sheltered housing: the warden's view', in Butler, A. (ed.), *Ageing, Recent Advances and Creative Responses*. London, Croom Helm.

Phillipson, C. and Strang, P. (1986). *Training and Education for an Ageing Society: New Perspectives for the Health and Social Services*. Health Education Council/ Department of Adult Education, University of Keele.

Phillipson, C. and Walker, A. (eds) (1986). *Ageing and Social Policy: A Critical Assessment*. Aldershot, Gower.

Phillipson, C. and Walker, A. (1987). 'The case for a critical gerontology', in di Gregorio, S. (ed.), *Social Gerontology: New Directions*. London, Croom Helm.

Philpott, S. (1977). 'The Montserratians: migration dependency and the maintenance of island ties in England', in Watson, J. (ed.), *Between Two Cultures: Migrants and Minorities in Britain*. Oxford, Basil Blackwell.

Platt, J. (1976). *Realities of Social Research*. London, Sussex University Press.

Plummer, K. (1983). *Documents of Life: An Introduction to the Problems and Literature of a Humanistic Perspective*. London, George Allen and Unwin.

Pollak, O. (1948). *Social Adjustment in Old Age*. New York, Social Science Research Council.

Power, M. and Kelly, S. (1981). 'Evaluating domiciliary volunteer care of the very old: possibilities and problems', in Goldberg, E. M. and Connelly, N. (eds), *Evaluative Research in Social Care*. London, Heinemann.

Pulling, J. (1987). *The Caring Trap*. Glasgow, Fontana.

Puner, M. (1974). *To the Good Long Life, What We Know About Growing Old*. London, Macmillan.

Pym, B. (1977). *Quartet in Autumn*. London, Macmillan.

Quadango, J. (1982). *Ageing in Early Industrial Society: Work, Family and Social Policy in 19th Century England*. London, Academic Press.

Qureshi, H. and Walker, A. (1986). 'Caring for elderly people: the family and the state', in Phillipson, C. and Walker, A. (eds), *Ageing and Social Policy: A Critical Assessment*. Aldershot, Gower.

Qureshi, H. and Walker, A. (1988). *The Caring Relationship: The Family Care of Elderly People*. London, Macmillan.

Rack, P. (1982). *Race, Culture and Mental Disorder*. London, Tavistock.

Radcliffe Richards, J. (1982). *The Sceptical Feminist*. Harmondsworth, Penguin.

Radical Statistics Health Group (1987). *Facing the Figures: What Really Is Happening to the National Health Service?* London, Radical Statistics.

Reichard, R., Livson, F. and Peterson, P. G. (1962). *Aging and Personality*. New York, John Wiley.

Rein, M. (1970). 'Problems in the definition and measurement of poverty', in Townsend, P. (ed.), *The Concept of Poverty*. London, Heinemann.

Rex, J. (1986). *Race and Ethnicity*. Milton Keynes, Open University Press.

Rex, J. and Moore, R. (1967). *Race, Community and Conflict: A Study of Sparkbrook*. Oxford, Oxford University Press.

Richardson, I. M. (1956). 'Retirement; a socio-medical study of 244 men'. *Scottish Medical Journal*, **1**, 381–91.

Riley, M. W. (1987). 'The significance of ageing in sociology'. *American Sociological Review*, **52**, 1–14.

Riley, M. W., Johnson, M. and Foner, A. (1972). *Aging and Society (3): A Sociology of Age Stratification*. New York, Russell Sage.

Riley, M. W., Foner, A. and Waring, J. (forthcoming). 'A sociology of age', in Smelser, N. J. and Burt, R. (eds), *Handbook of Sociology*. Berkeley, Sage.

Robb, B. (ed.) (1967). *Sans Everything: A Case to Answer*. London, Nelson.

Roberts, H. (ed.) (1981). *Doing Feminist Research*. London, Routledge and Kegan Paul.

Roberts, R. (1971). *The Classic Slum, Salford Life in the First Quarter of the Century*. Manchester, University of Manchester Press.

Robin, J. (1984). 'Family care of the elderly in a nineteenth century Devonshire parish'. *Ageing and Society*, **4**, 505–16.

Robinson, V. (1986). *Transients, Settlers and Refugees: Asians in Britain*. Oxford, Clarendon Press.

Robson, W. A. (1976). *Welfare State and Welfare Society: Illusion and Reality*. London, George Allen and Unwin.

Rose, A. M. (1964). 'A current theoretical issue in gerontology'. *Gerontologist*, **4**, 46–50.

Rose, E. J. B. (1969). *Colour and Citizenship: A Report on British Race Relations*. Oxford, Oxford University Press.

Rosenmayr, L. (1981). 'Objective and subjective perspectives of life span research'. *Ageing and Society*, **1**, 29–49.

Rosenmayr, L. and Kockeis, E. (1963). 'Propositions for a sociological theory of aging and the family'. *International Science Journal*, **XV**, 410–26.

Rosow, I. (1967). *Social Integration of the Aged*. New York, The Free Press.

Ross, J.-K. (1977). *Old People, New Lives: Community Creation in a Retirement Residence*. Chicago, University of Chicago Press.

Roth, J. (1966). 'Hired-hand research'. *American Sociologist*, **1**, 190–96.

Rowbotham, S. (1974). *Hidden from History: 300 Years of Women's Oppression and the Fight Against it*, Second Edition. London, Pluto.

Rowntree, B. S. (1947). *Old People: Report of a Survey Committee*. Oxford, Oxford University Press.

Rowntree, B. S. and Lasker, B. (1911). *Unemployment: A Social Study*. London, Macmillan.

Royal Commission on Population (1949). *Report*. London, HMSO.

Sahlins, M. D. (1968). *Tribesmen*. Englewood Cliffs, Prentice-Hall.

Scheidman, E. S. (1973). 'A national survey of attitudes towards death', in Scheidman, E. S. (ed.), *Death of Man*. New York, Quadrangle/New York Times.

Schwartz, M. S. and Schwartz, C. C. (1955). 'Problems of participant observation'. *American Journal of Sociology*, **60**, 343–53.

Shanas, E. (1971). 'Disengagement and work: Myth and reality', in *Work and Aging*. International Center of Social Gerontology.

Shanas, E., Townsend, P., Wedderburn, D., Friis, H., Milhoj, P. and Stehouwer, J. (1968). *Old People in Three Industrial Societies*. London, Routledge and Kegan Paul.

Shaw, J. (1971). *On Our Conscience, the Plight of the Elderly*. Harmondsworth, Penguin.

Shaw, L. S. (ed.) (1983). *Unplanned Careers: The Working Lives of Middle Aged Women*. Lexington, D. C. Heath.

Sheldon, J. H. (1948). *The Social Medicine of Old Age, Report of an inquiry in Wolverhampton*. Oxford, Oxford University Press.

Shephard, R. J. (1978). *Physical Activity and Ageing*. London, Croom Helm.

Sidell, M. (1986). 'Coping with confusion: the experience of sixty elderly people and their informal and formal carers'. Ph.D. Thesis. Norwich, University of East Anglia.

Silman, A., Evans, J. and Loysen, E. (1987). 'Blood pressure and migration: a study of Bengali immigrants in East London'. *Journal of Epidemiology and Community Health*, **41**, 152–5.

Simmons, L. W. (1945). *The Role of the Aged in Primitive Society*. New Haven, Yale University Press.

Simmons, L. W. (1960). 'Ageing in pre-industrial societies', in Tibbitts, C. (ed.), *Handbook of Social Gerontology*. Chicago, University of Chicago Press.

Simpson, I., Back, K. W. and McKinney, J. C. (1966). 'Orientations towards work and retirement and self-evaluation in retirement', in Simpson, I. and McKinney, J. C. (eds), *Social Aspects of Ageing*. North Carolina, Durham University Press.

Snellgrove, D. R. (1963). *Elderly Housebound: A Report on Elderly People who are Incapacitated*. Luton, White Crescent Press.

Sontag, S. (1975). 'The double standard of aging', in Bart, P. (ed.), *No Longer Young: The Older Woman in America*. Michigan, Wayne State University, Institute of Gerontology.

Sontag, S. (1983). *Illness as Metaphor*. Harmondsworth, Penguin.

Spackman, A. (1987). 'The middle-age dilemma: what to do with mother'. *Independent*, 10 August, 10.

Stacey, M. (1981). 'The division of labour revisited, or overcoming the two Adams', in

Abrams, P., Deem, R., Finch, J. and Rock, P. (eds), *Development and Diversity: British Sociology, 1950–1980*. London, George Allen and Unwin.

Stearns, P. (1977). *Old Age in European Society: The Case of France*. London, Croom Helm.

Stearns, P. N. (ed.) (1982). *Old Age in Pre-industrial Society*. New York, Holmes and Meier.

Sternheimer, S. (1985). 'The vanishing babushka: a roleless role for older soviet women', in Blau, Z. (ed.), *Current Perspectives on Aging and the Lifecycle, Volume 1: Work, Retirement and Social Policy*. Greenwich, Connecticut, JAI Press.

Stone, L. (1982). *The Family, Sex and Marriage in England 1500–1800*. Harmondsworth, Penguin.

Streib, G. F. (1983). 'The frail elderly: research dilemmas and research opportunities'. *Gerontologist*, **23**, 40–44.

Sykes, G. M. and Matza, D. (1957). 'Techniques of neutralisation: a theory of delinquency'. *American Sociological Review*, **22**, 664–70.

Sykes, M. (1985). 'Discrimination in discourse', in Van Dijk, T. A. (ed.), *Handbook of Discourse Analysis (4), Discourse Analysis in Society*. London, Academic Press.

Szinovacz, M. (1982). 'Research on women's retirement', in Szinovacz, M. (ed.), *Women's Retirement: Policy Implications of Recent Research*. London, Sage.

Taylor, H. (1979). 'A sociology of ageing?', in *Old Age: A Register of Social Research 1978–79*, compiled by H. Todd. London, Centre for Policy on Ageing.

Taylor, H. (1980). 'Old age research: a priority at the present time?', in *Old Age: A Register of Social Research 1979–80*, compiled by H. Todd. London, Centre for Policy on Ageing.

Taylor, H. (1983). *The Hospice Movement in Britain: Its Role and Future*. London, Centre for Policy on Ageing.

Taylor, H. (1985). Book Review of Clench, P., *Managing to Care in Community Services for the Terminally Ill. Ageing and Society*, **5**, 136–8.

Taylor, R. and Ford, G. (1983). 'Inequality in old age: an examination of age, sex and class differences in a sample of community elderly'. *Ageing and society*, **3**, 183–208.

Terkel, S. (1977). *Working*. Harmondsworth, Penguin.

Thane, P. (1978). 'The muddled history of retiring at 60 and 65'. *New Society*, 3 August, 234–6.

Thatcher, R. (1981). 'Centenarians in England and Wales'. *Population Trends*, **25**, 11–14.

Thomas, K. (1976). 'Age and authority in early modern England'. *Proceedings of the British Academy*, **LXII**, 205–48.

Thomas, K. (1978). *Religion and the Decline of Magic*. London, Peregrine.

Thompson, P. (1978). *The Voice of the Past: Oral History*. Oxford, Oxford University Press.

Thompson Rogers, G. (1985). 'Nonmarried women approaching retirement: who are they and when do they retire?' in Blau, Z. (ed.), *Current Perspectives on Aging and the Lifecycle (1): Work, Retirement and Social Policy*. Greenwich, JAI Press.

Thomson, A., Lowe, C. and McKeown, T. (1951). *The Care of the Ageing and Chronic Sick*. Edinburgh, E. & S. Livingstone.

Thomson, D. (1984). 'The decline of social welfare: falling state support for the elderly since early Victorian times'. *Ageing and Society*, **4**, 451–82.

Thomson, D. (1986). 'Welfare and the historians', in Bonfield, L., Smith, R. M. and

Wrightson, K. (eds), *The World We Have Gained: Histories of Population and Social Structure*. Oxford, Basil Blackwell.

Tinker, A. (1981). *The Elderly in Modern Society*. London, Longman.

Tinker, A. (1984). *Staying at Home: Helping Elderly People*. London, HMSO.

Titmuss, R. M. (1970). 'Foreword' to Goldberg, E. M., *Helping the Aged: A Field Experiment in Social Work*. London, George Allen and Unwin.

Titmuss, R. M. (1974). *Social Policy*. London, George Allen and Unwin.

Tonnies, F. (1955). *Community and Association*. London, Routledge and Kegan Paul.

Townsend, P. (1952). 'The purpose of the institution', in Tibbits, C. and Donahue, W. (eds), *Social and Psychological Aspects of Aging*. New York, Columbia University Press.

Townsend, P. (1957). *The Family Life of Old People, An Inquiry in East London*. London, Routledge and Kegan Paul.

Townsend, P. (1958). 'A society for people', in Mackenzie, N. (ed.), *Conviction*. London, MacGibbon and Kee.

Townsend, P. (1962). *The Last Refuge*. London, Routledge and Kegan Paul.

Townsend, P. (1973). *The Social Minority*. London, Allen Lane.

Townsend, P. (1979). *Poverty in the United Kingdom, A Survey of Household Resources and Standards of Living*. Harmondsworth, Penguin.

Townsend, P. (1981). 'The structured dependency of the elderly: a creation of social policy in the twentieth century'. *Ageing and Society*, **1**, 5–28.

Townsend, P. (1986). 'Ageism and social policy', in Phillipson, C. and Walker, A. (eds), *Ageing and Social Policy: A Critical Assessment*. Aldershot, Gower.

Townsend, P. and Davidson, N. (1982). *Inequalities in Health*. Harmondsworth, Penguin.

Townsend, P. and Wedderburn, D. (1965). *The Aged in The Welfare State*. London, Bell.

Treasury (1984). *The Next Ten Years; Public Expenditure and Taxation into The 1990s*. Cmnd. 9189. London, HMSO.

Tunstall, J. (1966). *Old and Alone*. London, Routledge and Kegan Paul.

Unruh, D. R. (1983). *Invisible Lives: Social Worlds of the Aged*. Beverly Hills, Sage.

Vallery-Masson, J. (1981). 'Retirement and morbidity: a three year longitudinal study of a French managerial population'. *Age and Ageing*, **10**, 271–6.

Vaughan, D. (1987). *Uncoupling: Turning Points in Intimate Relationships*. London, Methuen.

Verbrugge, L. (1985). 'An epidemiological profile of older women', in Haug, M., Ford, A. and Sheafor, M. (eds), *The Physical and Mental Health of Aged Women*. New York, Springer.

Victor, C. (1987). *Old Age in Modern Society: A Textbook of Social Gerontology*. London, Croom Helm.

Waerness, K. (1984). 'Caring as women's work in the welfare state', in Holter, H. (ed.), *Patriarchy in a Welfare Society*. Oslo, Universitetsforlaget.

Wainwright, P. and Burnip, S. (1983). 'QUALPACS at Burford'. *Nursing Times*, 2 February, 30–33; 17 August, 26–7.

Walker, A. (1980). 'The social origins of impairment, disability and handicap'. *Medicine in Society*, **6**, 18–26.

Walker, A. (1981). 'Towards a political economy of old age'. *Ageing and Society*, **1**, 73–94.

Walker, A. (1983). 'Care for elderly people: a conflict between women and the state', in

Finch, J. and Groves, D. (eds), *A Labour of Love: Women, Work and Caring*. London, Routledge and Kegan Paul.

Walker, A. (1985). 'Care of elderly people', in Berthoud, R. (ed.), *Challenges to Social Policy*. Aldershot, Gower.

Walker, A. (1986). 'Pensions and the production of poverty in old age', in Phillipson, P. and Walker, A. (eds), *Ageing and Social Policy: A Critical Assessment*. Aldershot, Gower.

Walker, A. (1987). 'The poor relation: poverty among old women', in Glendinning, C. and Millar, J. (eds), *Women and Poverty in Britain*. Brighton, Wheatsheaf.

Wall, R. (1984). 'Residential isolation of the elderly, a comparison over time'. *Ageing and Society*, 4, 483–503.

Watson, J. (ed.) (1977). *Between Two Cultures: Migrants and Minorities in Britain*. Oxford, Basil Blackwell.

Way, A. and Fennell, G. (1987). *Sheltered Housing for Elderly People: A Bibliography 1976–1987*. Oxford, Anchor Housing Association.

Webb, B. and Stimson, G. (1976). 'People's accounts of medical encounters', in Wadsworth, M. and Robinson, D. (eds), *Studies in Everyday Medical Life*. London, Martin Robertson.

Weightman, G. (1977). 'Poor man's Harley Street'. *New Society*, 20 October, 118–19.

Wenger, G. C. (1984). *The Supportive Network, Coping with Old Age*. London, George Allen and Unwin.

Wheeler, R. (1986). 'Housing policy and elderly people', in Phillipson, C. and Walker, A. (eds), *Ageing and Social Policy: A Critical Assessment*. Aldershot, Gower.

Whitehead, M. (1987). *The Health Divide: Inequalities in Health in the 1980s*. London, The Health Education Authority.

Wilensky, H. (1961). 'The uneven distribution of leisure'. *Social Problems*, 9, 32–56.

Willcocks, D. (1982). 'Gender and the care of elderly people in Part III accommodation'. Paper presented to the Annual Conference of the British Sociological Association, University of Manchester.

Willcocks, D., Peace, S. and Kellaher, L. (1987). *Private Lives in Public Places: A Research-Based Critique of Residential Life in Local Authority Old People's Homes*. London, Tavistock.

Williams, R. (1981a). 'Logical analysis as a qualitative method I: themes in old age and chronic illness'. *Sociology of Health and Illness*, 3, 140–64.

Williams, R. (1981b). 'Logical analysis as a qualitative method II: conflict of ideas and the topic of illness'. *Sociology of Health and Illness*, 3, 165–87.

Willmott, P. (1987). *Friendship Networks and Social Support*. London, Policy Studies Institute.

Worsley, P. (ed.) (1987). *The New Introducing Sociology*, 3rd edition. Harmondsworth, Penguin.

Wright, F. (1986). *Left to Care Alone*. Aldershot, Gower.

Wrigley, E. A. (1969). *Population and History*. London, Weidenfeld and Nicolson.

Zorbaugh, H. W. (1929). *The Gold Coast and the Slum*. Chicago, University of Chicago Press.

Index

DATE DUE

2/09/09

DEC 1 7 2011